TRAN NGUYEN

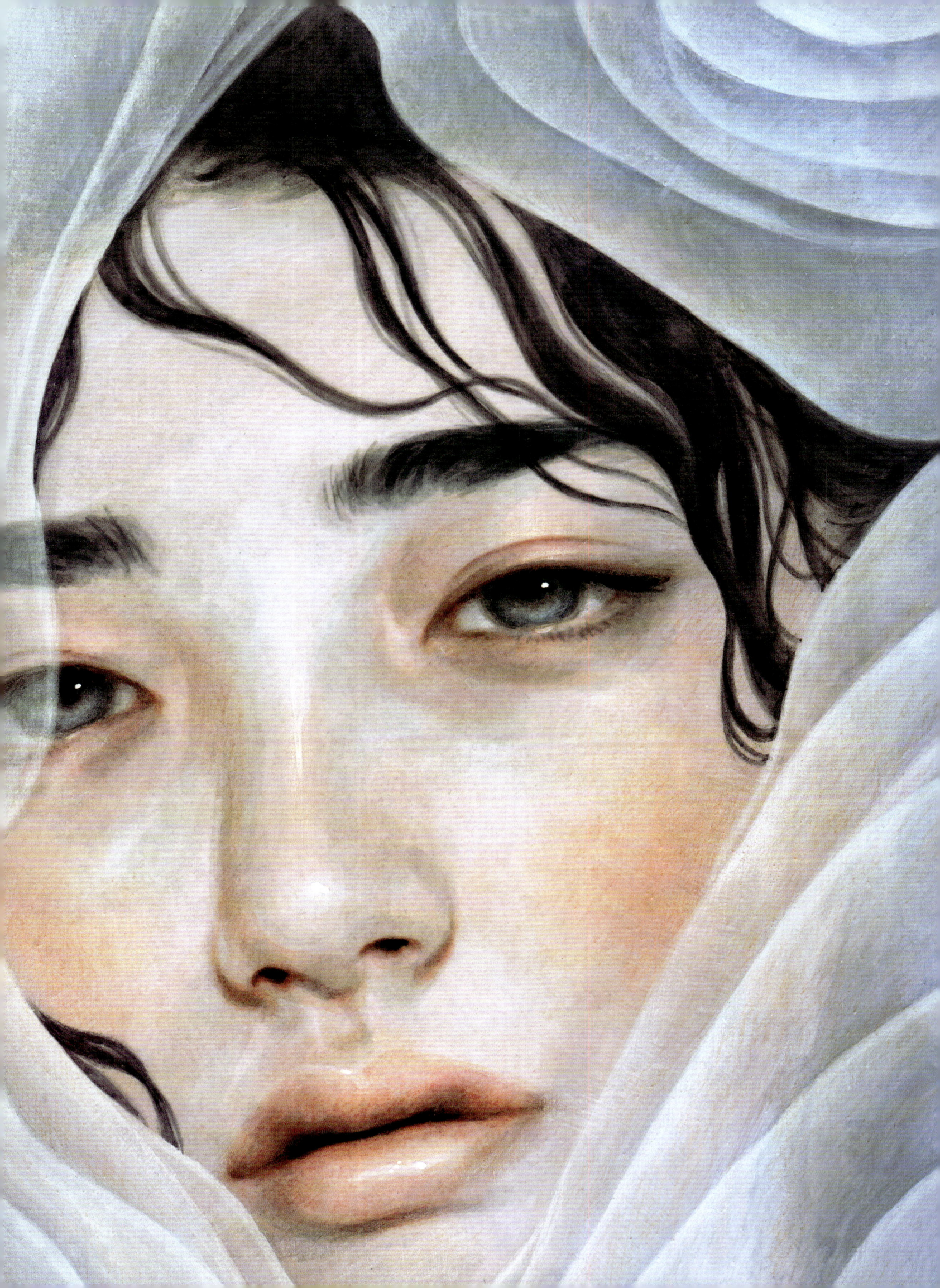

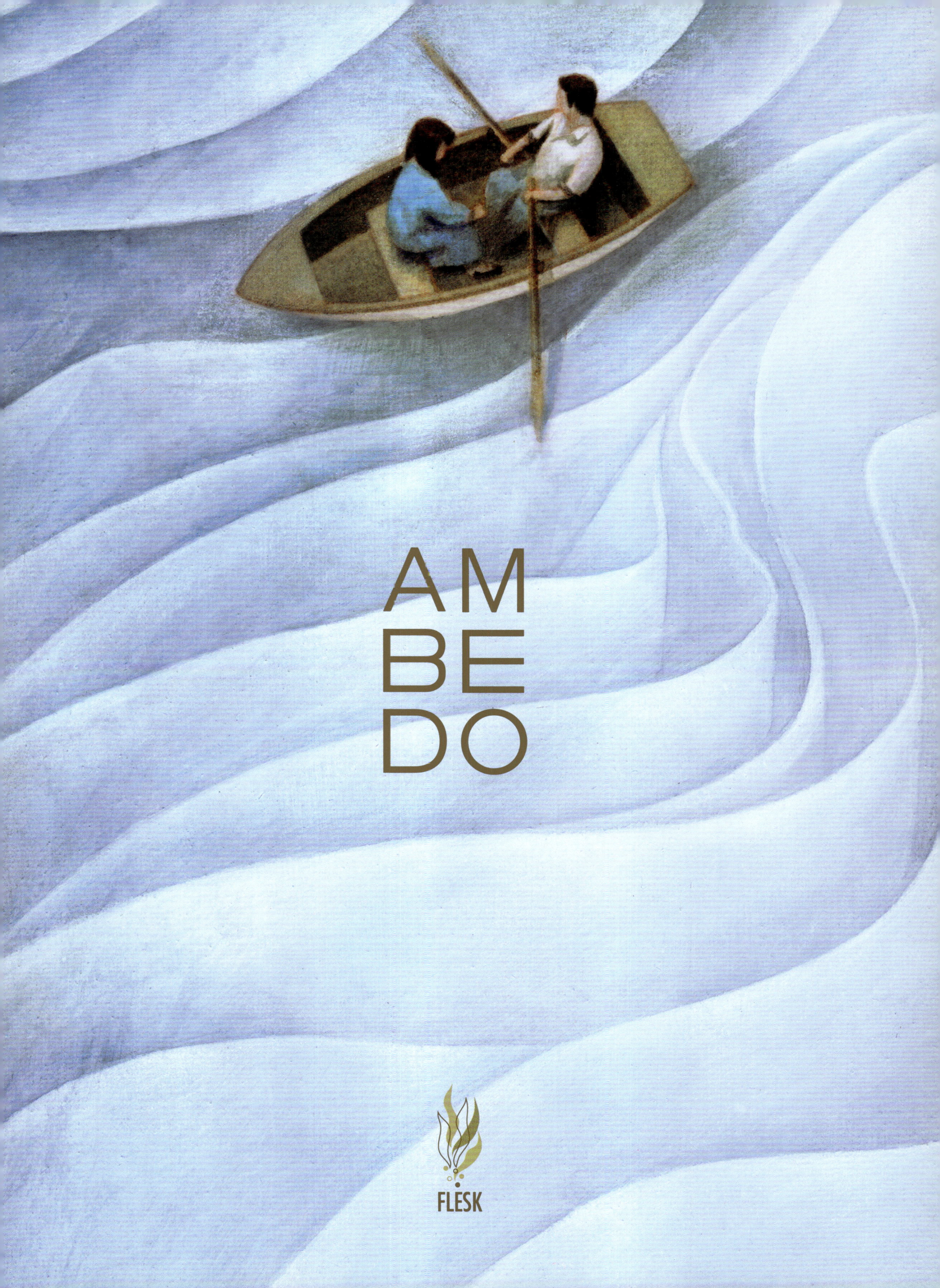

Designed by John Fleskes and Tran Nguyen
Copyedited by Martin Timins
Production assistance by Vicky Lien
First Printing, October 2025
ISBN: 978-1-64041-096-1
Library of Congress Control Number: 2024949224
Printed in China
Asia One Printing Limited, Hong Kong
fleskpublications.com
mynameistran.com

CONTENTS

AMBEDO

n. a kind of melancholic trance in which you become completely absorbed in vivid sensory details. Etymology: From albedo, a physics term that describes the proportion of light reflected by a substance (*from Latin, 'whiteness'*). Ambedo refers to the tendency both to reflect and to absorb.

—written by John Koenig

INTRODUCTION

The following is a collection of paintings and drawings dating from 2009 to 2018. It showcases the work I've done for gallery exhibitions and commercial illustration projects. In the span of almost a decade, my approach to art-making has transformed significantly. Through years of trial and error, I've learned to refine my technique of painting with acrylics and colored pencils, established my artistic style and found my way through the complex inner workings of being a freelance artist.

In 2009, I graduated from Savannah College of Art and Design and took my first steps into the world of fine art. A gallery in Culver City, California, called ThinkSpace presented me with the opportunity to showcase in its upcoming exhibitions that year. Starting out, I contributed to its small group shows, which quickly escalated to two-person shows and then to having my own solo opening.

Toward the end of 2010, I branched out of the California fine-art scene and began exhibiting with galleries across the United States and other countries. I createc my *Constellar* trilogy for the Jonathan LeVine Gallery in New York City and also completed a large series of paintings for my solo show at Roq La Rue in Seattle, Washington. As I contributed to more exhibitions, my *curriculum vitae* grew, establishing a presence in the gallery world.

I experimented with different techniques while painting these new bodies of work, leading to my current style. The gallery section of this book reveals a gradual though noticeable change in the overall mood and treatment of my painting technique. My early works carry an earthy, brown tone made with timid paint strokes. Over the years, I've fine-tuned my technique of mixing acrylics and colored pencils to yield a more polished execution.

The way I interpret and visually explain ideas also has changed tremendously. By exploring a variety of motifs and themes in the past decade, I've established personal symbols that interlace with one another to illustrate my story. Most of my inspiration is deeply rooted in my childhood memories and my family's experiences growing up in Augusta, Georgia. When possible, I try to leave little crumbs of my narrative in the paintings. Art can be a wonderful tool that facilitates growth and healing, especially when it originates from an intimate and undisguised place. My personal paintings—which are what my gallery work is mostly comprised of—have helped me to elevate my artistic voice and find fulfillment in what I do.

While painting for gallery shows, I took a leap into commercial illustration. I began creating visuals for books and magazines, television, brand packaging and advertisements. In marrying my gallery work with communications art, I redirected my fine-art aesthetic to tell someone else's story.

In 2012, with the help of my agent, I was commissioned to create my first magazine cover for a publication called *Angels on Earth*. Gingerly, I laid the foundations of my illustration portfolio and started receiving work from larger publishers, such as *Playboy* and the *Smithsonian*. One of my most treasured projects is the *#3890Tigers* campaign, launched by Tiger Beer and the World Wildlife Fund. The objective was to bring together art and technology to fight the illegal tiger trade and spread awareness of the decimated number of wild tigers left in the world. This 2017 project fueled my artistic passion and gave me the opportunity to be part of a cause larger than myself.

I'm currently working on a mixture of gallery and commercial projects as well as trying to fit in a few experimental ventures here and there. My art is still growing, and I intend to let it branch out as far as it can to other industries and unknown territory. I expect the next decade of my career to be filled with just as much growth, failure, struggle and creative fulfillment.

—*Tran Nguyen*

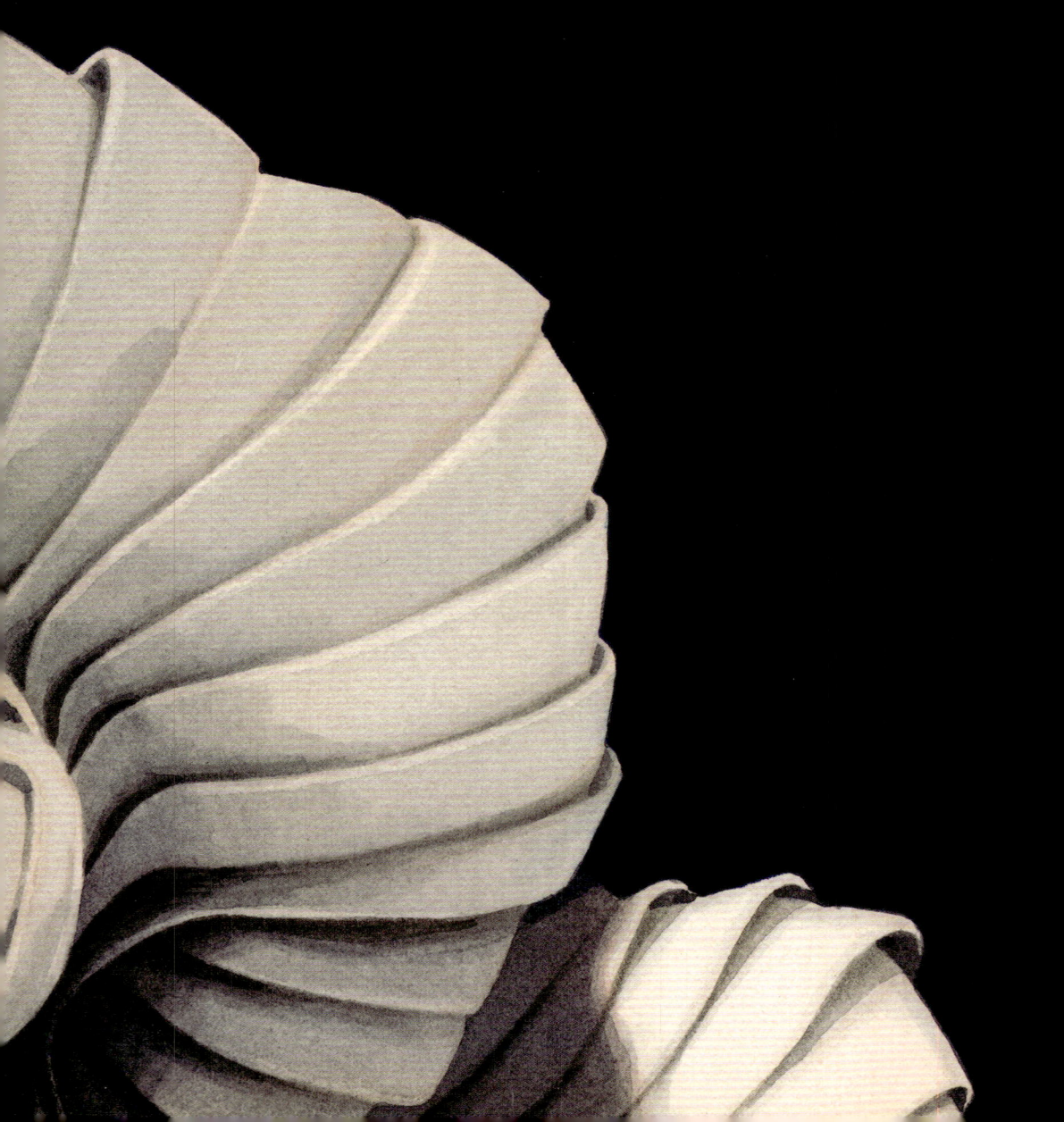

GA

LLERY

ART CREATED FOR GALLERY EXHIBITIONS, INCLUDING GROUP,
MULTI-PERSON AND SOLO SHOWS.

PORTRAITS OF THE UNKNOWN

2009

Exhibited at ThinkSpace Art Gallery in Culver City, California, *Portraits of the Unknown* was my first large body of work created for an exhibition. It was also the first of many series that explore themes focusing on therapeutic imagery. This concept came to fruition after I read Bruce L. Moon's *Art & Soul: Reflections on an Artistic Psychology*, which discusses the many facets of image-making and the act of healing through art.

This collection touches primarily on the emotional aesthetic of death and its effect on everyday existence. My goal is to visually circumnavigate the apprehension surrounding death, having each painting depict different ways to embrace it. It also showcases the many phases in a person's lifetime—the welcoming of relationships, their goodbyes and the in-betweens.

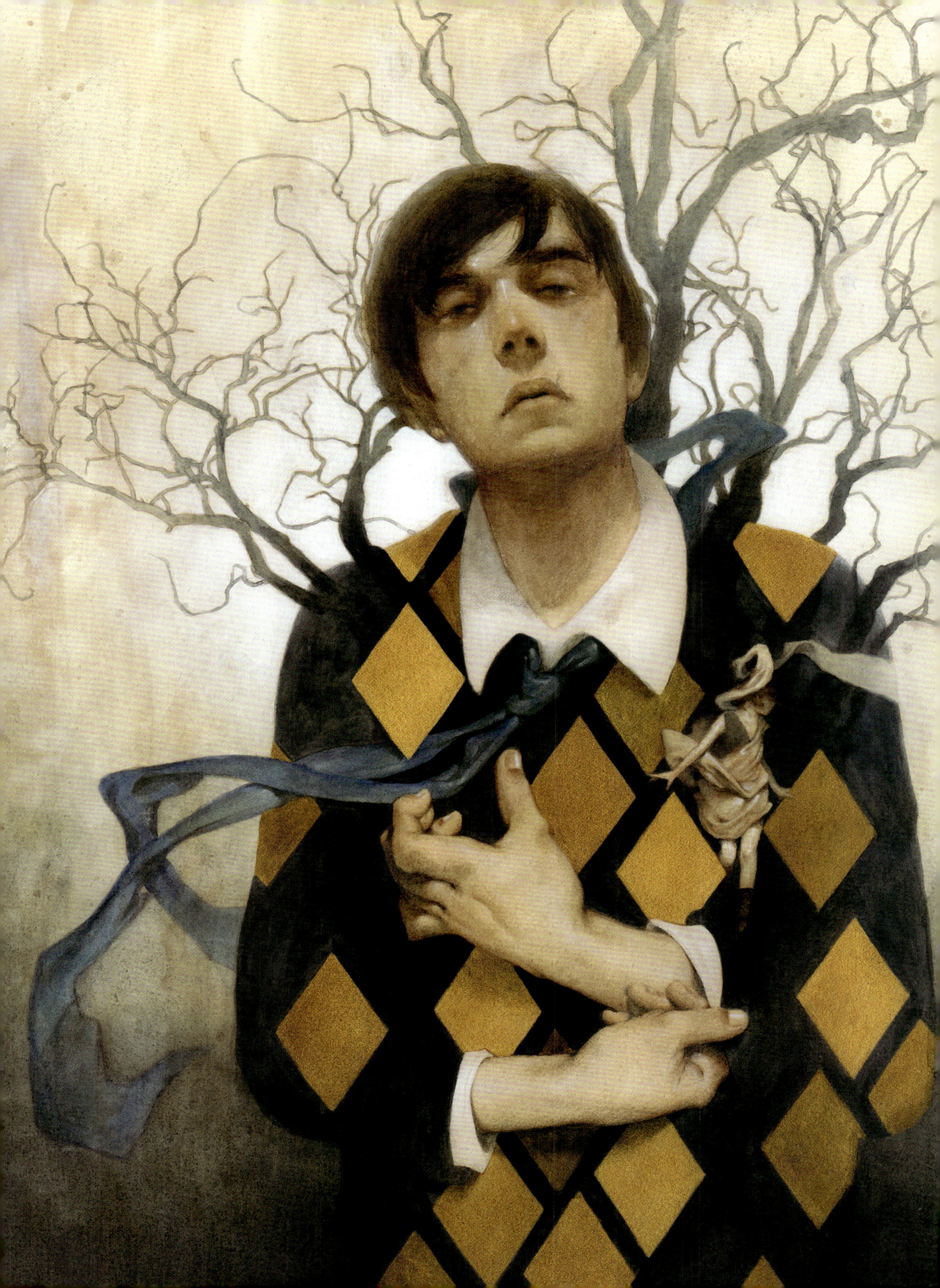

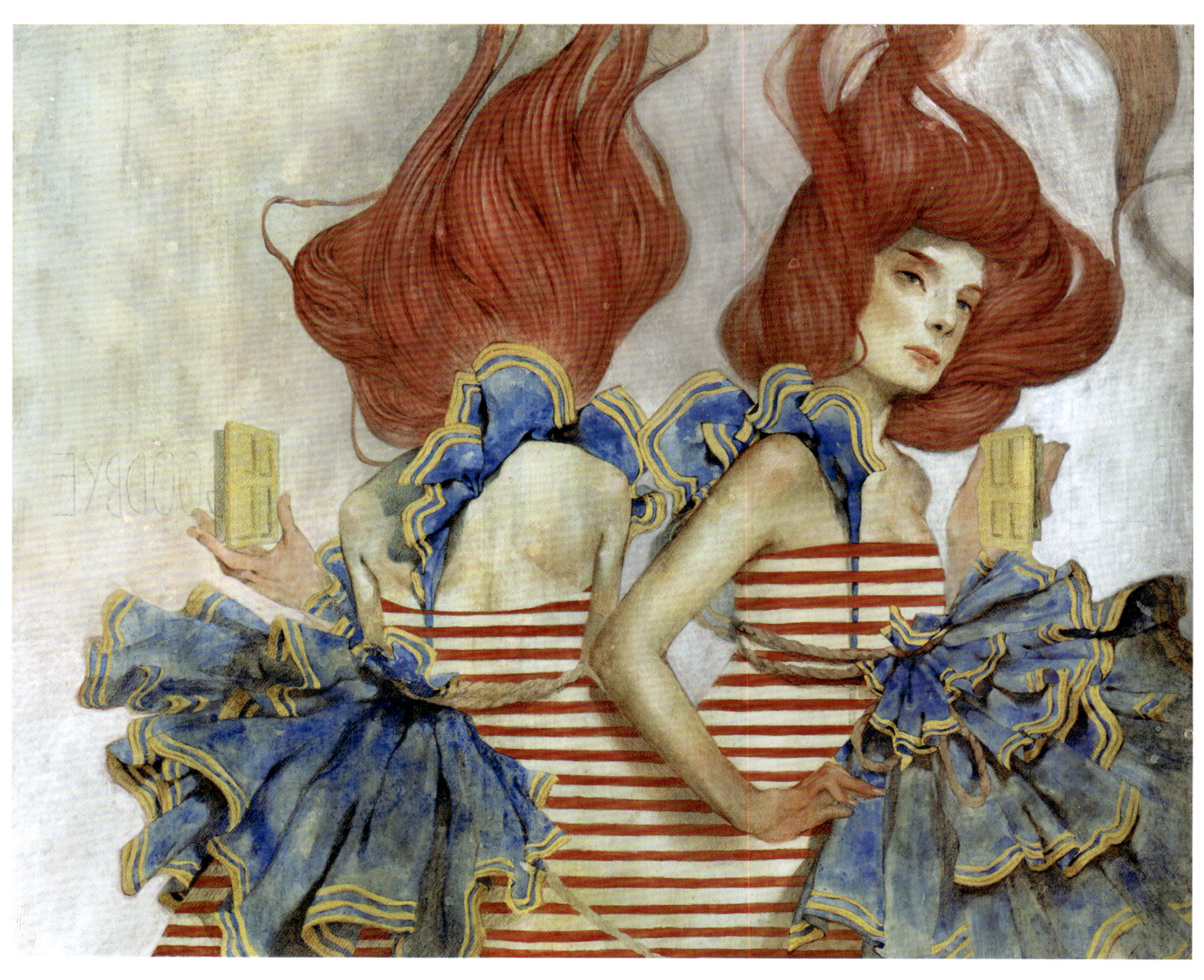

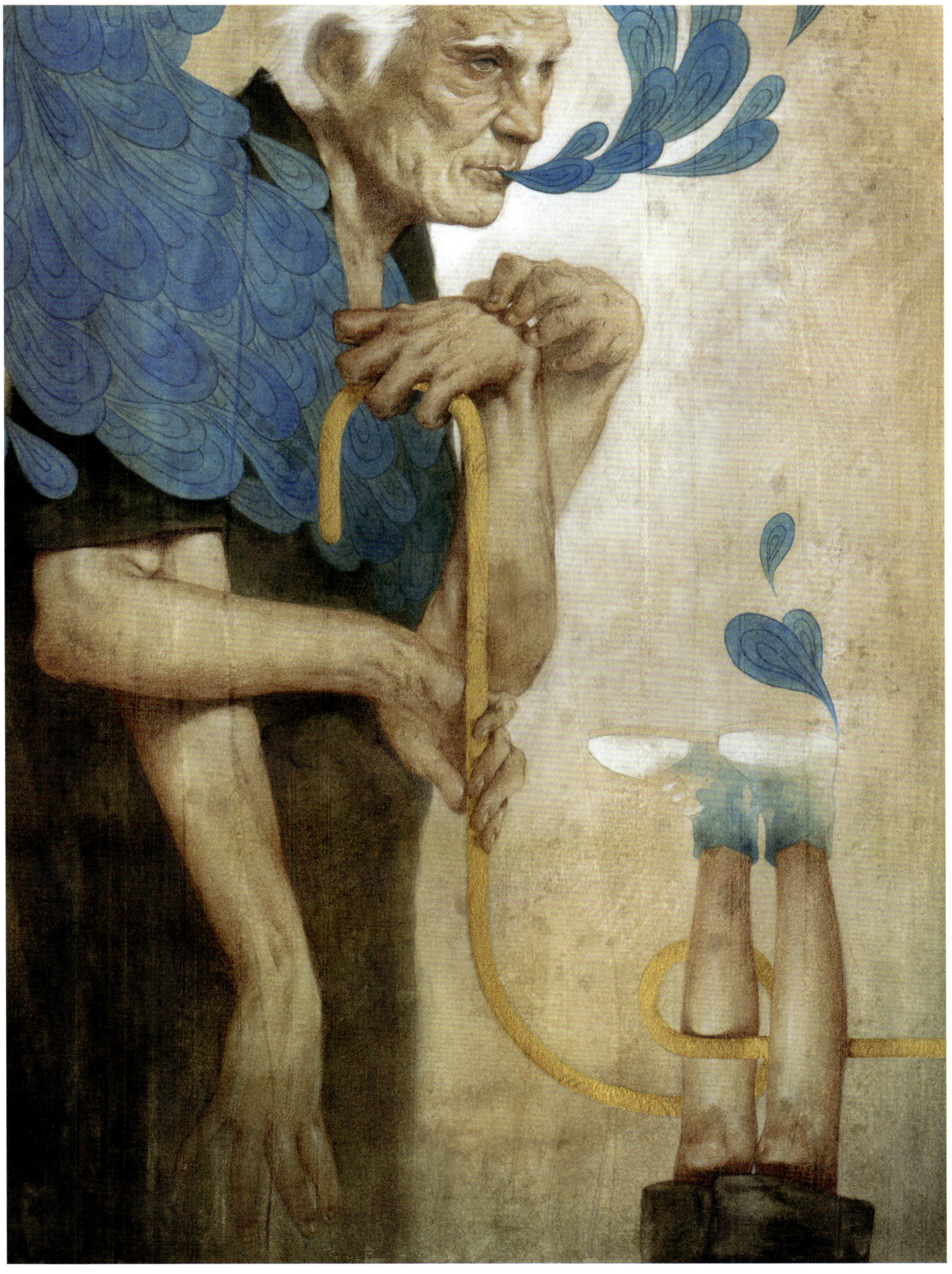

NURTURING THE UNEASED SOUL

2010

In further elaboration of the previous exhibition, this collection romanticizes the more common and universal sorrows that we all face daily. It's an even deeper dive into therapeutic imagery, particularly the exploration of melancholia, where the emotions of· longing, wonder and anxiety are found. My intent is to have each painting illustrate ordeals that the psyche endures, such as existential emptiness and mental illness. I find that these sentiments can desaturate our lively spirit yet, simultaneously, be essential to personal growth.

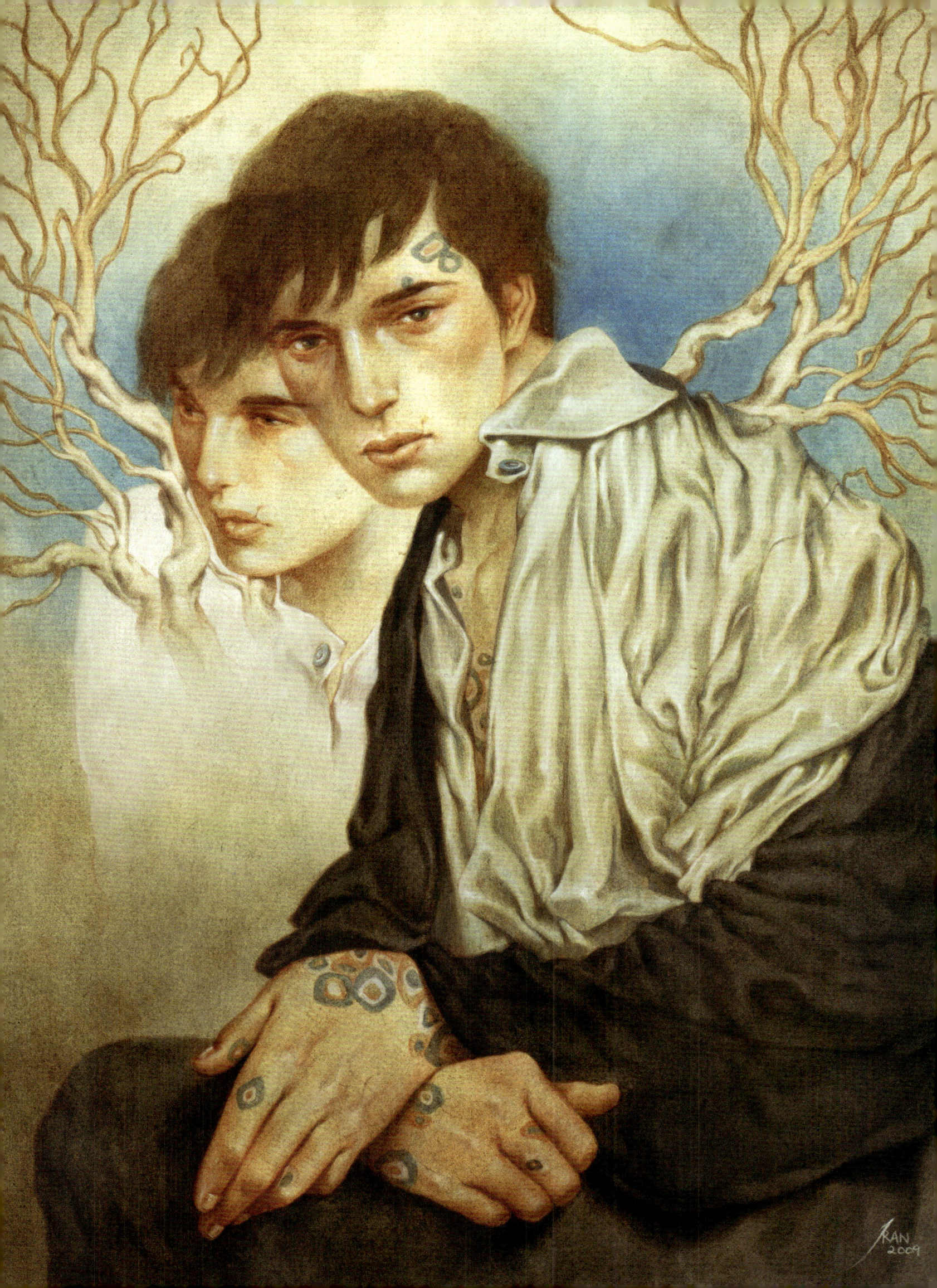

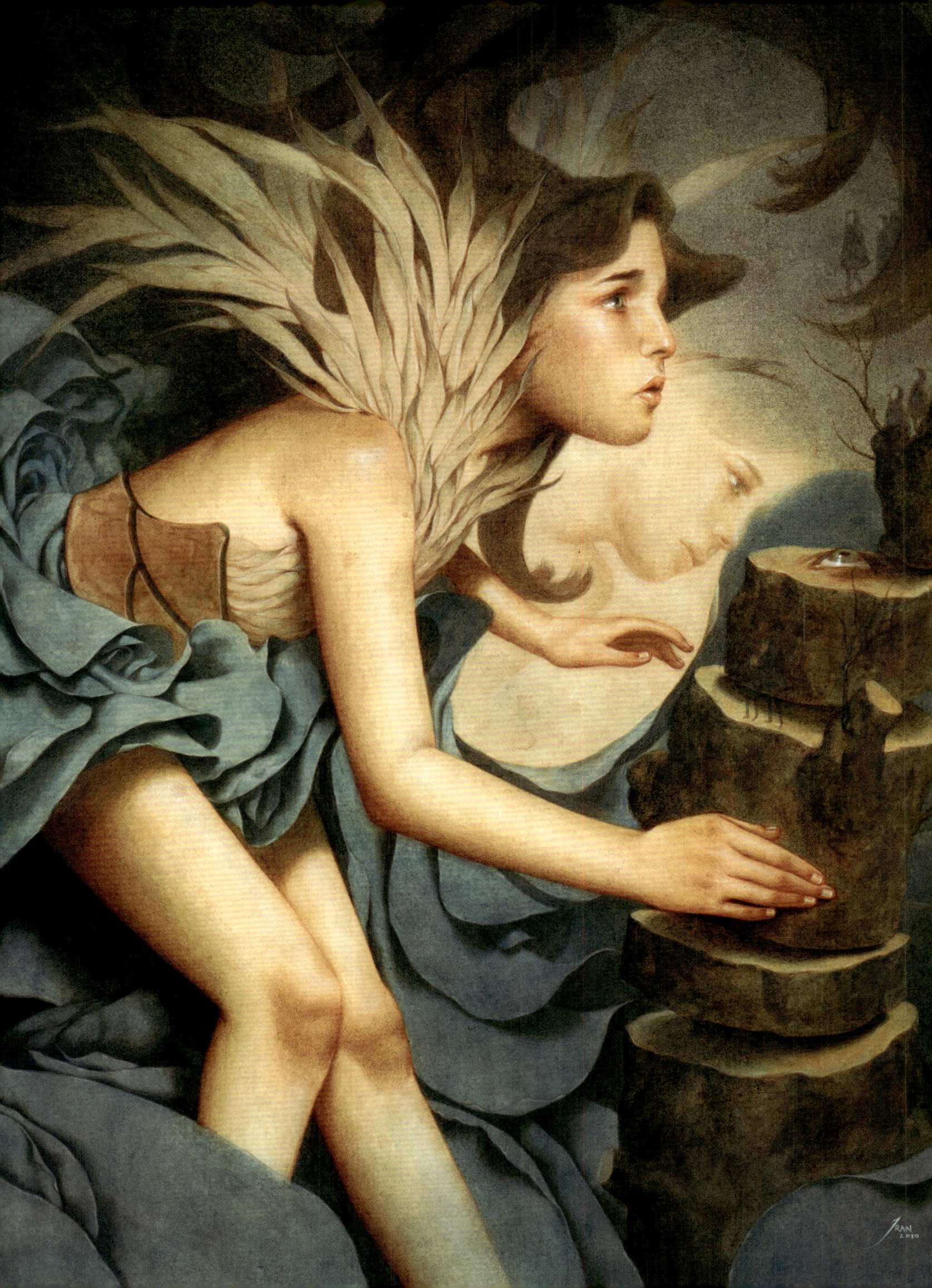

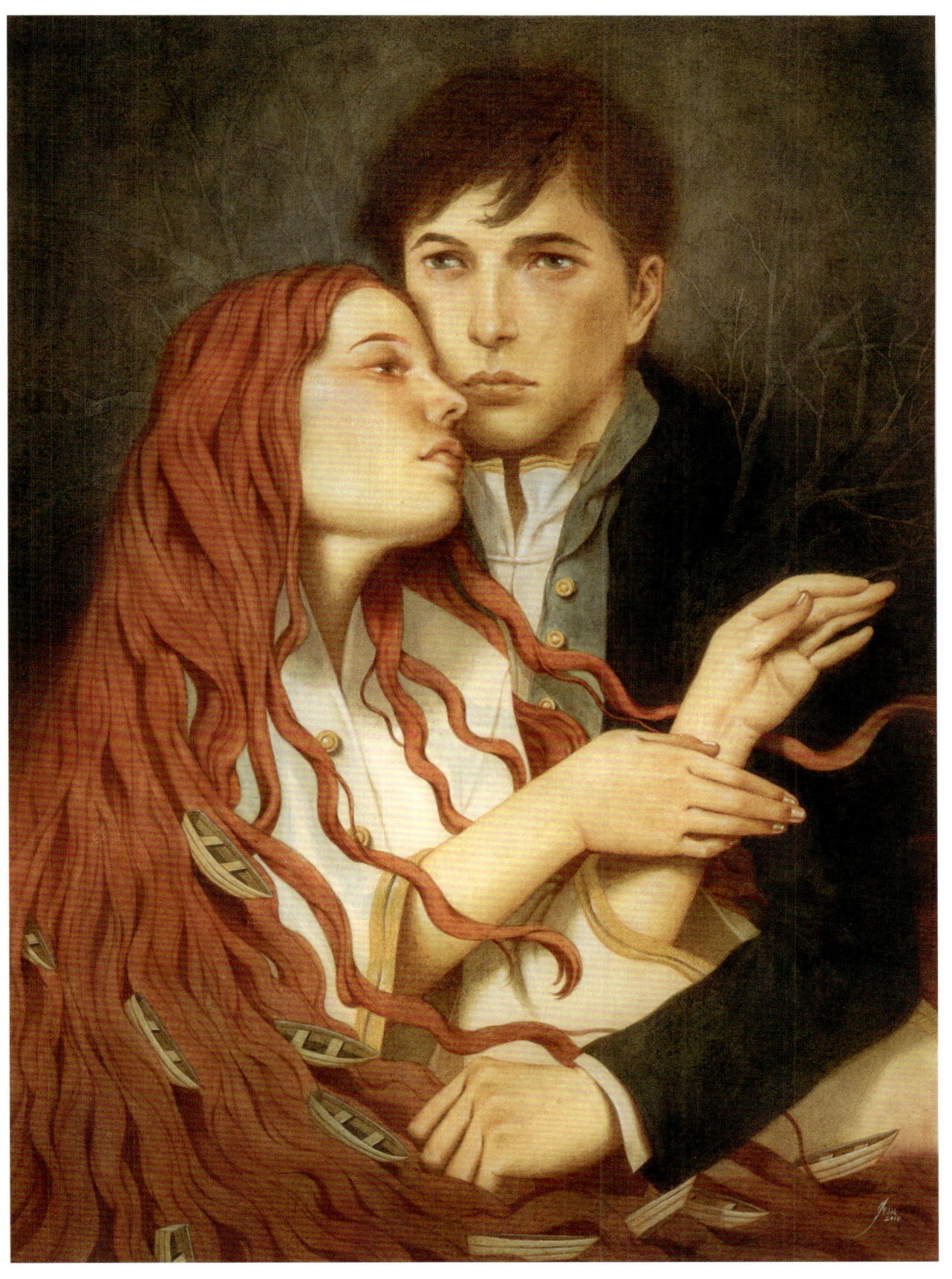

above
AND SHE SAID TO HIM
acrylic & colored pencil on paper, 12" x 16", 2010

left
AND OUR WORLD CAME TUMBLING AFTER
acrylic & colored pencil on paper, 12" x 16", 2010

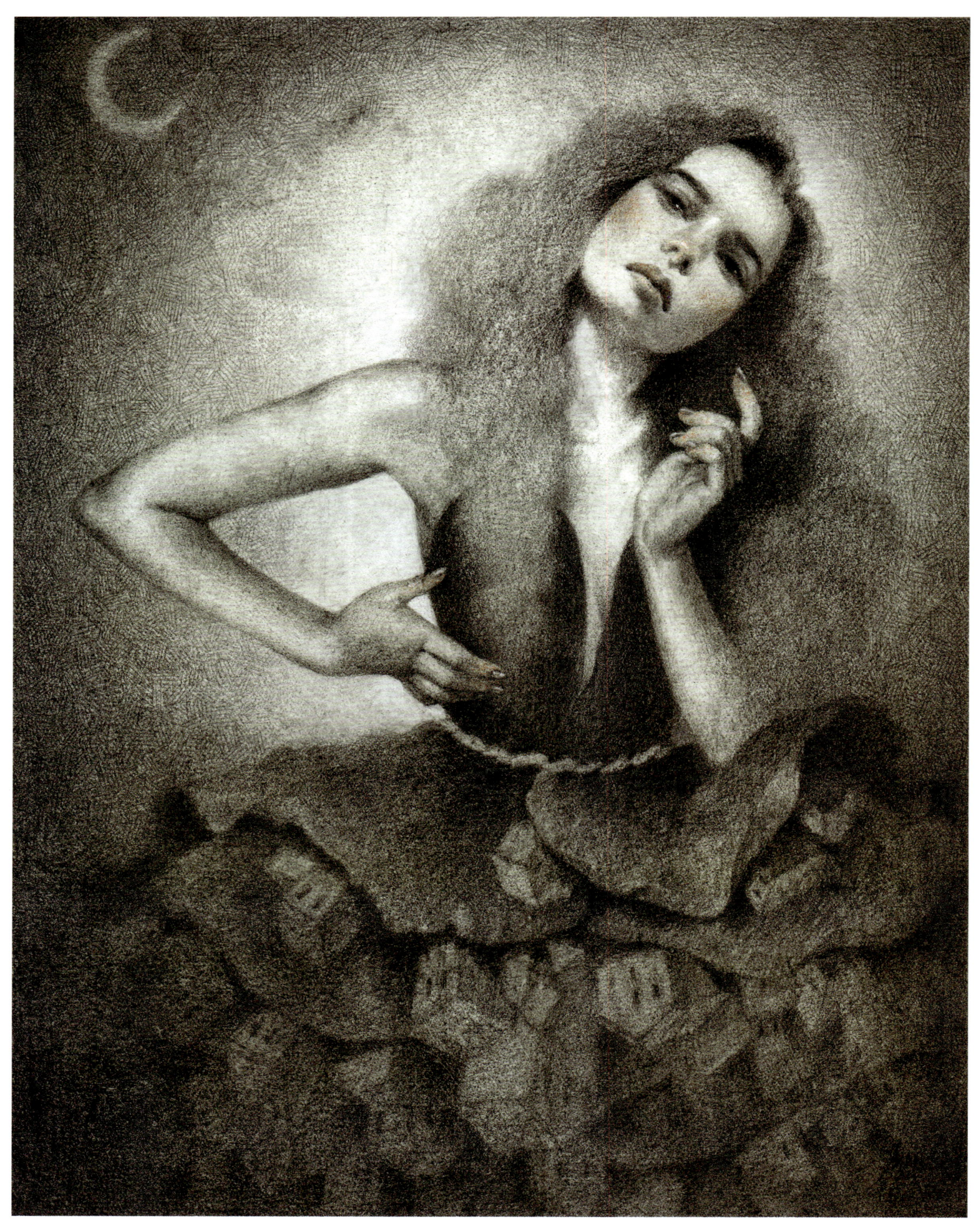

IN THE STATE OF A VAGABOND
graphite & colored pencil on paper, 8" x 10", 2010

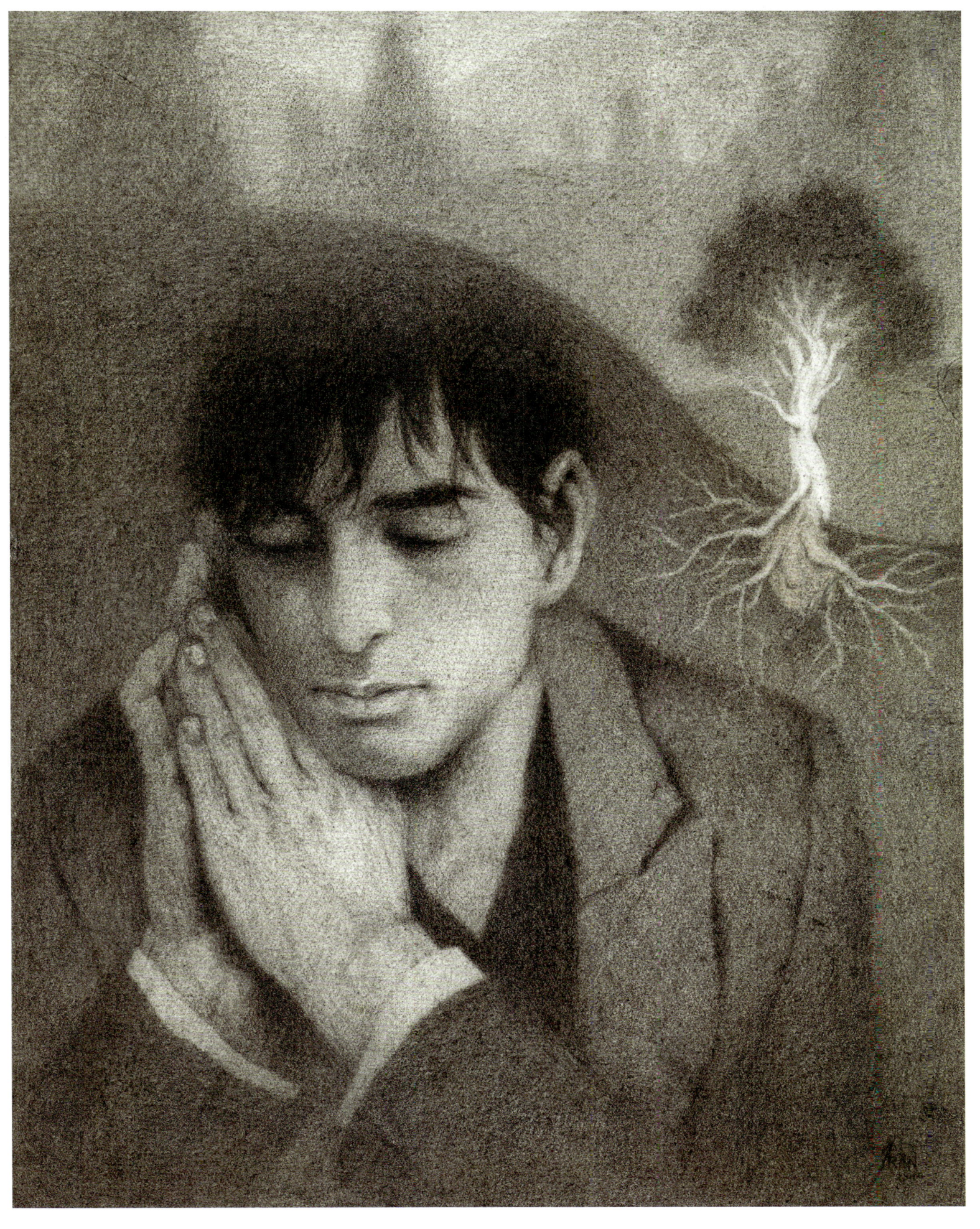

BURIED UNDER A BURDEN TREE
graphite & colored pencil on paper, 8" x 10", 2010

DO NOT BREATHE IN THE MOON
acrylic & colored pencil on paper, 16" x 20", 2010

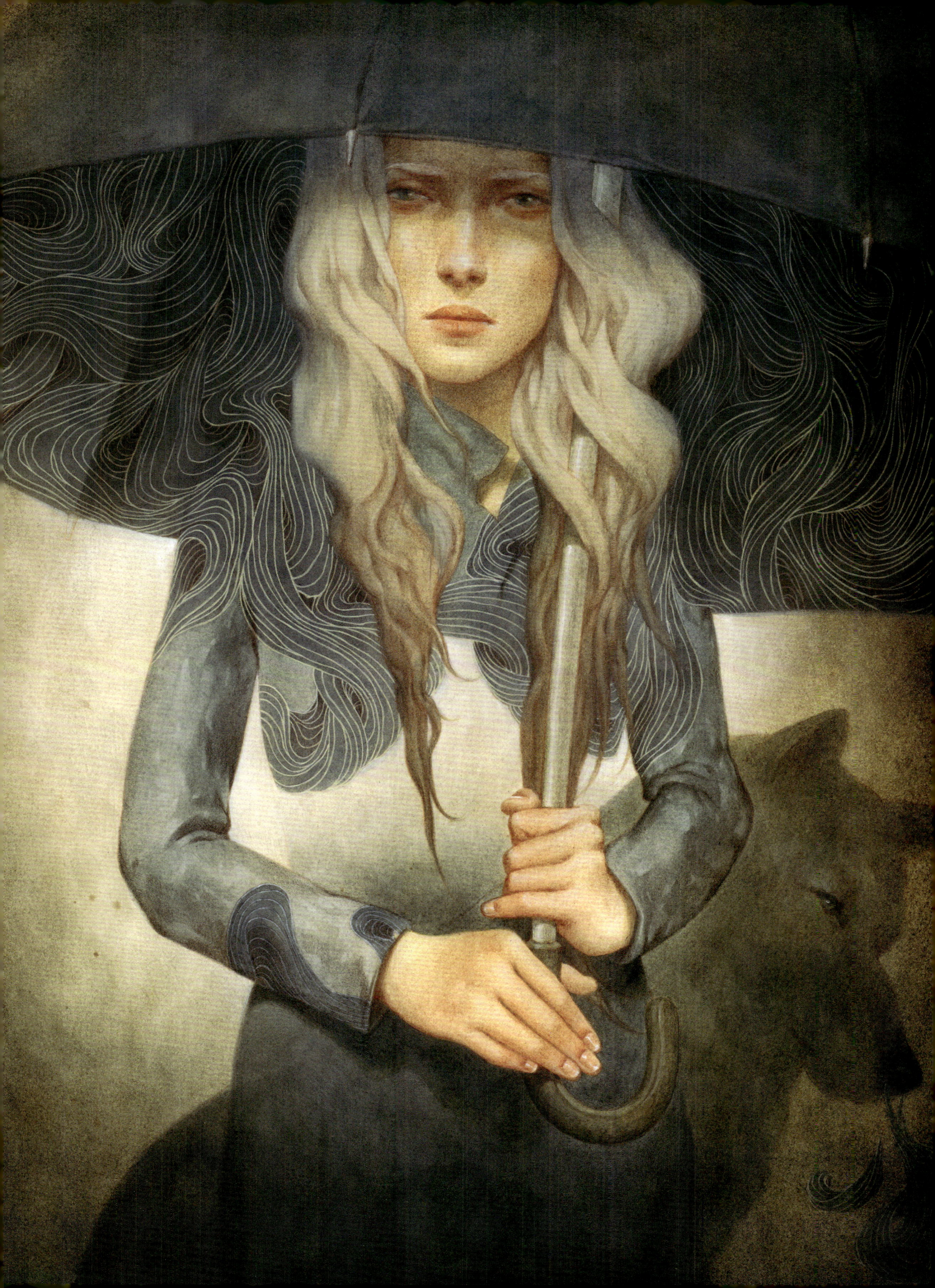

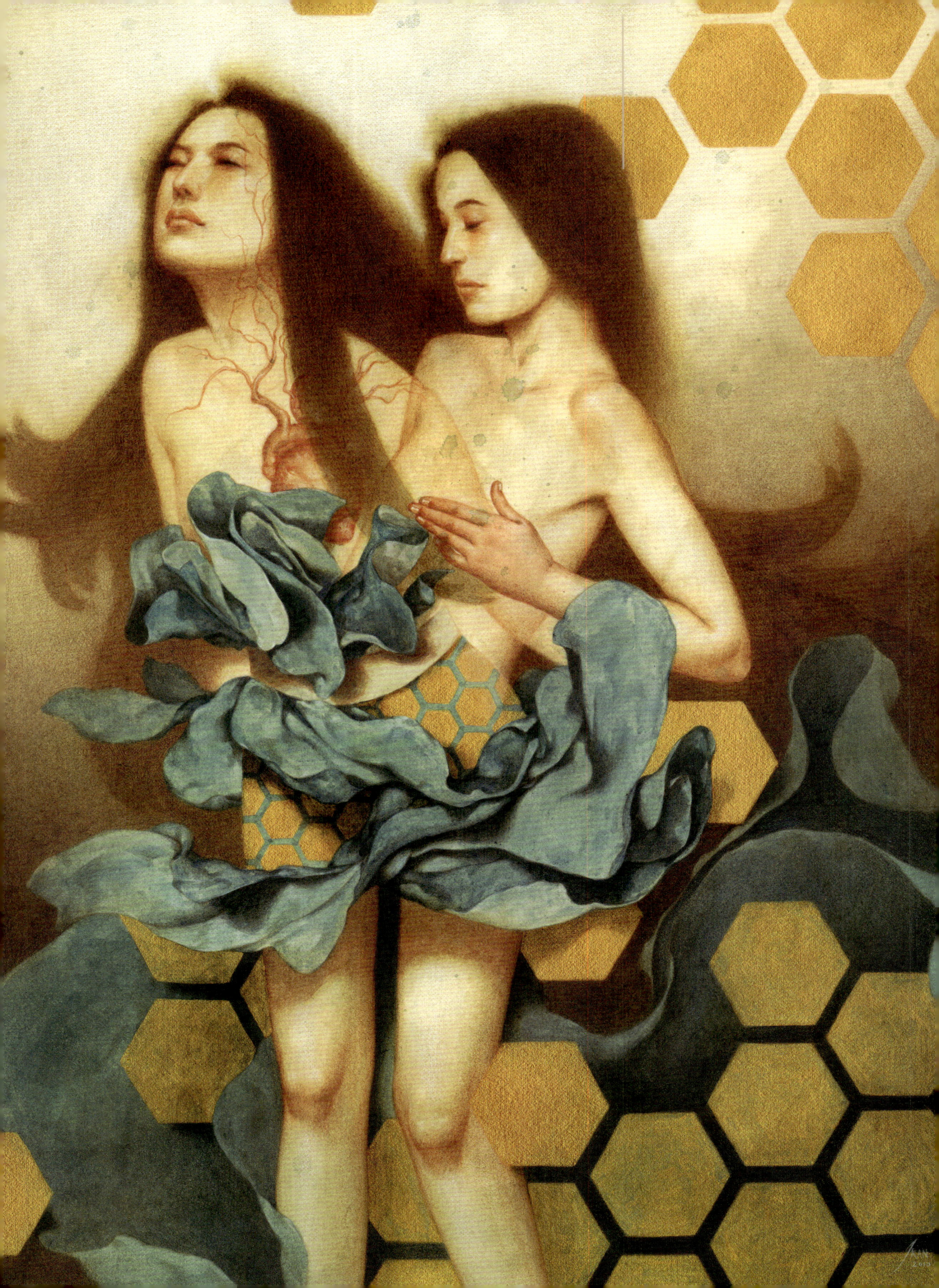

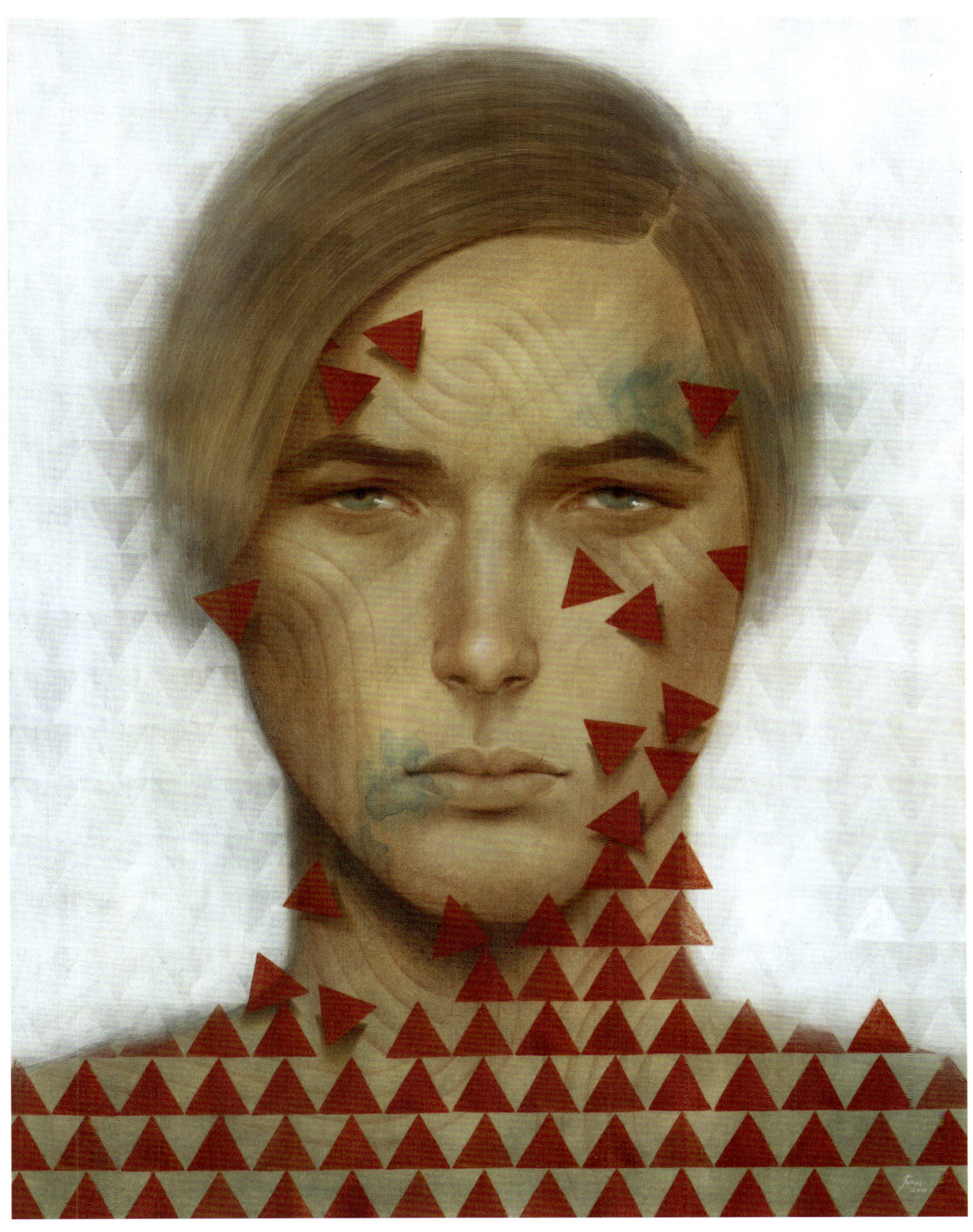

above
REARRANGING YOUR CLUTTERED MIND
acrylic & colored pencil on paper, 16" x 20", 2010

left
PARTING FROM YOUR WAYWARD HEART
acrylic & colored pencil on paper, 12" x 16", 2010

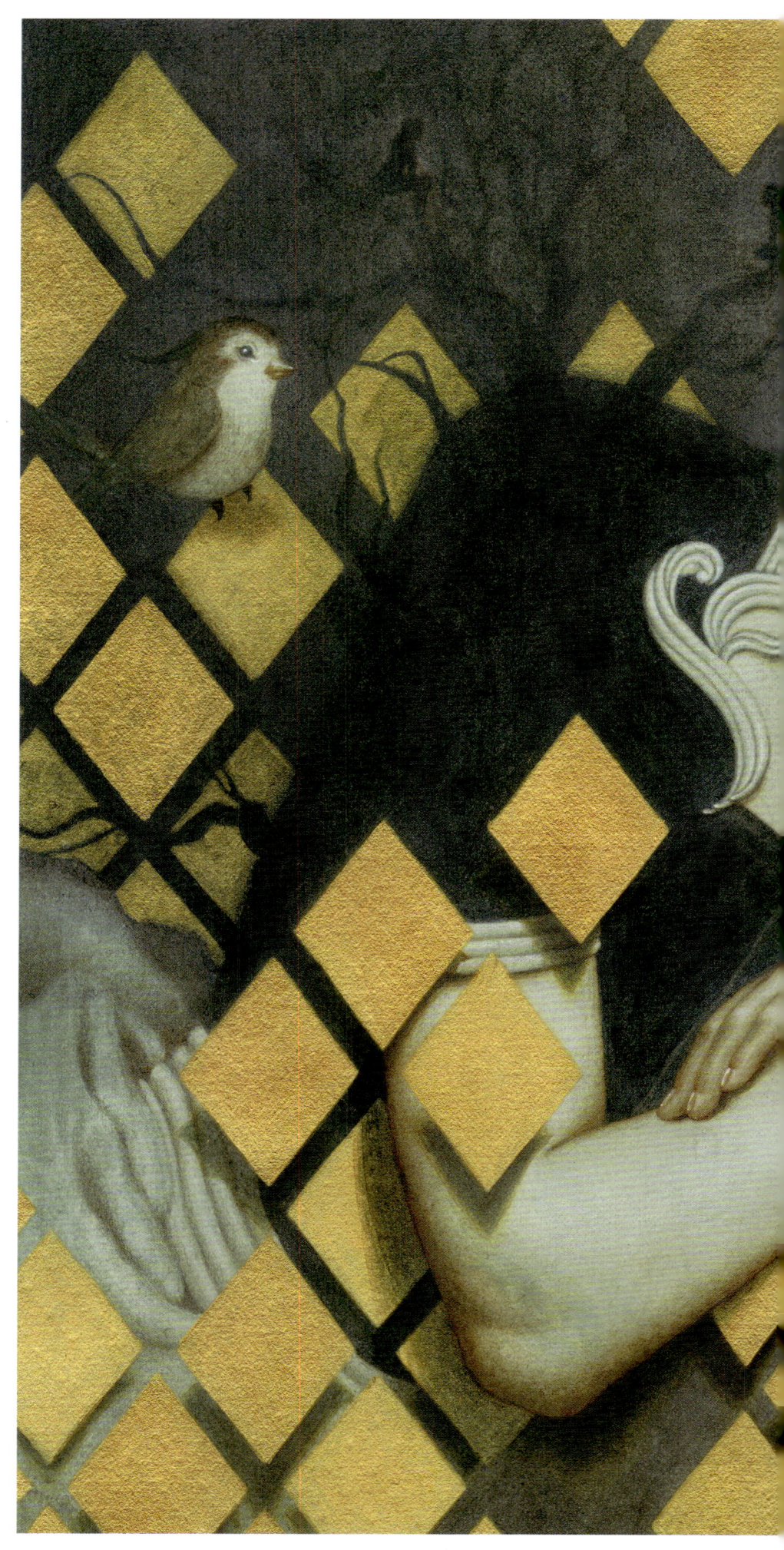

THE COLOR CF A COLORLESS SOUL
acrylic & colored pencil on paper, 15.5" x 11.5", 2010

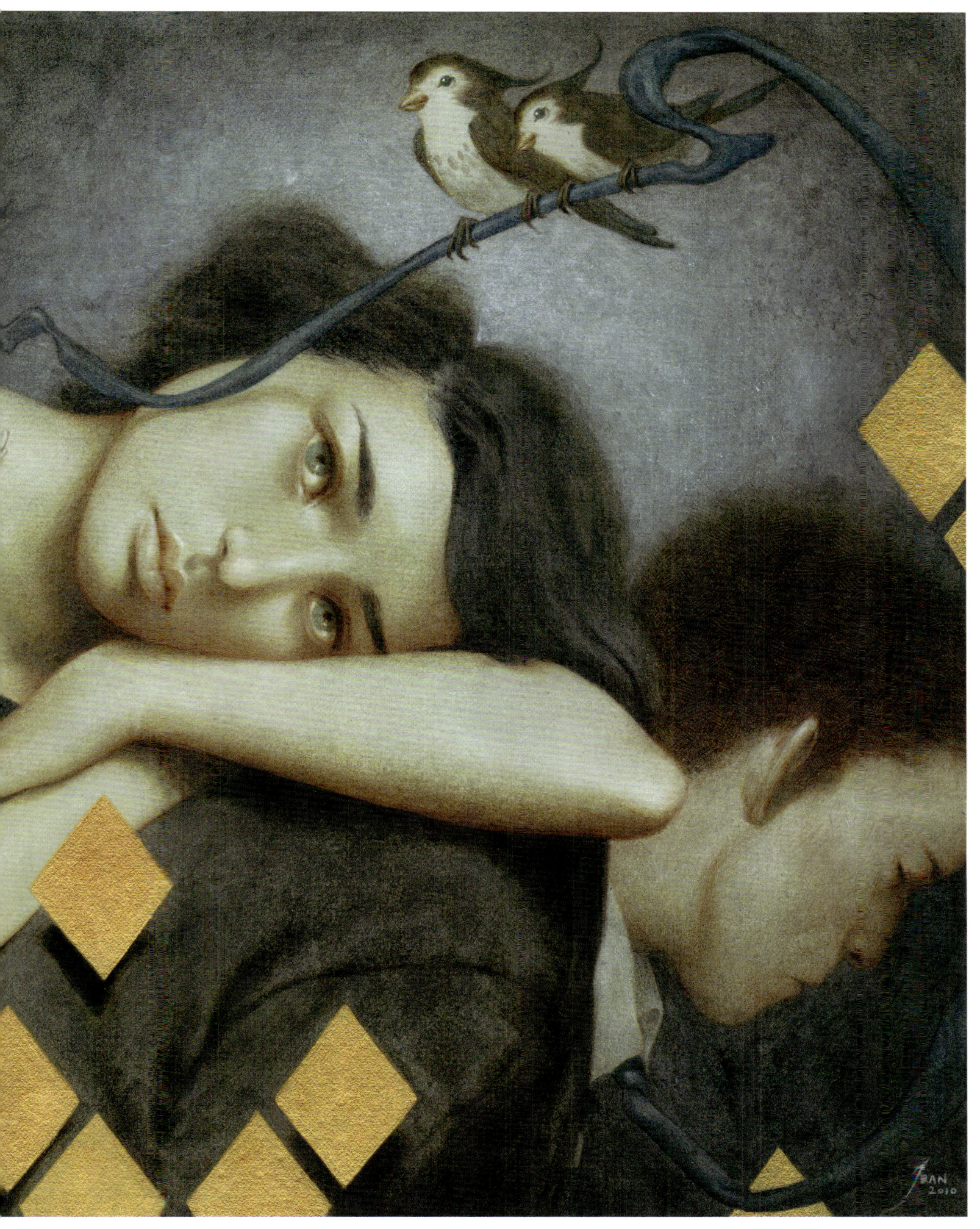

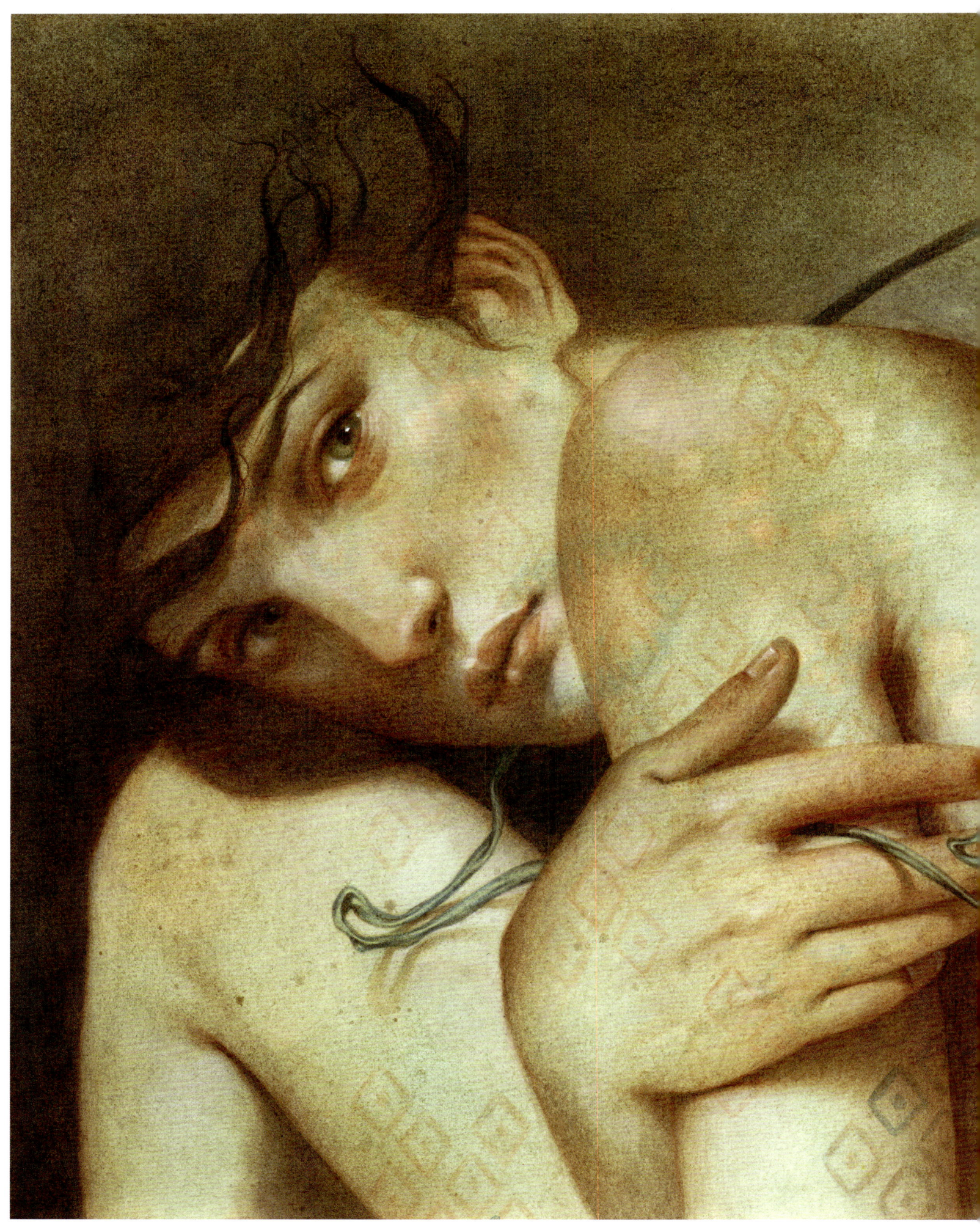

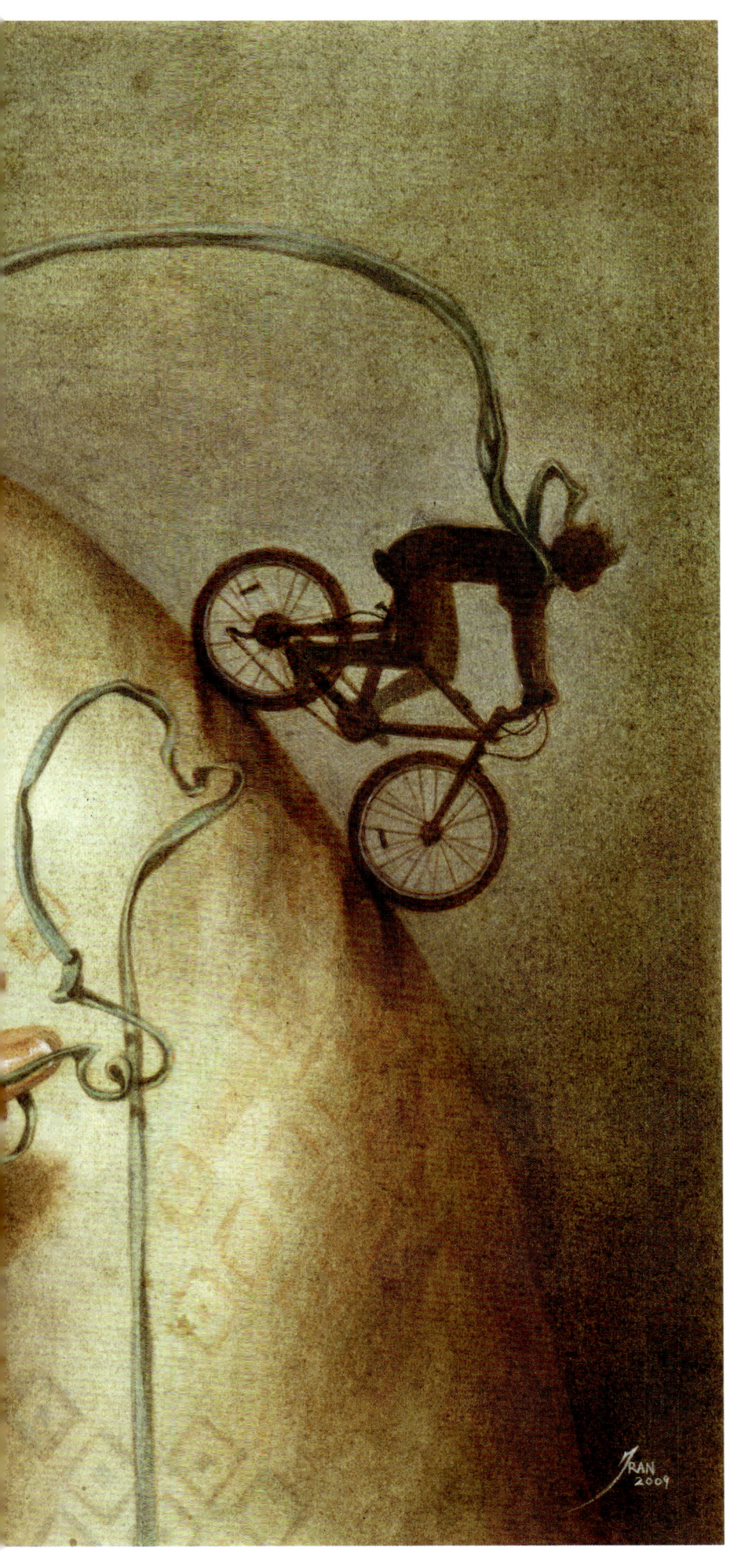

CONSTELLAR

2010

Unlike the other series, *Constellar* is a trilogy that explores the fantastical side of melancholy. It was exhibited at Jonathan LeVine Gallery in New York City as part of a large group show. It's a departure into psychological landscapes that blend reality with things that are reminiscent of a distant dream. With a more lighthearted touch, the paintings narrate tales of celestial love, an unbounded future and sage-lit caverns.

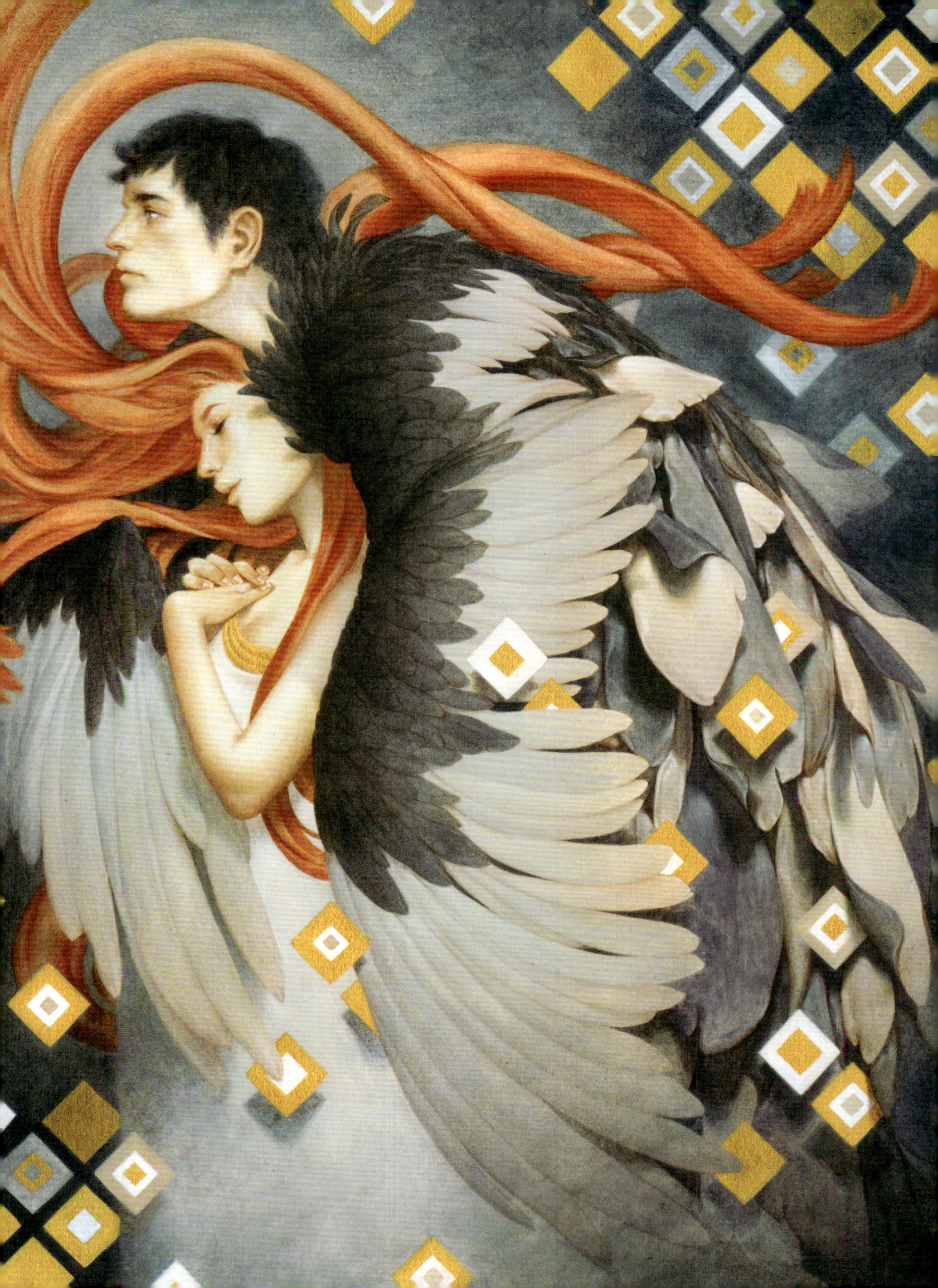

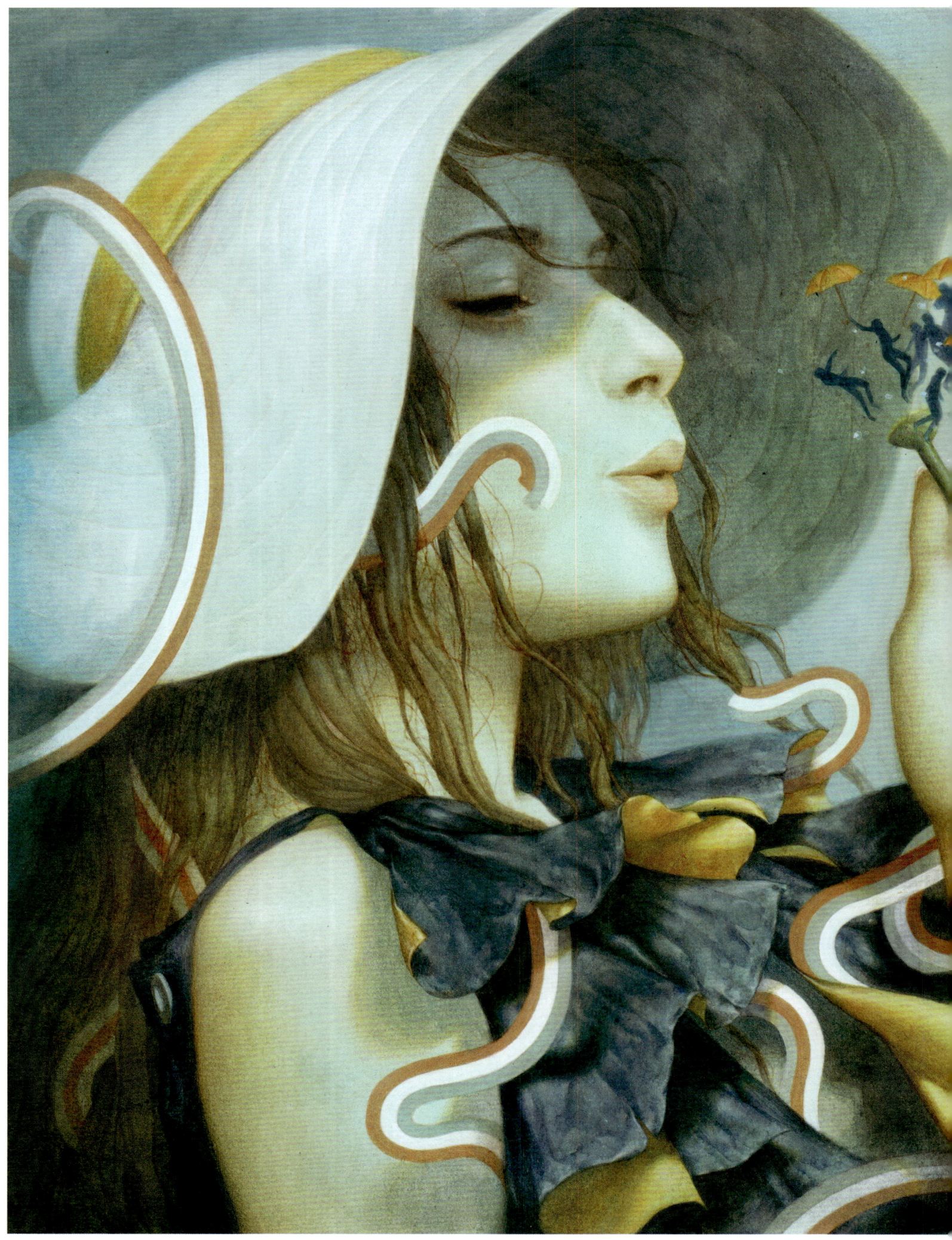

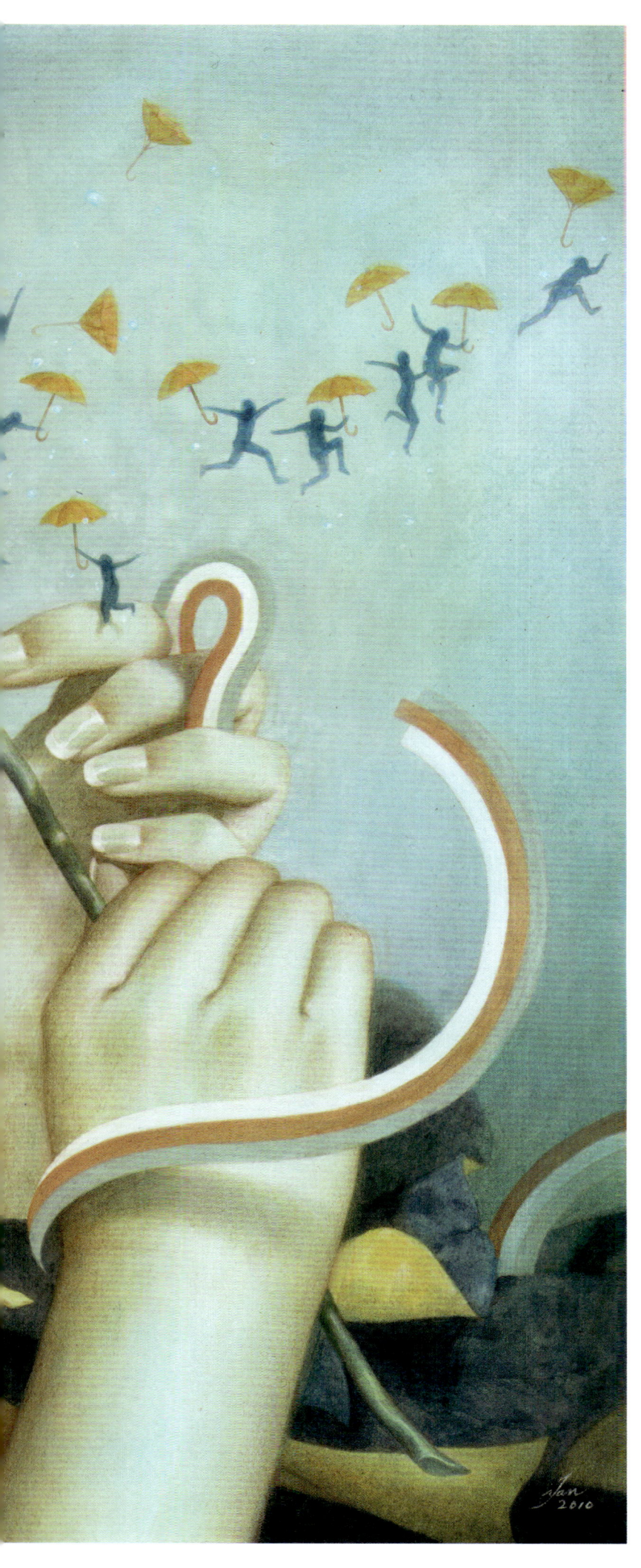

IF THE WORLD KEEPS CHURNING, TURNING
acrylic & colored pencil on paper, 13" x 16", 2010

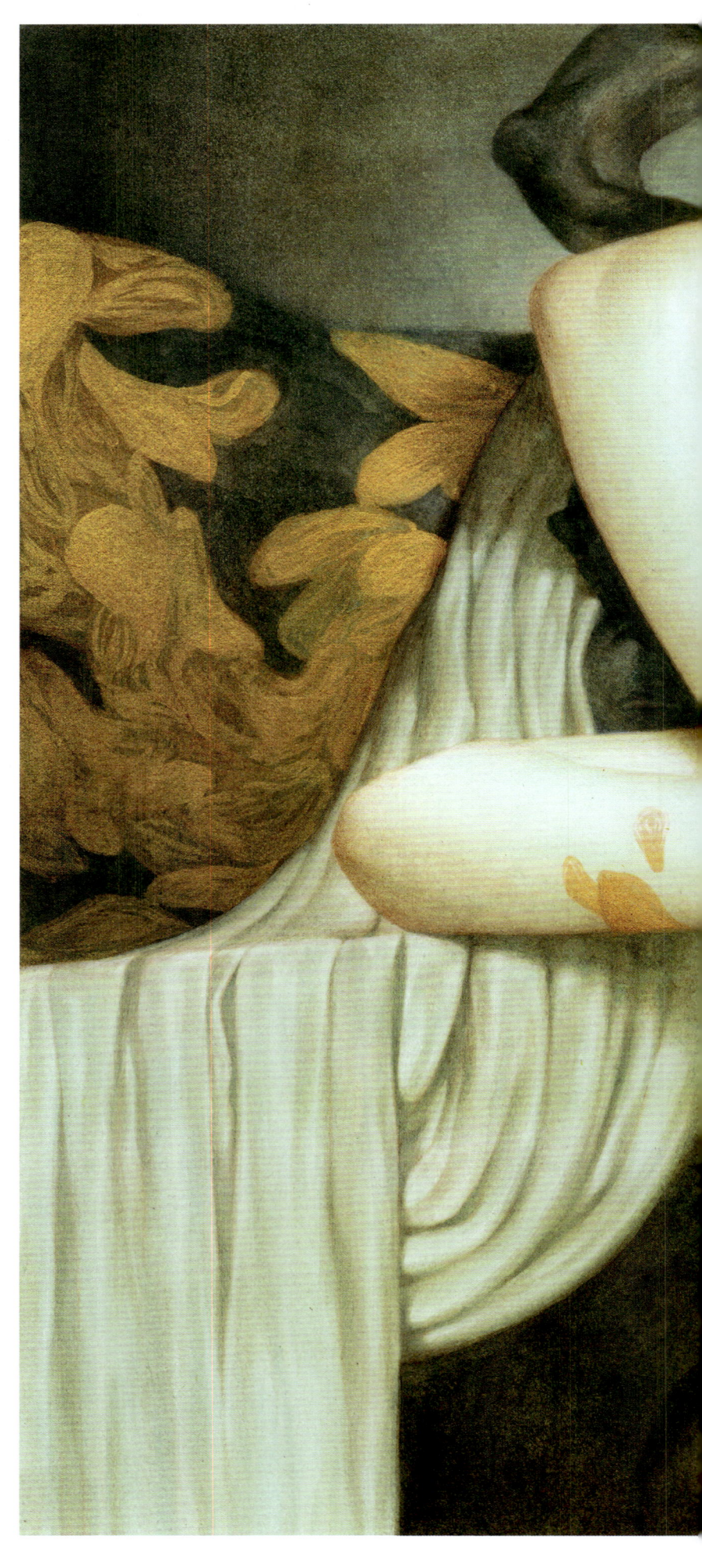

WHEN YOU LEAVE BEHIND A FRAGMENTED MEMORY
acrylic & colored pencil on paper, 12˝ x 16˝, 2010

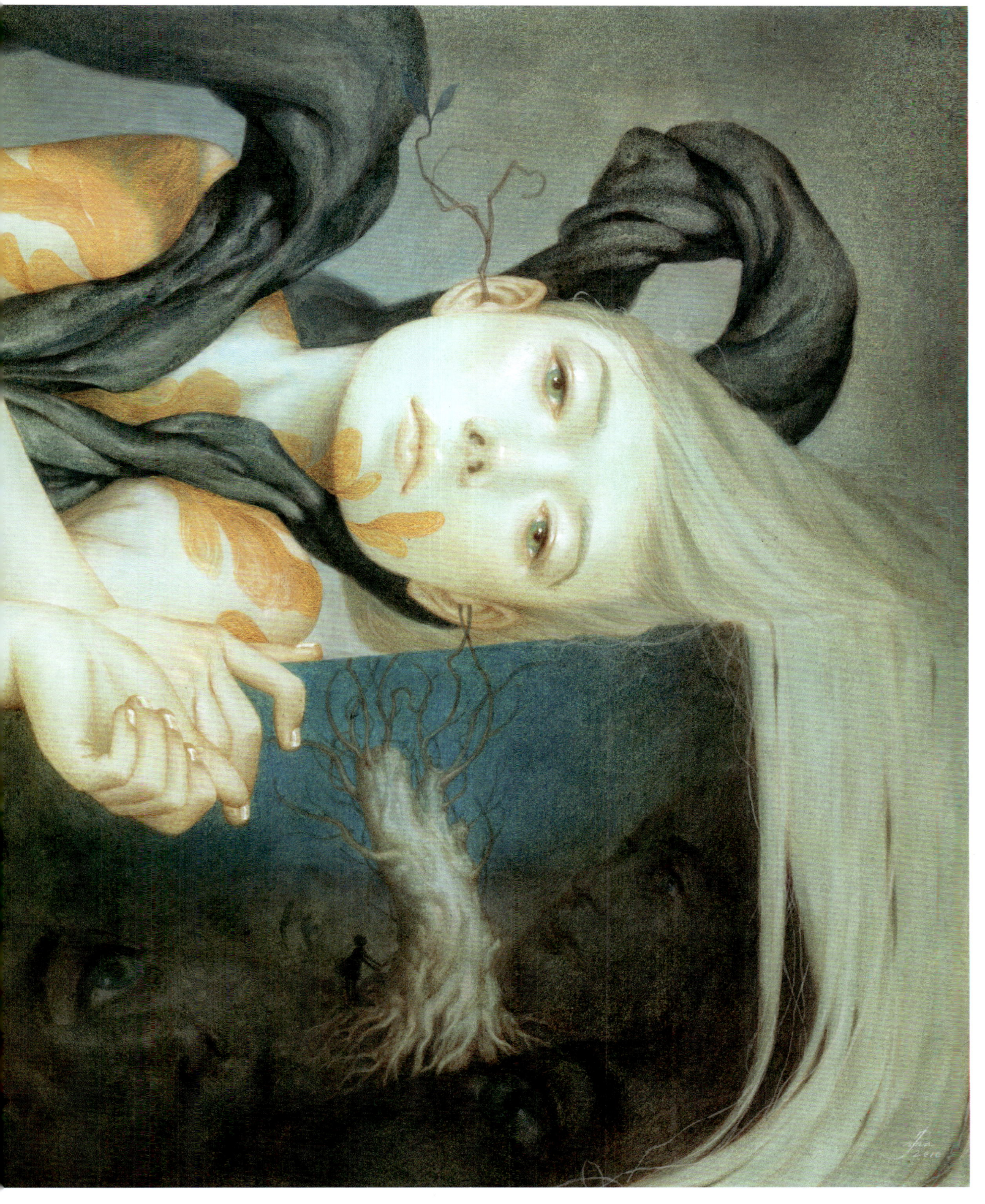

THE SYNAPSE BETWEEN HERE & THERE

2011

By definition, a synapse is *the region at which a nerve impulse passes from one neuron (here) to another (there)*. It's where raw and visceral responses originate in the brain.

This collection of thirteen paintings—one of my largest bodies of work—was completed for my third solo exhibition and showcased at ThinkSpace Art Gallery. The concept behind it focuses on the kindling condition of the mind and its inner workings. I wanted to abstractly depict the mind as it responds to stimuli by giving form to the impulsion, which is represented by billowing fabric and floating geometric shapes. This is also when I painted *Treading to an Untrimmed Memory* and found my love for larger-than-life figures.

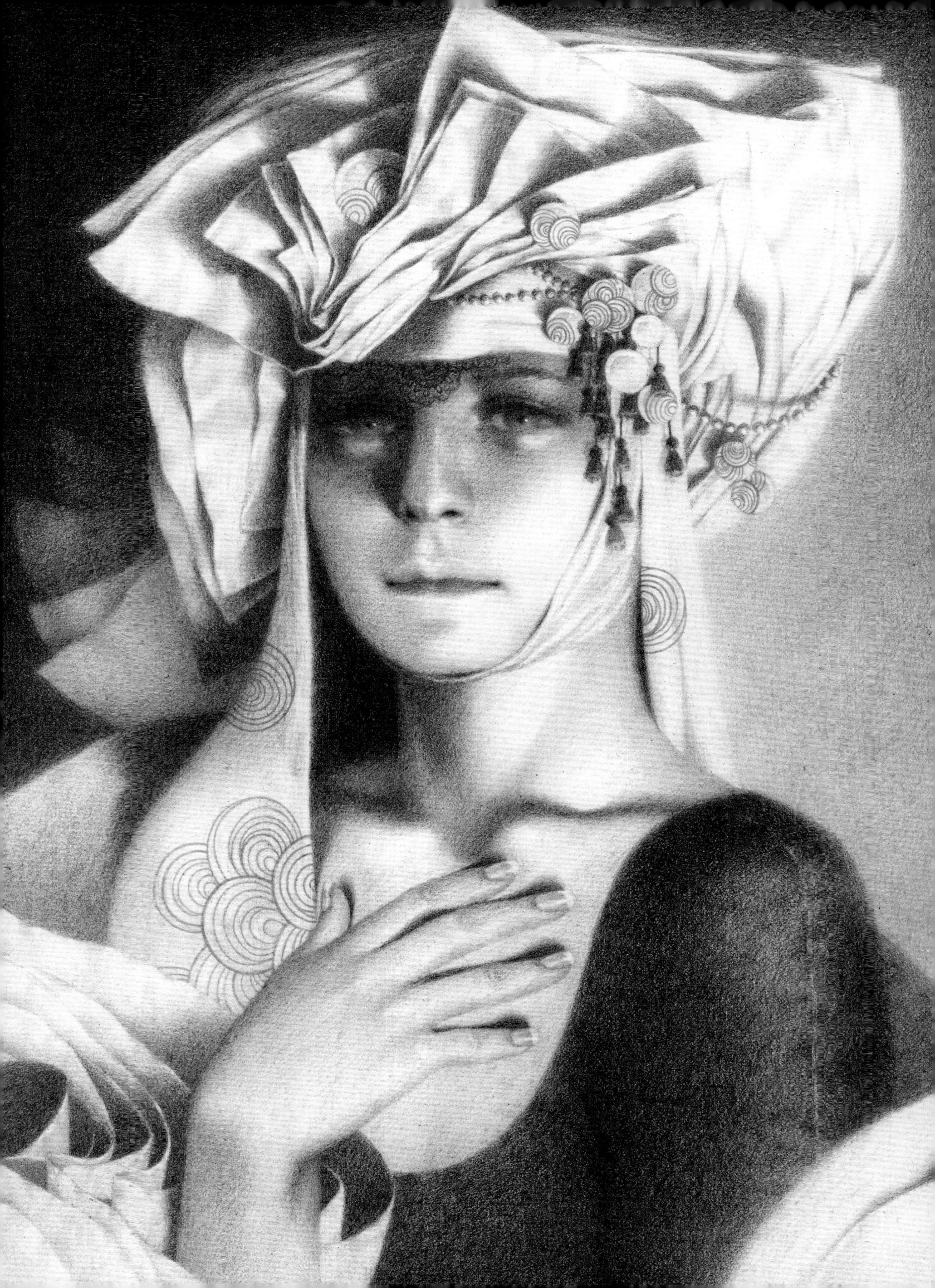

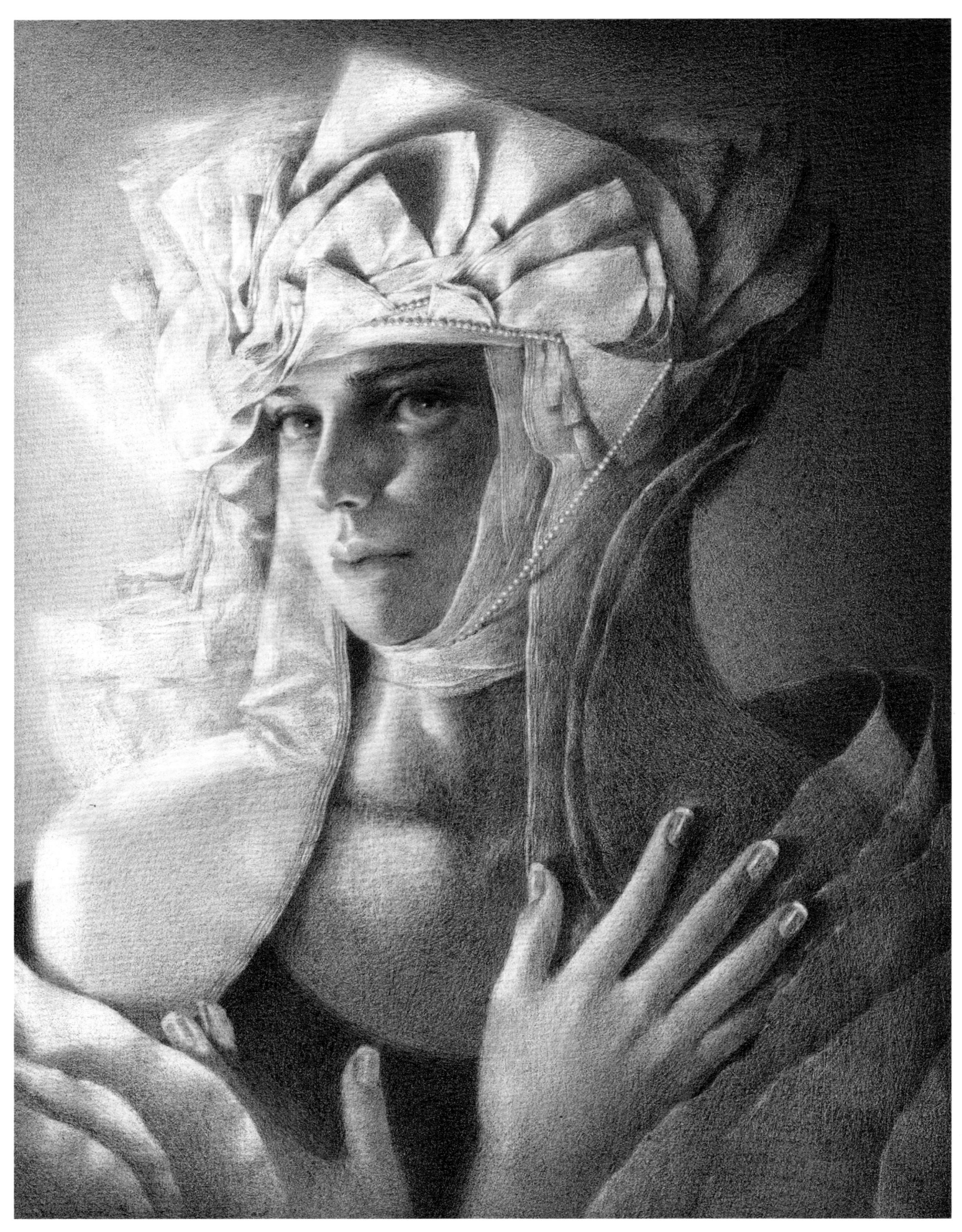

IT FEELS LIKE A PALLID EMPATHY
graphite on paper, 11" x 14", 2011

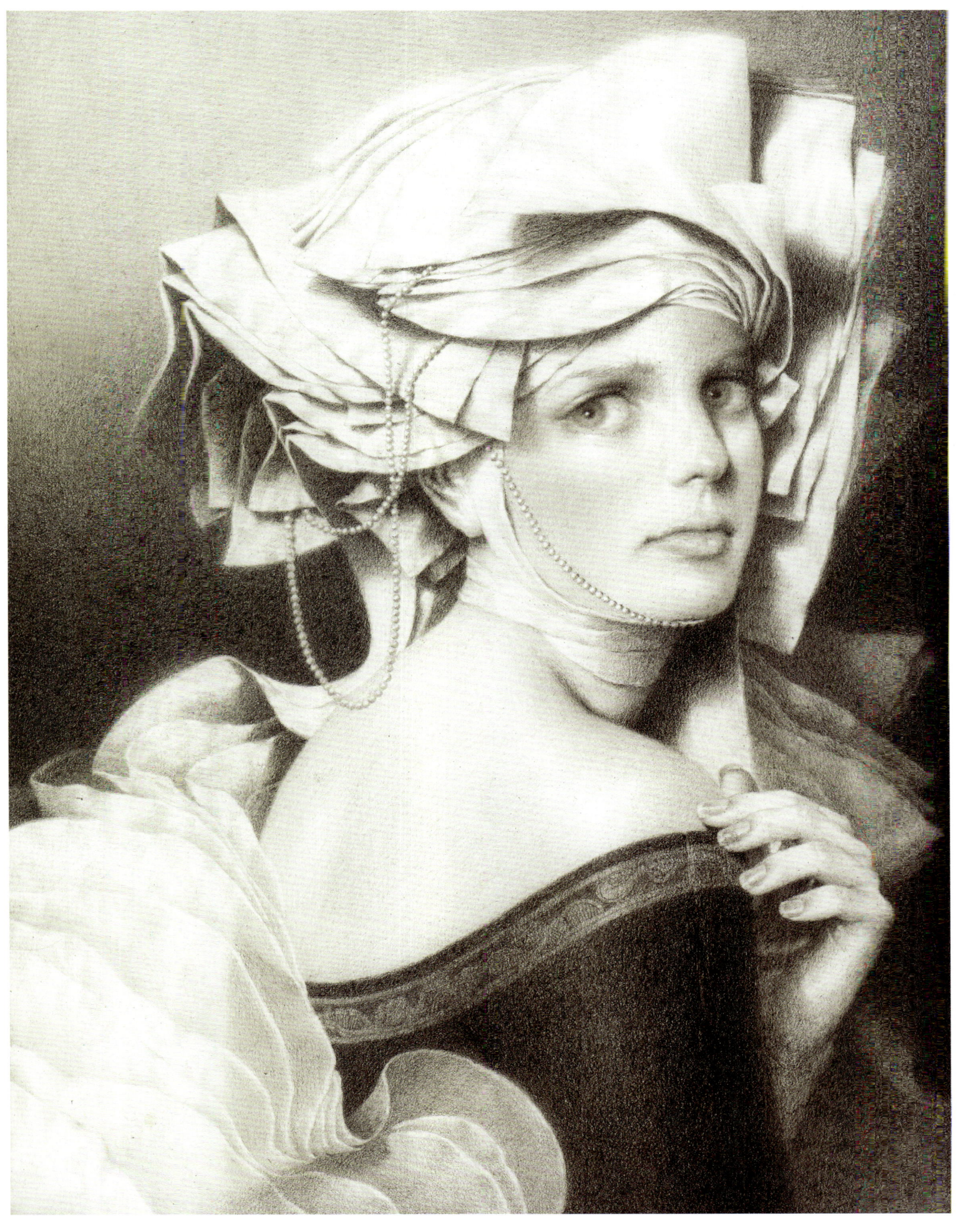

CONFRONTED WITH AN OVER-EXPOSED MARQUEE
graphite on paper, 11" x 14", 2011

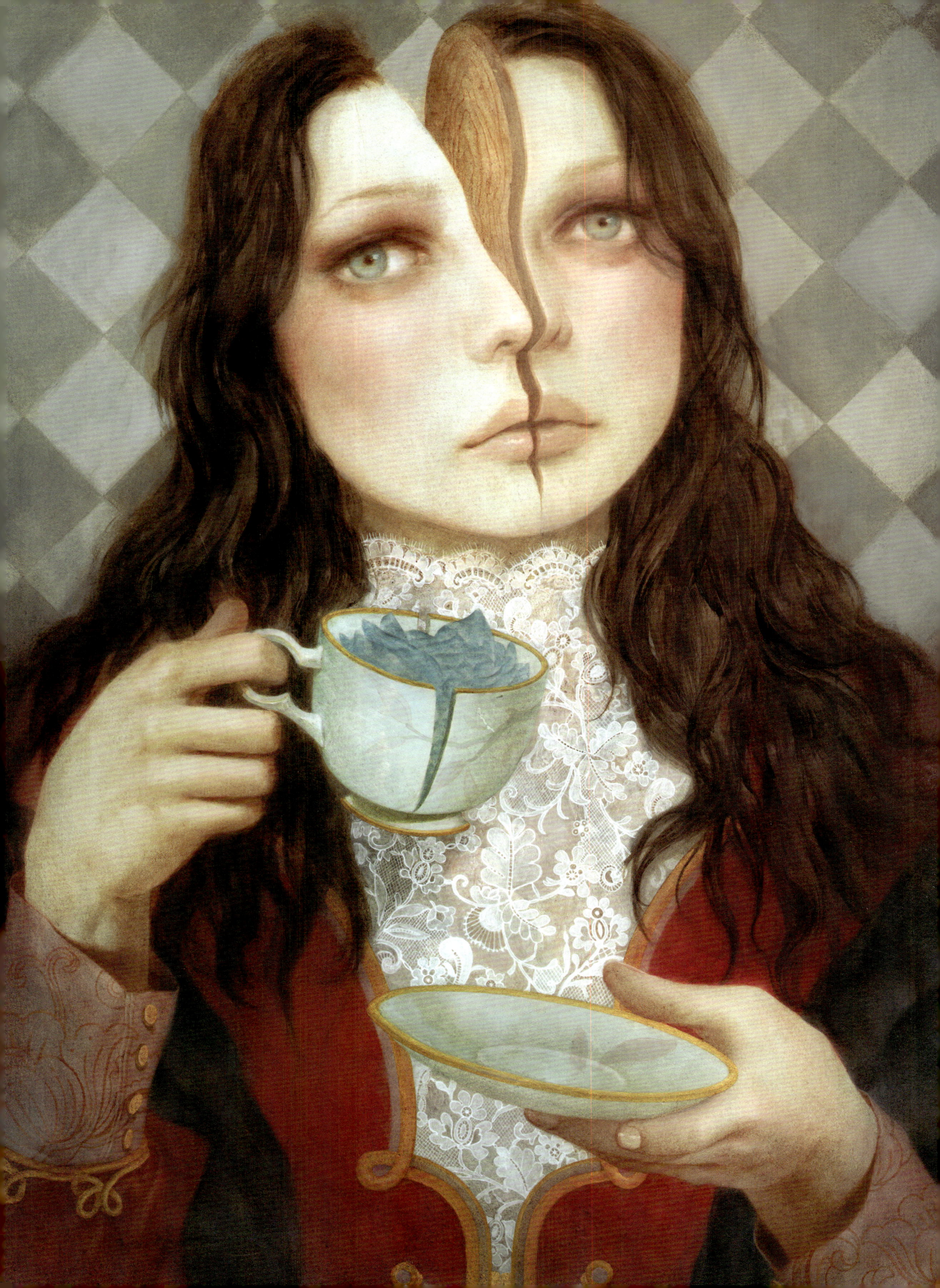

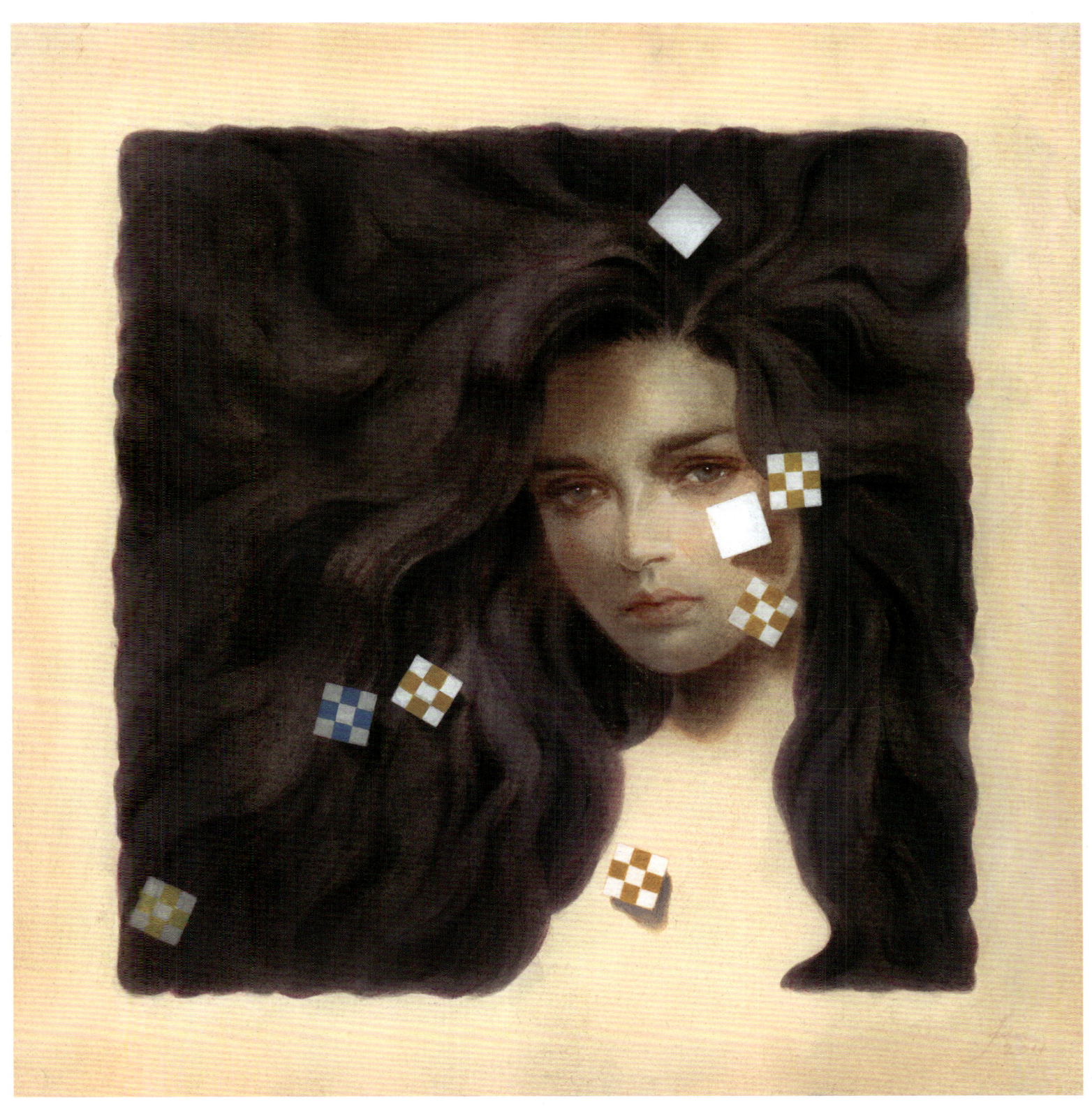

IN THE CORNERS OF YOUR EQUILATERAL MIND
acrylic & colored pencil on paper, 10" x 13", 2011

left
I CAME ACROSS A WILTING COGNITION
acrylic & colored pencil on paper, 18" x 25", 2011

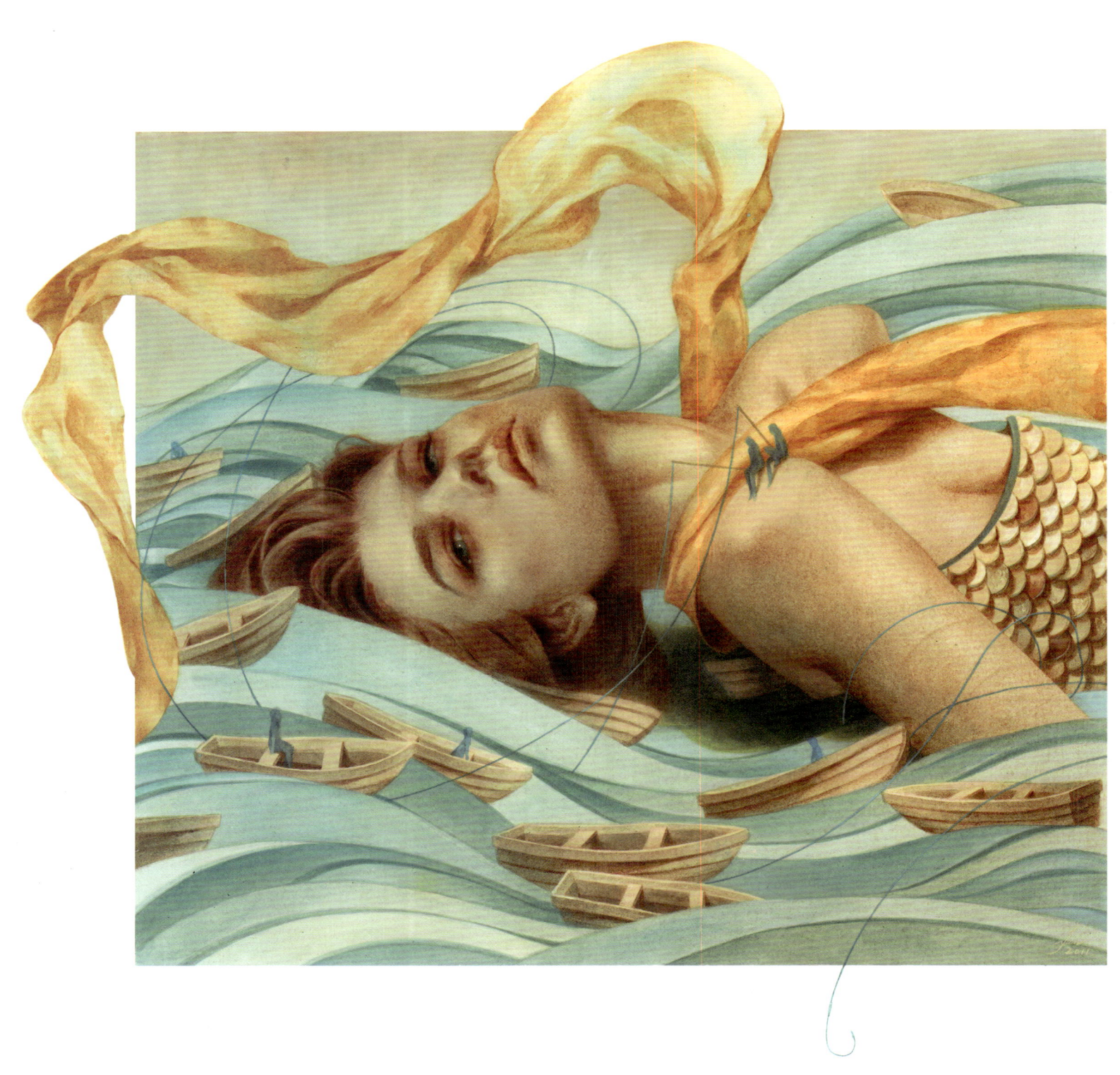

CAST INTO A RIPPLED MENTALITY
acrylic & colored pencil on paper, 14" x 18", 2011

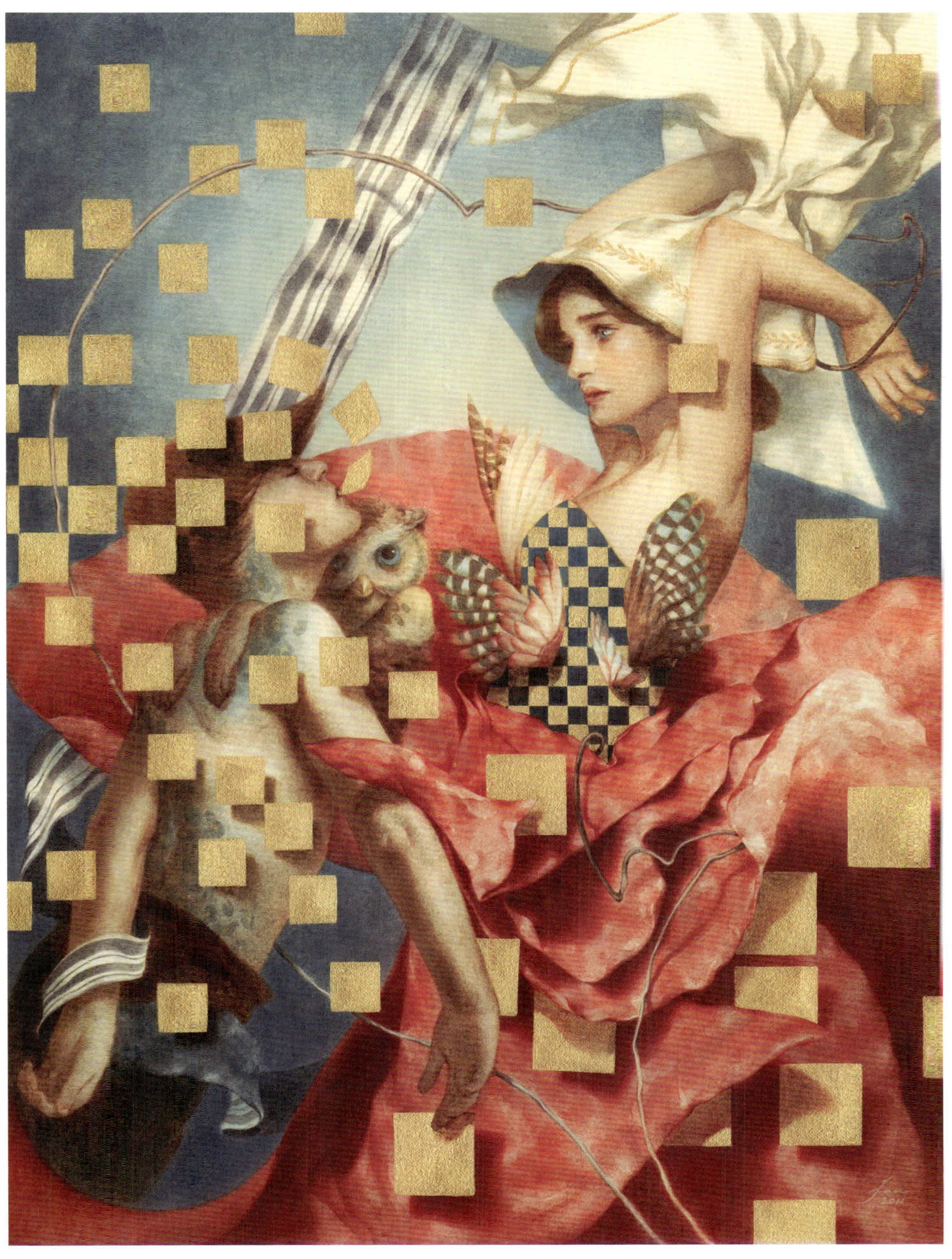

LIVING PARALLEL TO AN INFECTIOUS PIGMENT
acrylic & colored pencil on paper, 13" x 17", 2011

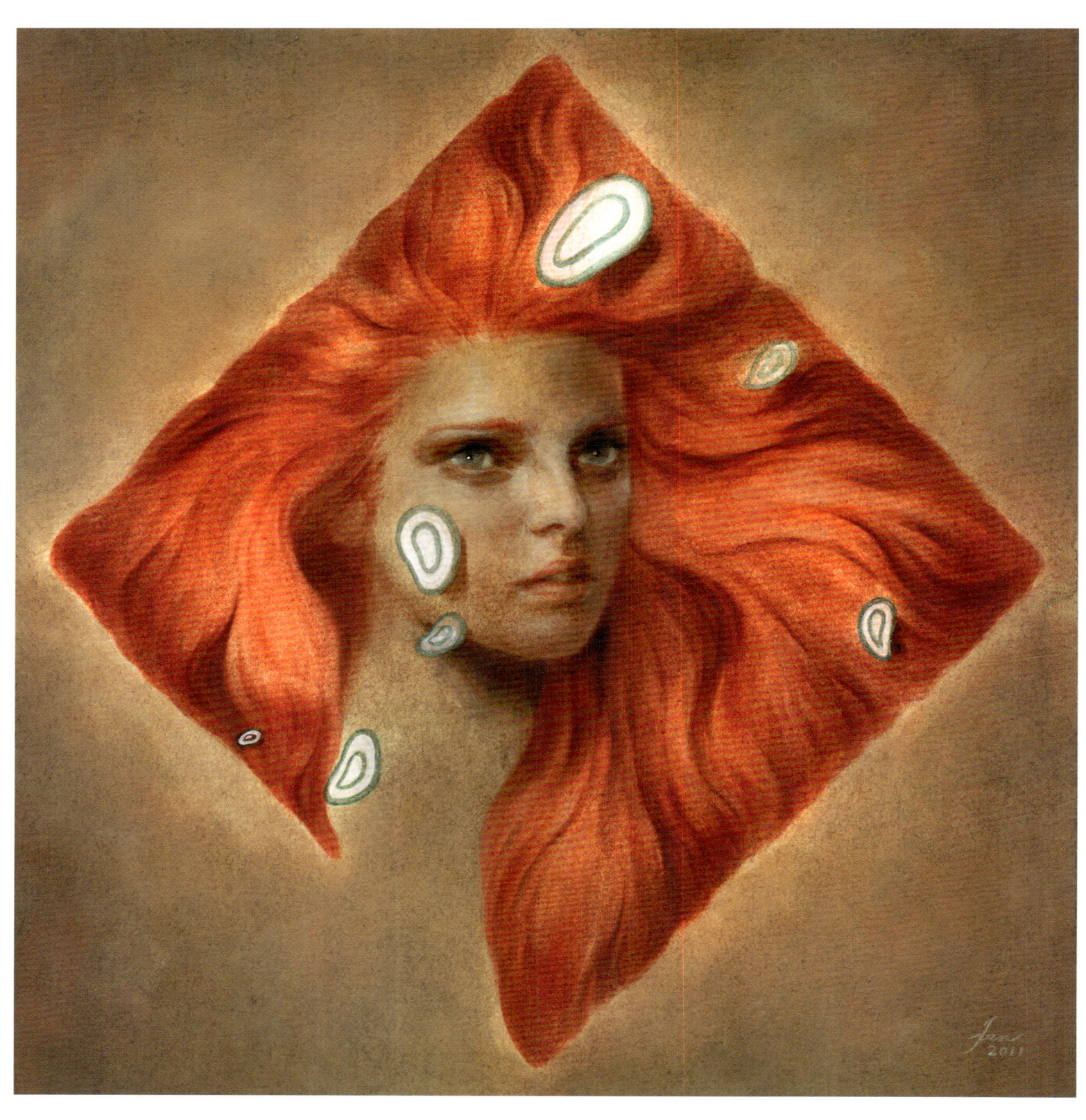

MY CONVERSATION WITH AN ANGULAR THOUGHT
acrylic & colored pencil on paper, 10" x 10", 2011

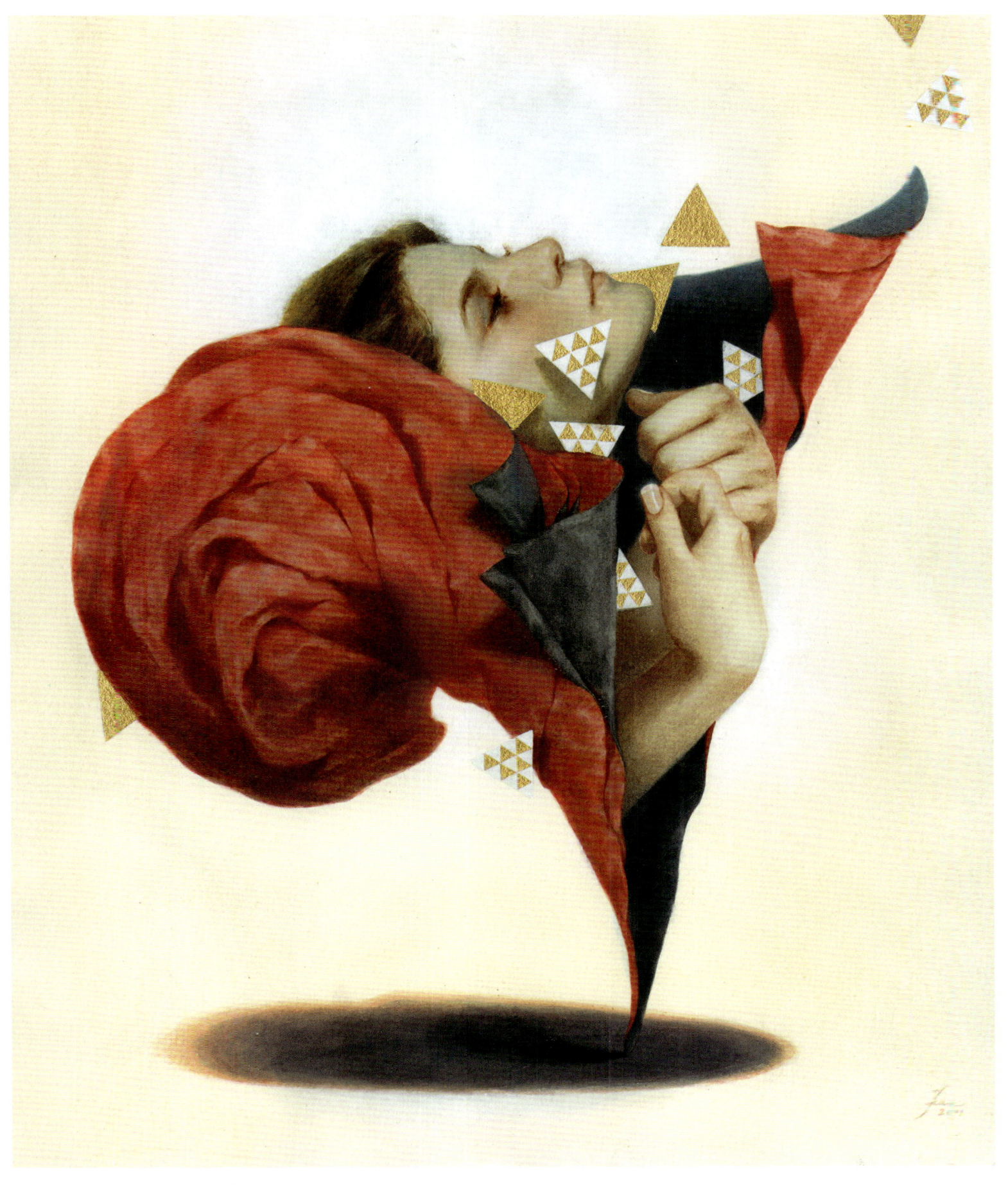

SEARCHING FOR AN UNCHARTED HYPOTENUSE
acrylic & colored pencil on paper, 12" x 14", 2011

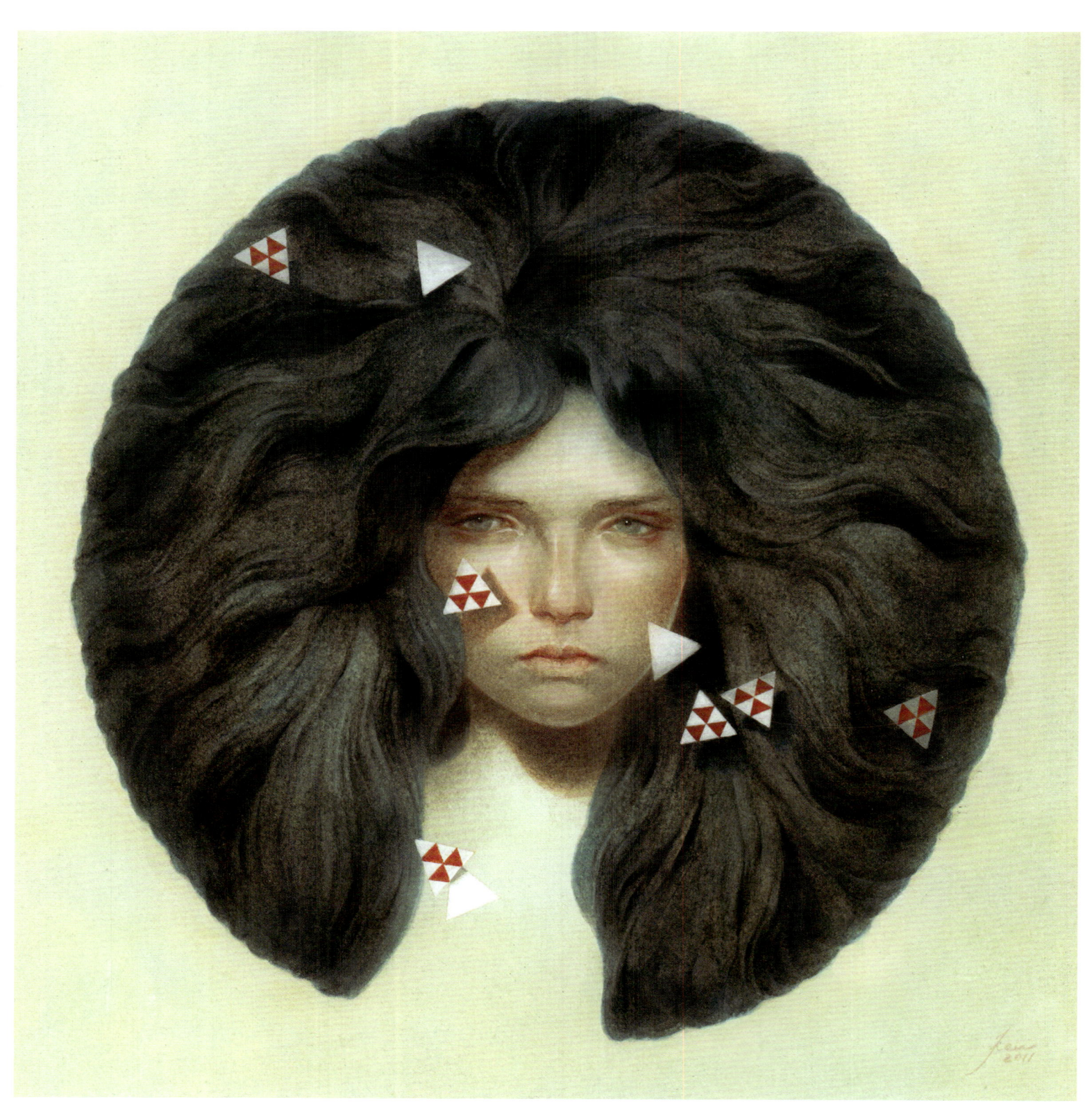

THE DIAMETER OF A DIM ENDEAVOR
acrylic & colored pencil on paper, 10" x 10", 2011

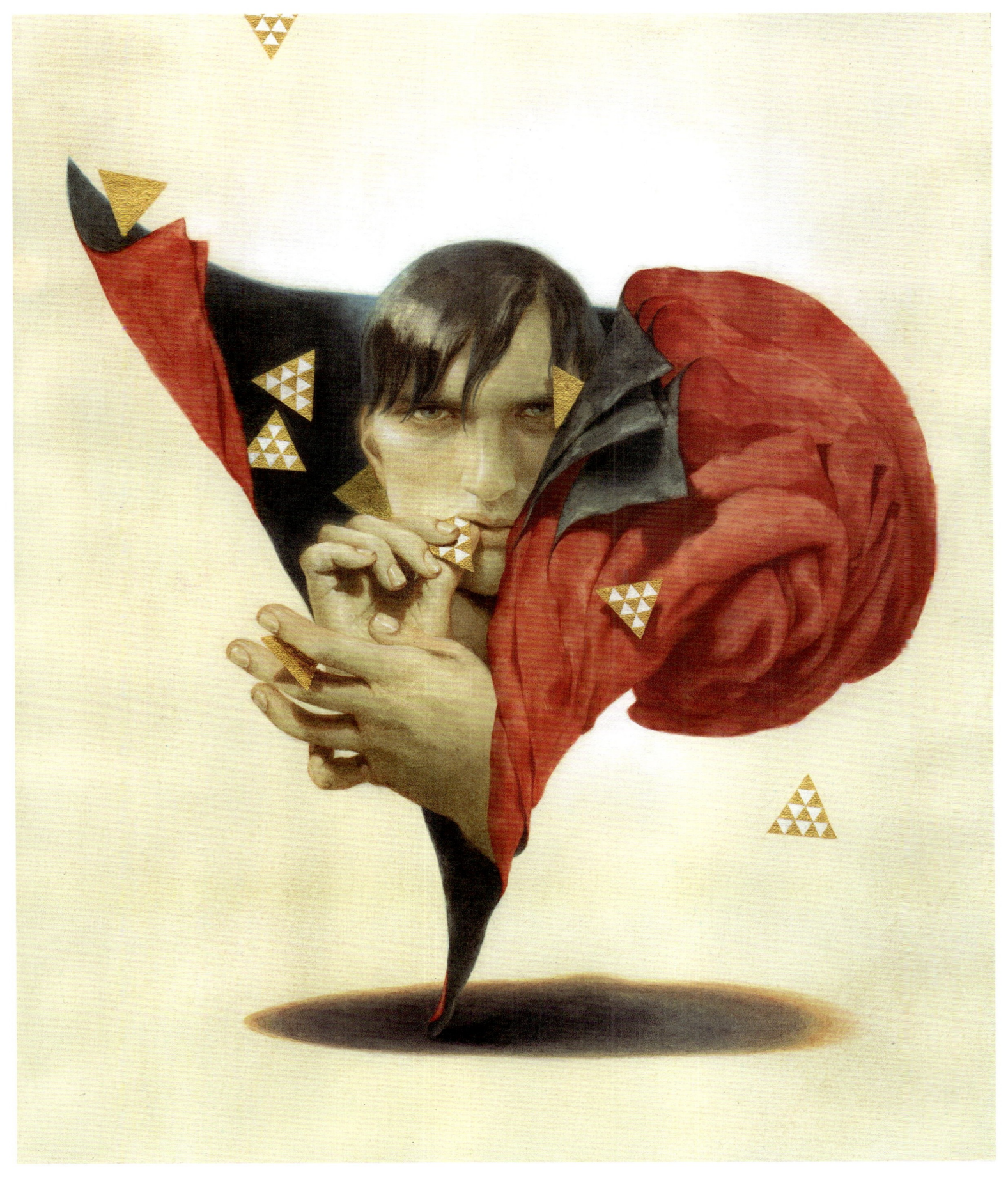

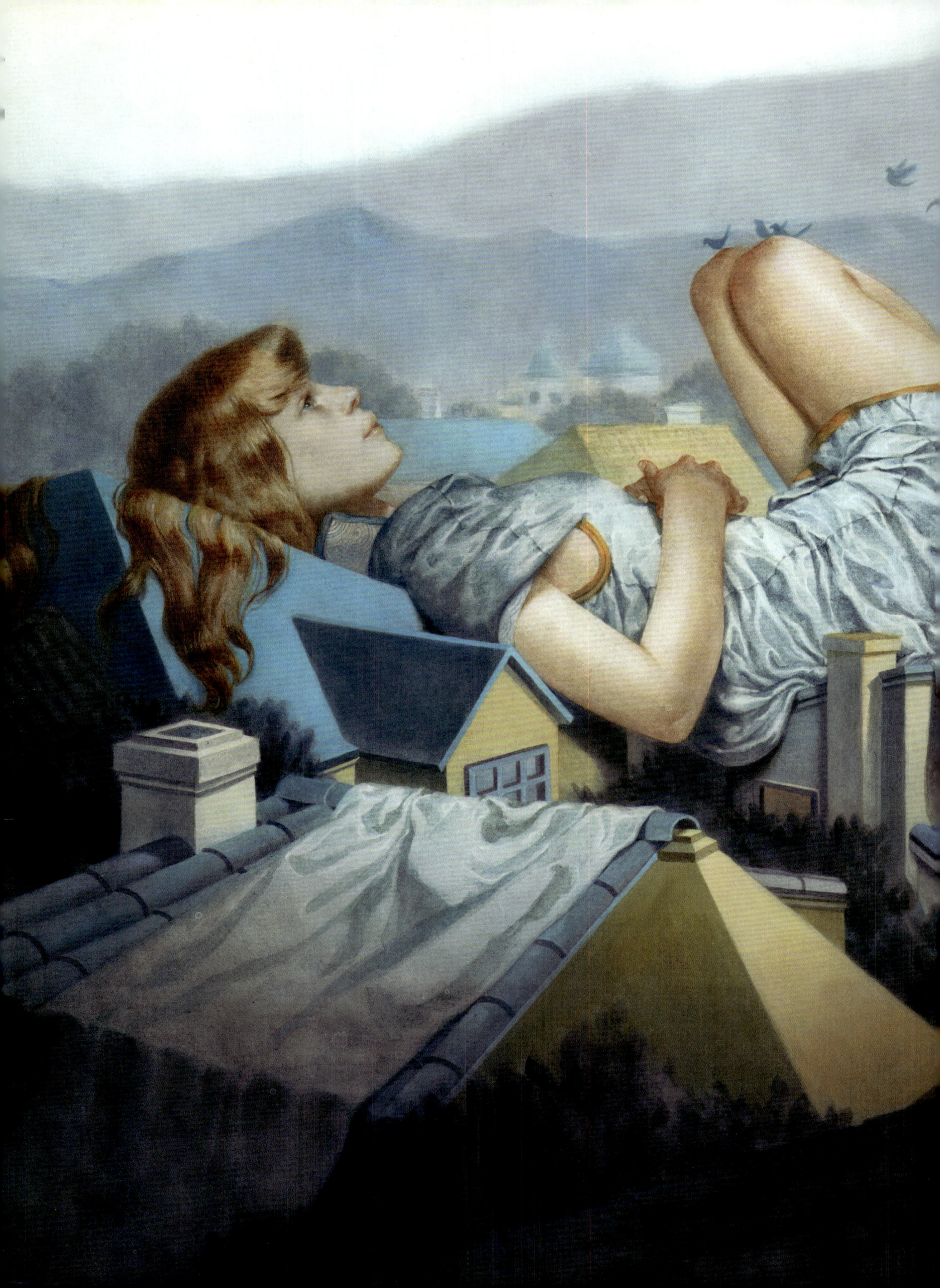

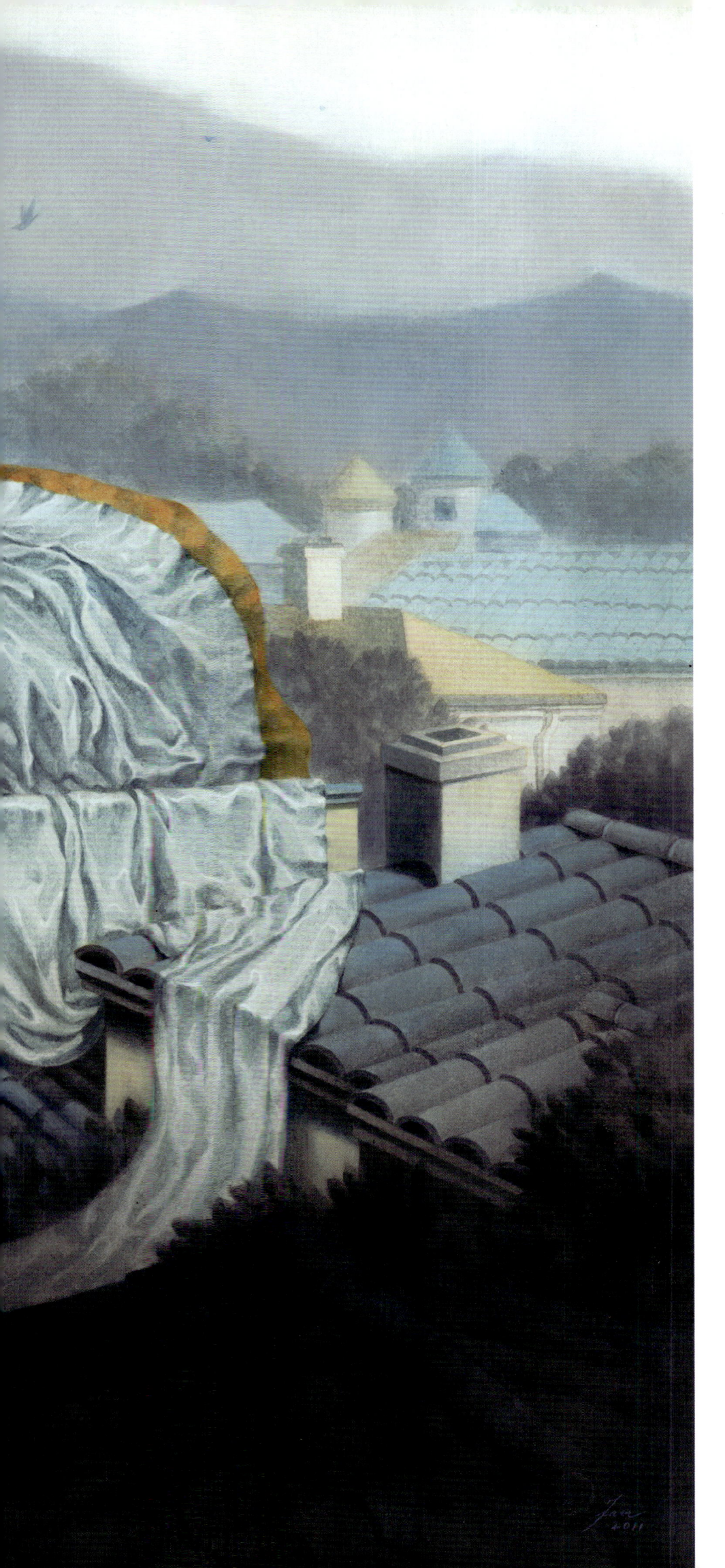

TREADING THROUGH AN UNTRIMMED MEMORY
acrylic & colored pencil on paper
21" x 17.6", 2011

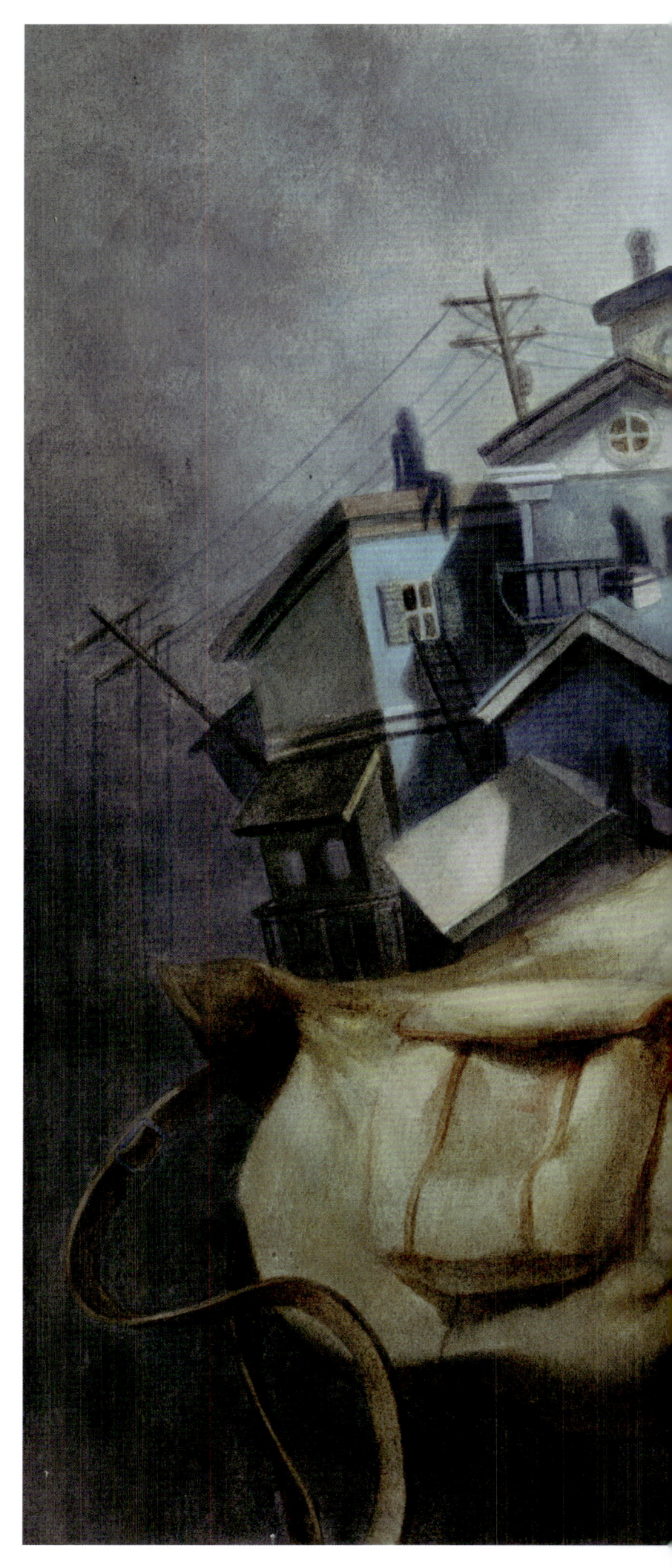

WHEN THE WORLD ISN'T LOOKING
acrylic & colored pencil on paper, 12" x 15", 2011

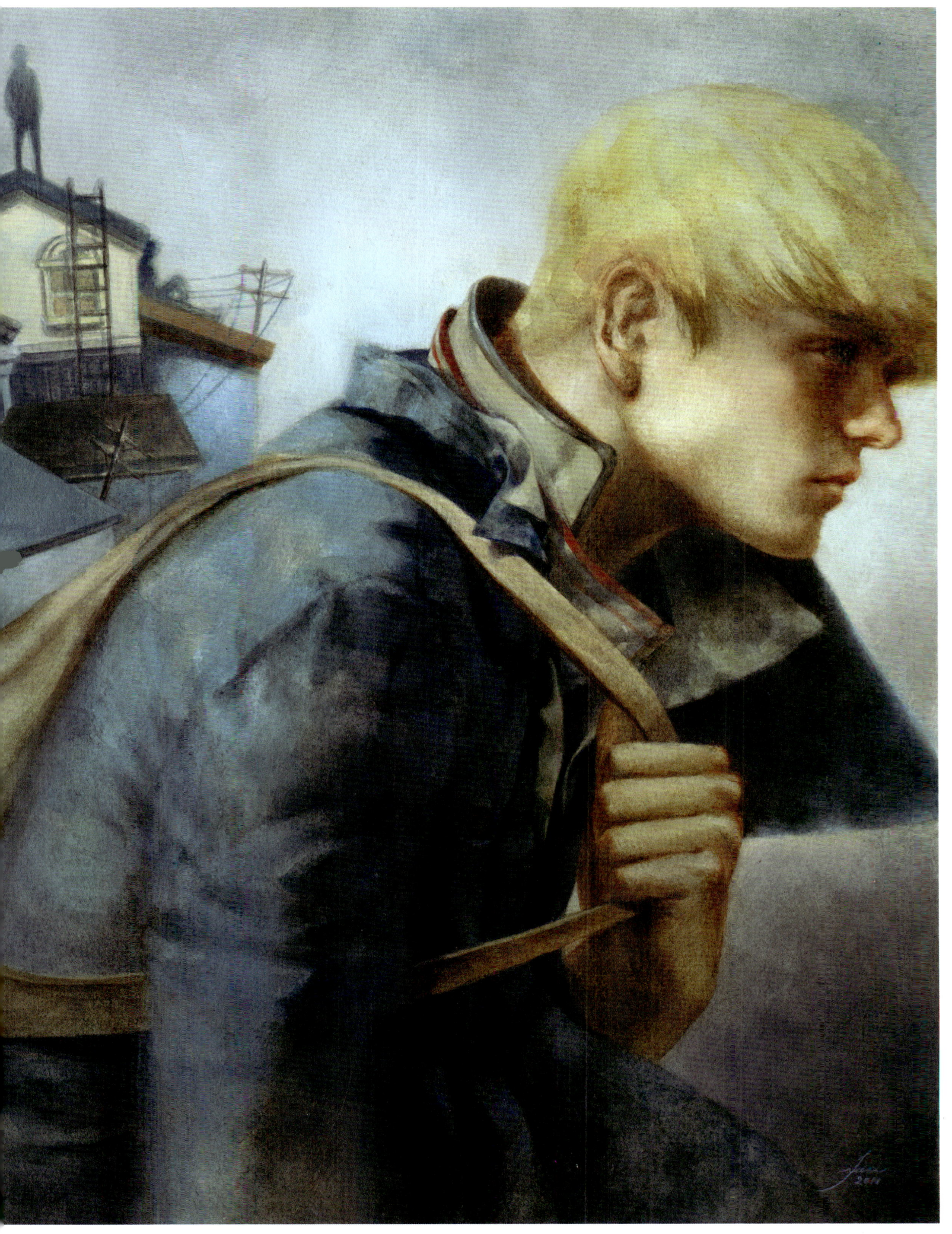

BORROWED MEMORIES

2012

Borrowed Memories is an homage to my early-2009 painting titled *Our Flutter-some Ordeal*, which is based on the idea of metamorphosis. I find myself constantly transforming in the way I think and live. The series is my highly romanticized portrayal of the changing from one form to another.

The figures in the paintings are found enveloped by cocoons made from abstract shapes. The shapes inter-mingle with the figures, and it's left unclear whether they're emerging from or pupating into its surrounding. I wanted each chrysalis to convey the many facets of one's self and the forever-changing identities that come into existence.

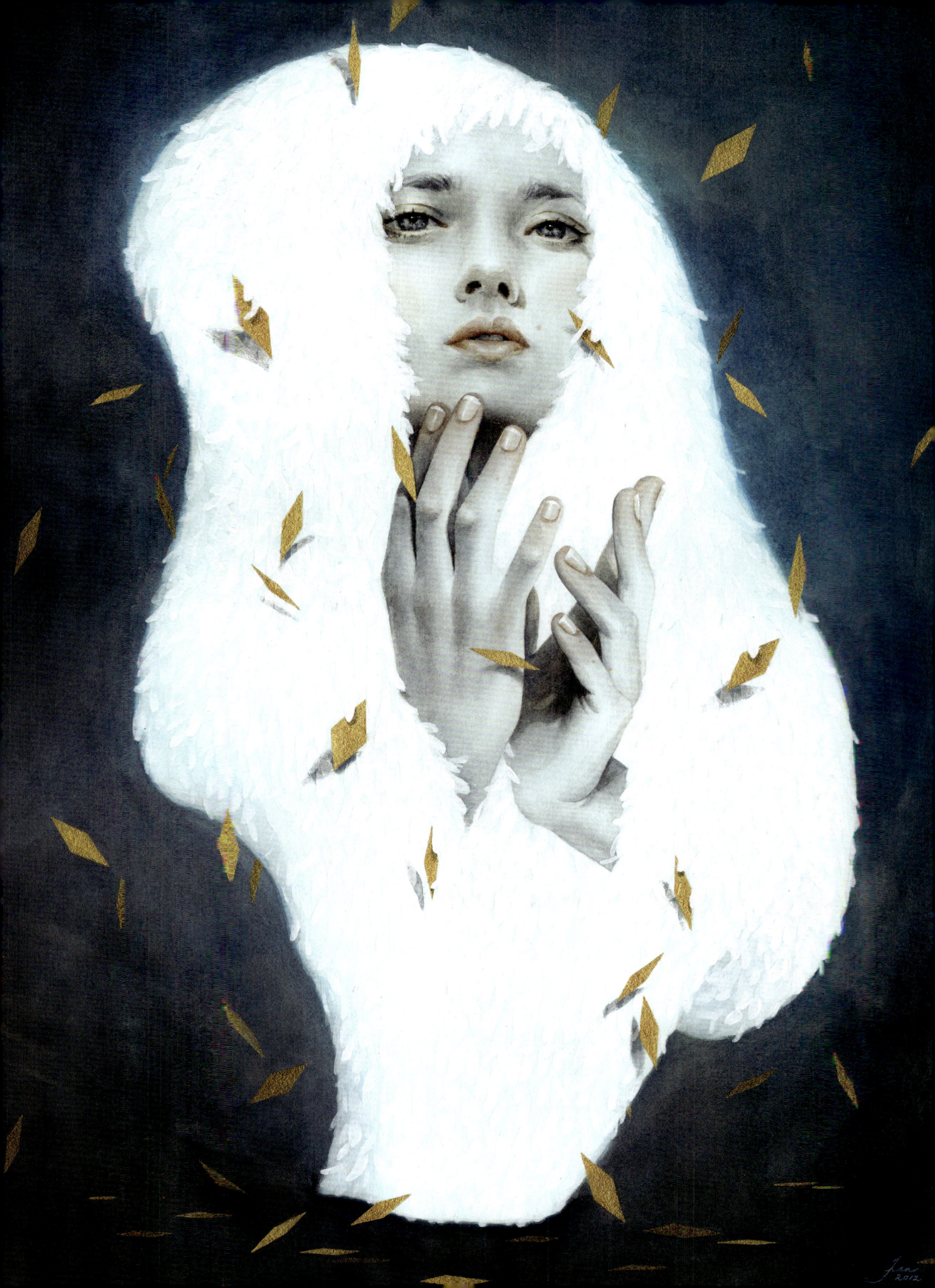

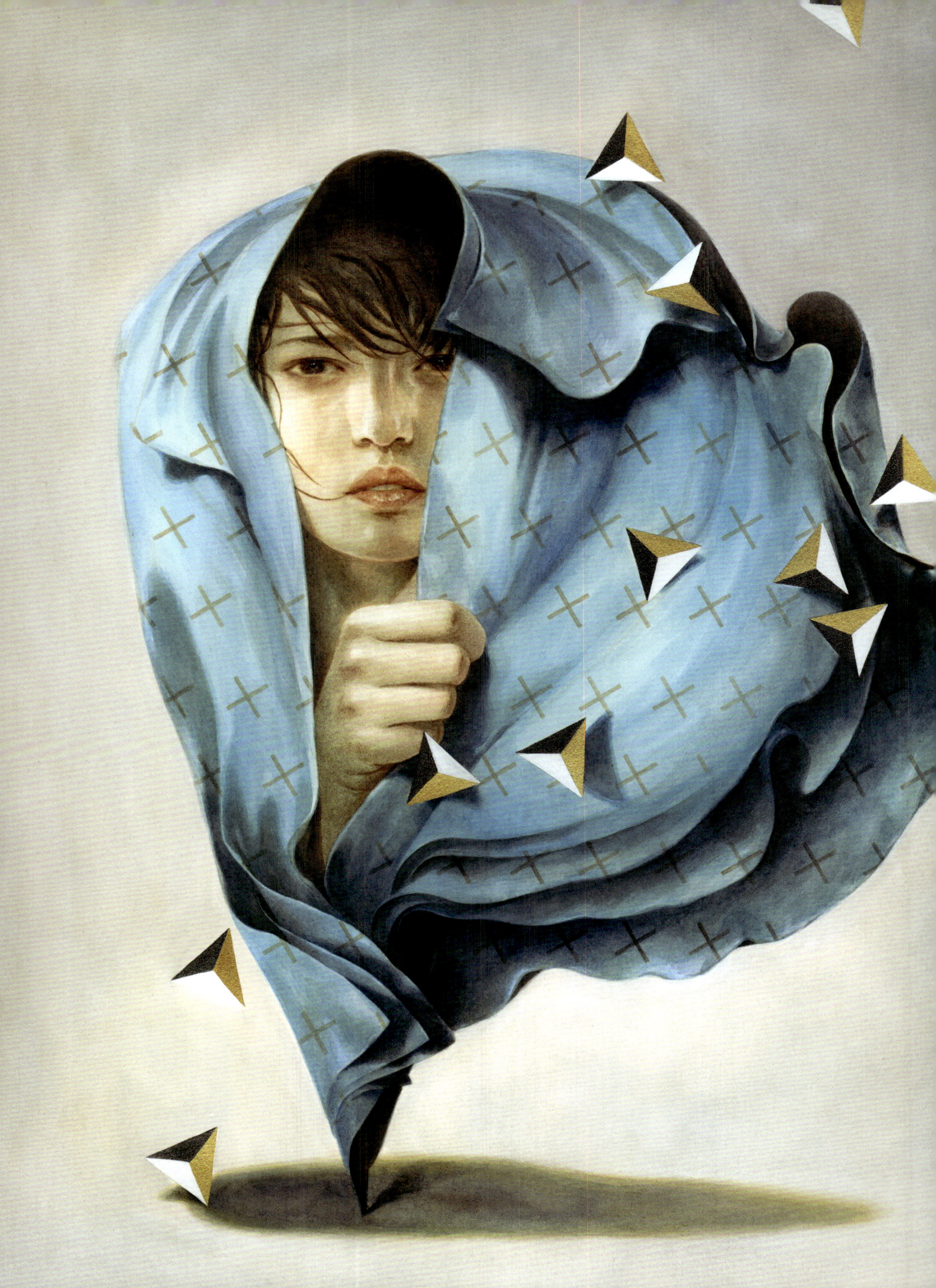

A CHROMATIC COCOON
acrylic & colored pencil on paper 18 x 21, 2012

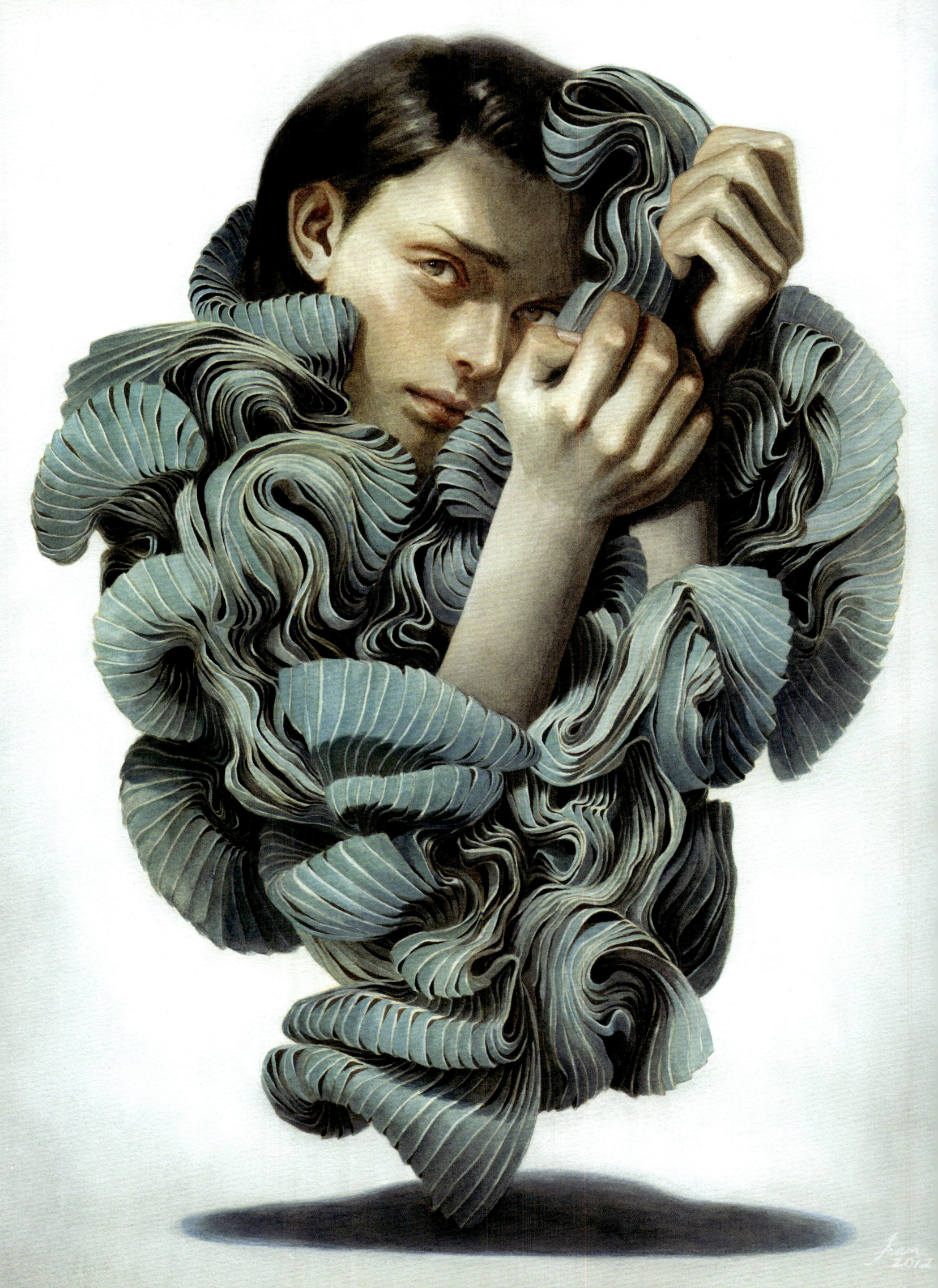

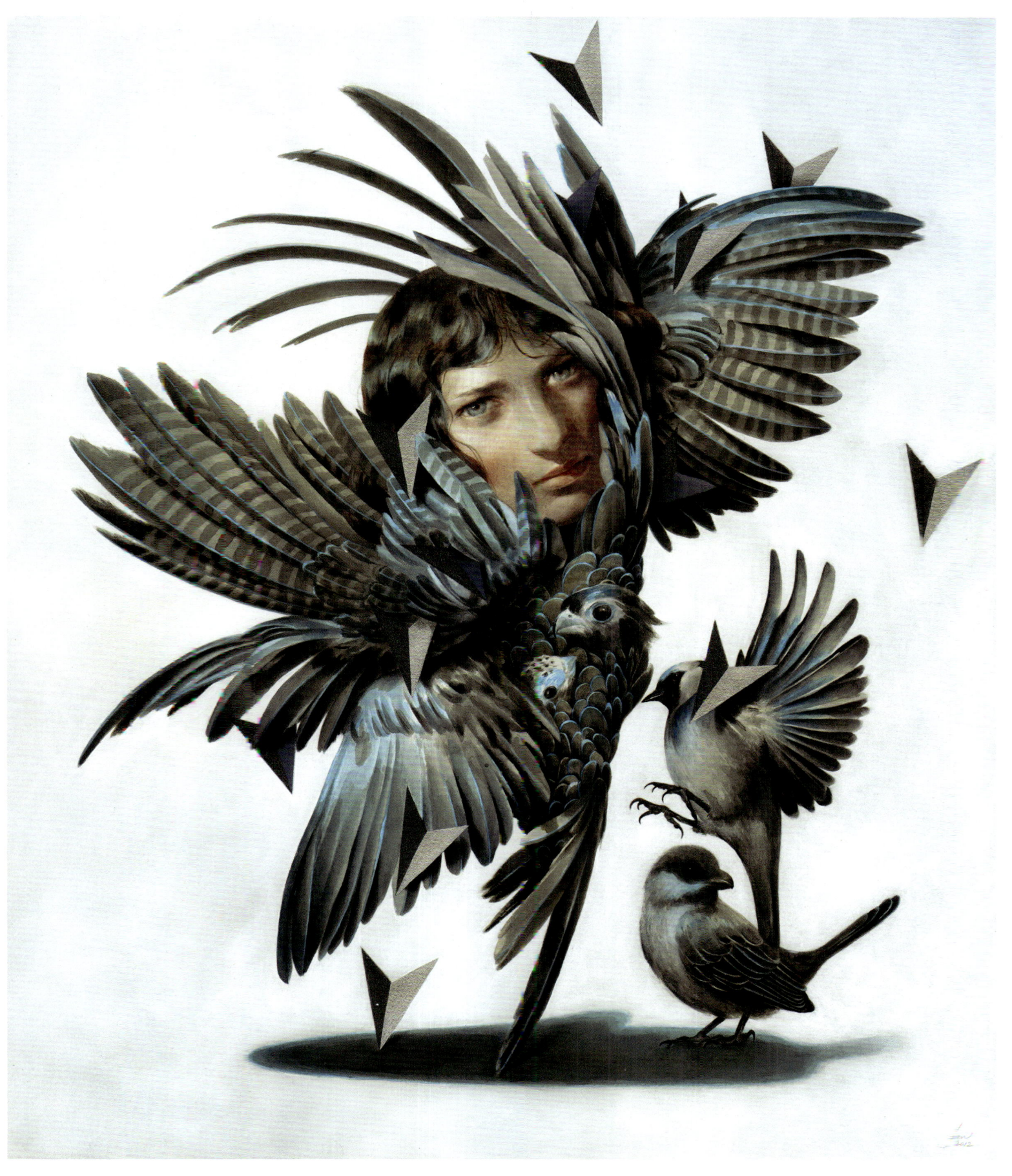

above
FABRICATION & ITS TETHERED FACE
acrylic & colored pencil on paper, 20" x 23", 2012

left
ENVELOPED BETWEEN A PLEATED THOUGHT
acrylic & colored pencil on paper, 12" x 15", 2012

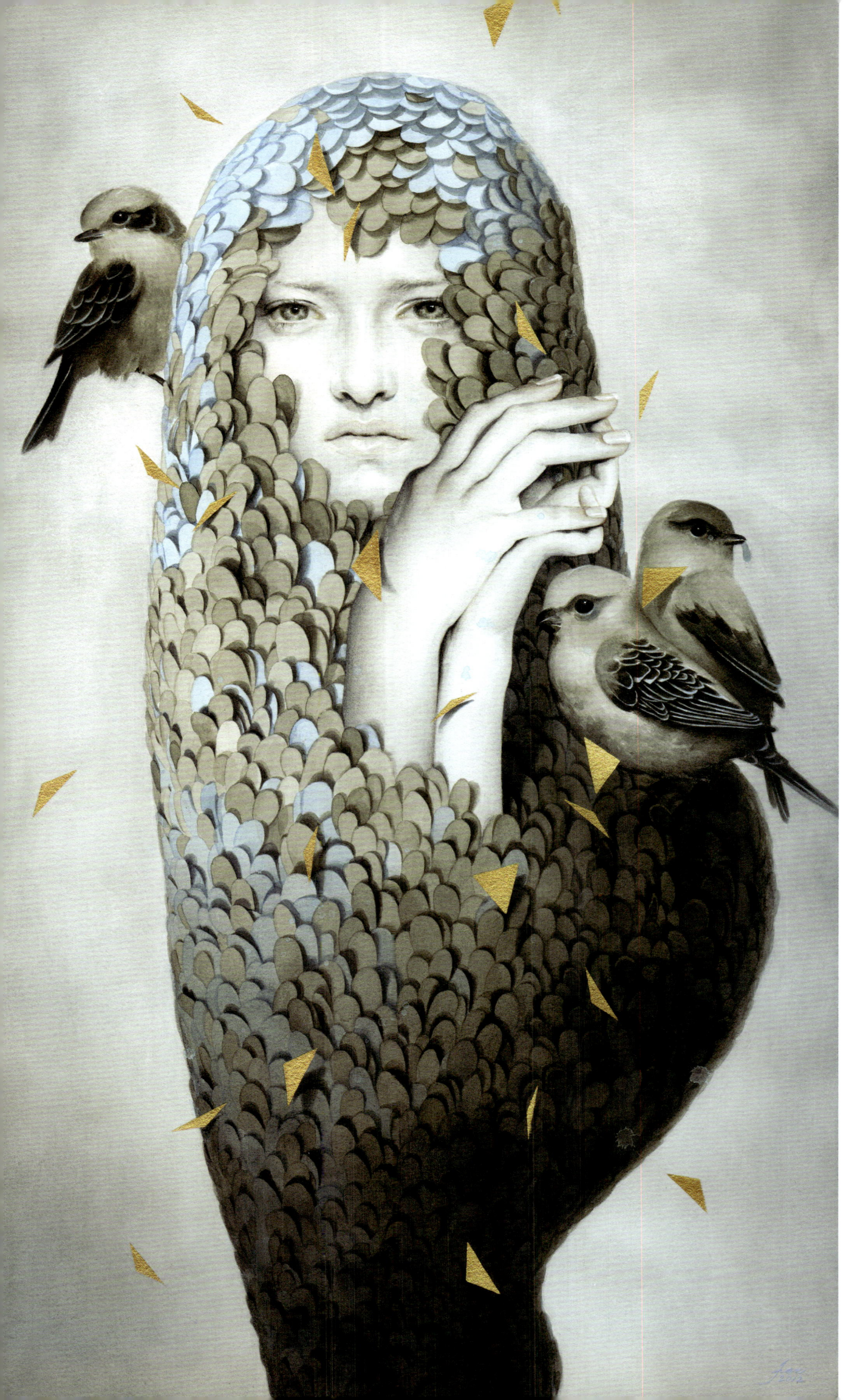

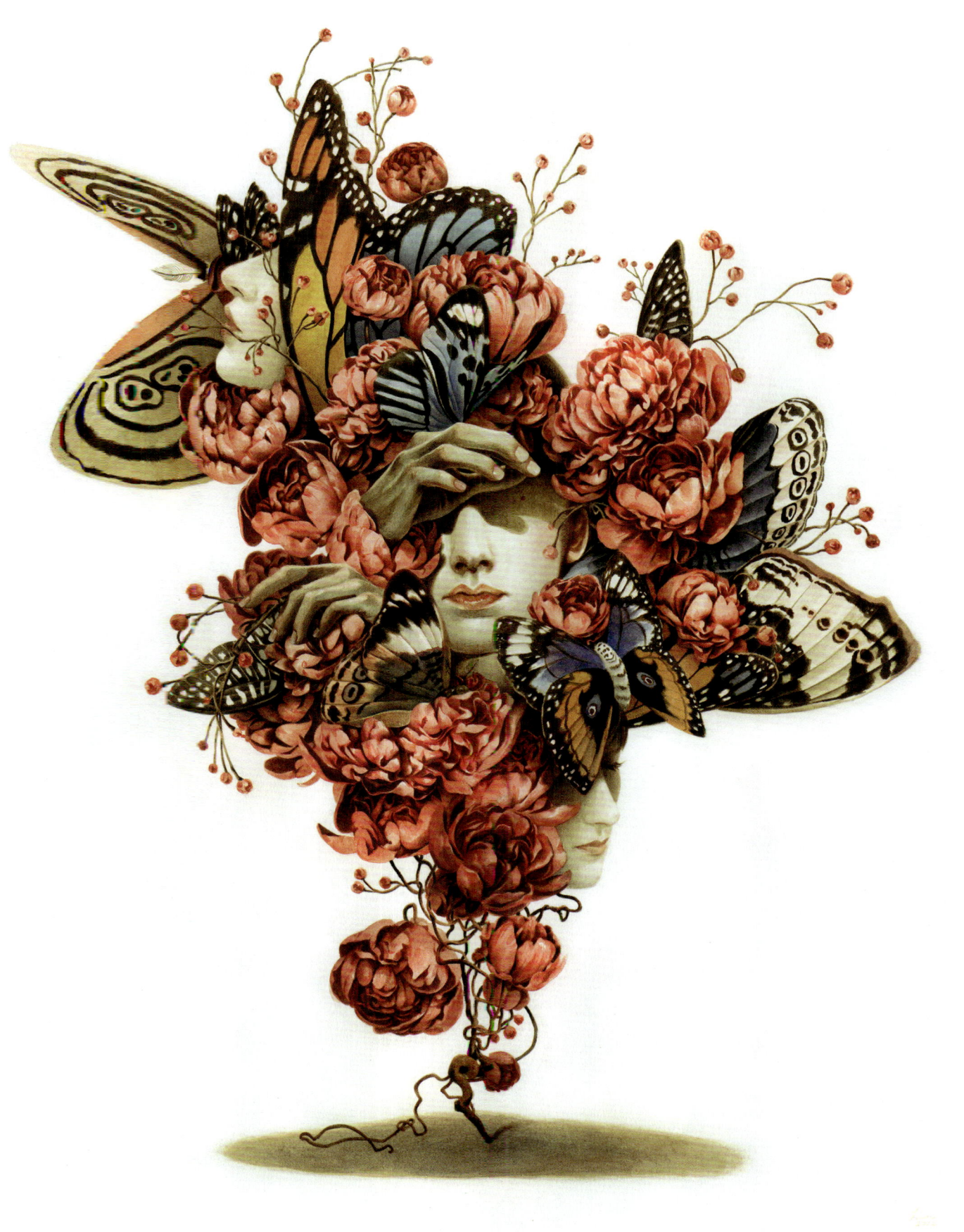

above
WANDERING ACROSS A BORROWED BELIEF
acrylic & colored pencil on paper, 20" x 26", 2012

left
NESTLED WITHIN A PALLID DISPOSITION
acrylic & colored pencil on paper, 12" x 20", 2012

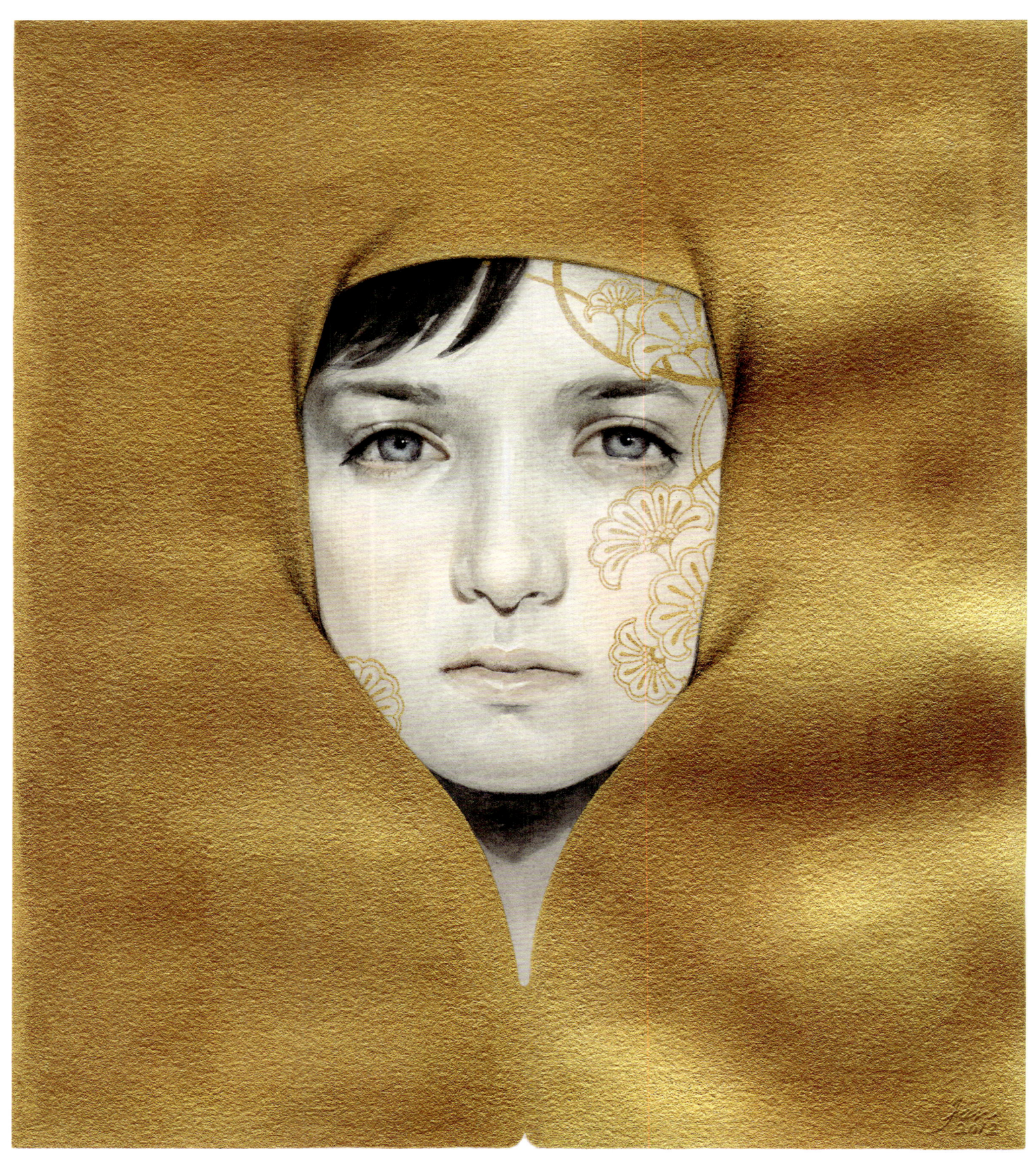

WHEN WE SUCCUMB TO A GOLDEN MOMEN™
acrylic & colored pencil on paper, 11" x 12", 2012

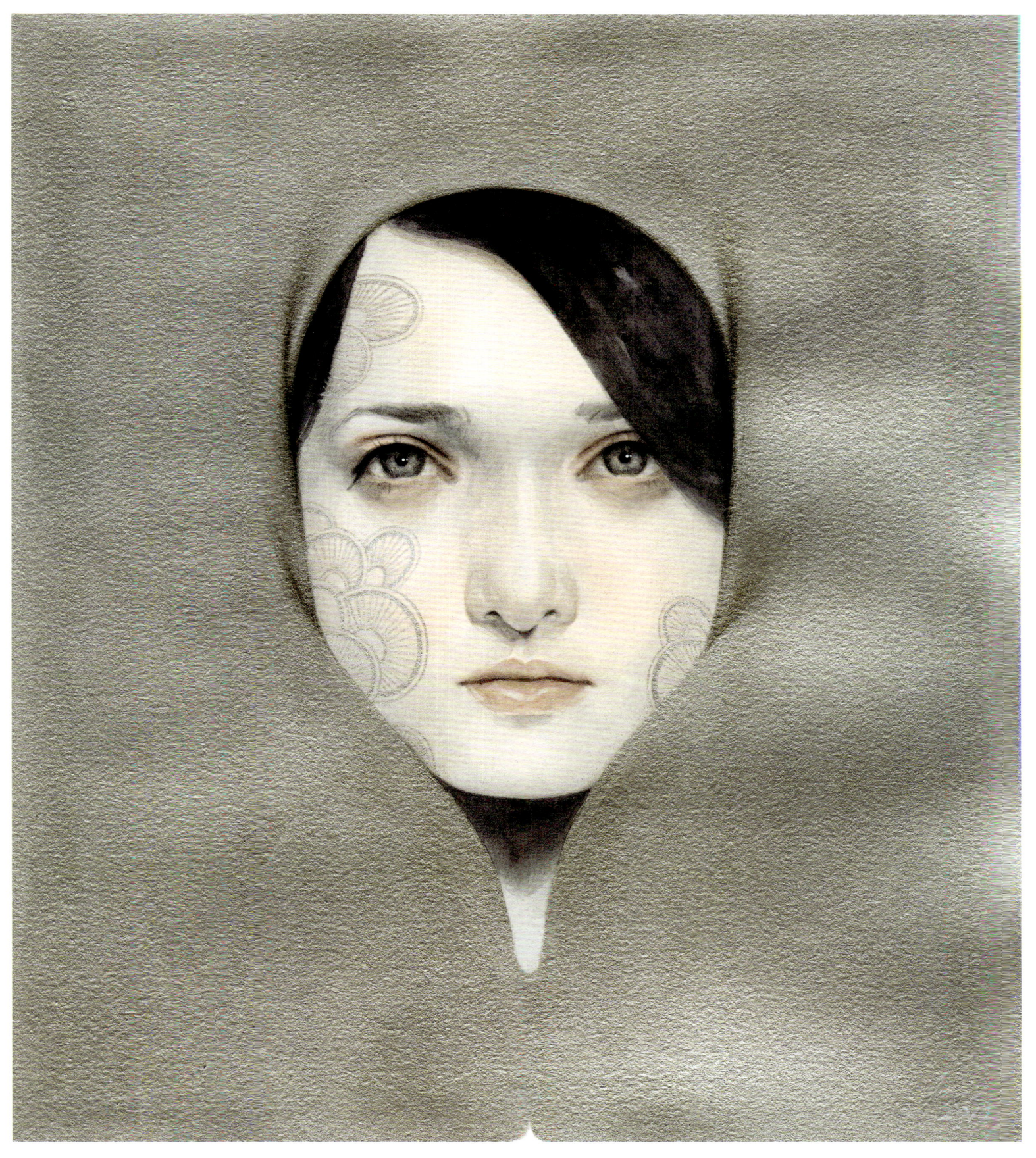

THE PLACE PROCURED FROM OUR YESTERYEARS

2013

The paintings in this collection are my visual manifestation of nostalgia, which is a derivative branch of melancholy. Its narrative is told through a larger-than-life presence with hues of brown and blue. The inhabitants in *The Place Procured From Our Yesteryears* appear spectral as they wander through neighborhoods of old, cherished memories and find themselves reliving moments in their past.

Nostalgia is often described as a sentimental longing for places in our yesteryears. I tend to find myself stuck between these blurred lines of now and then, and my hope is for this sequence of softly rendered paintings to invite the viewer to bridge the two.

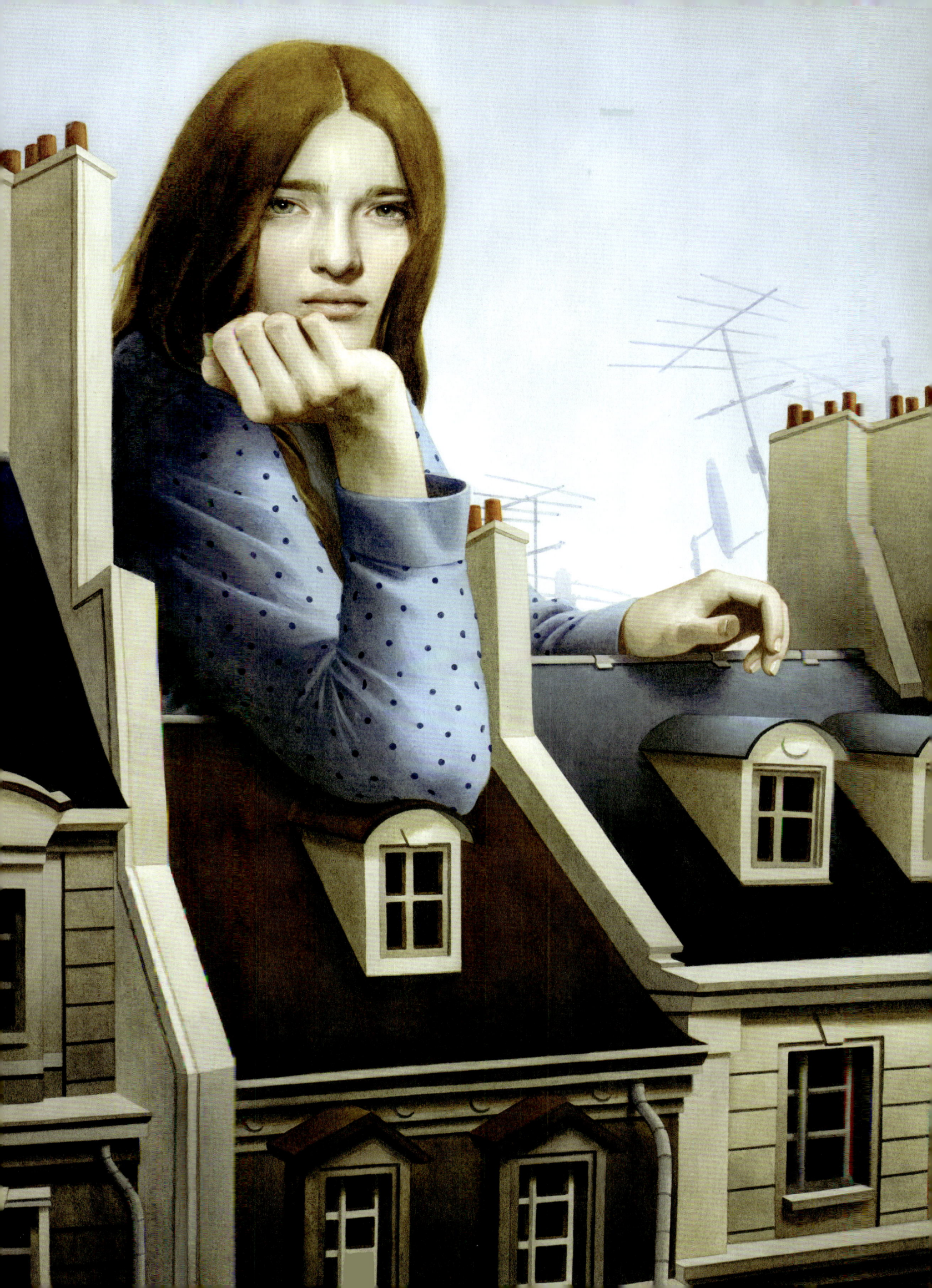

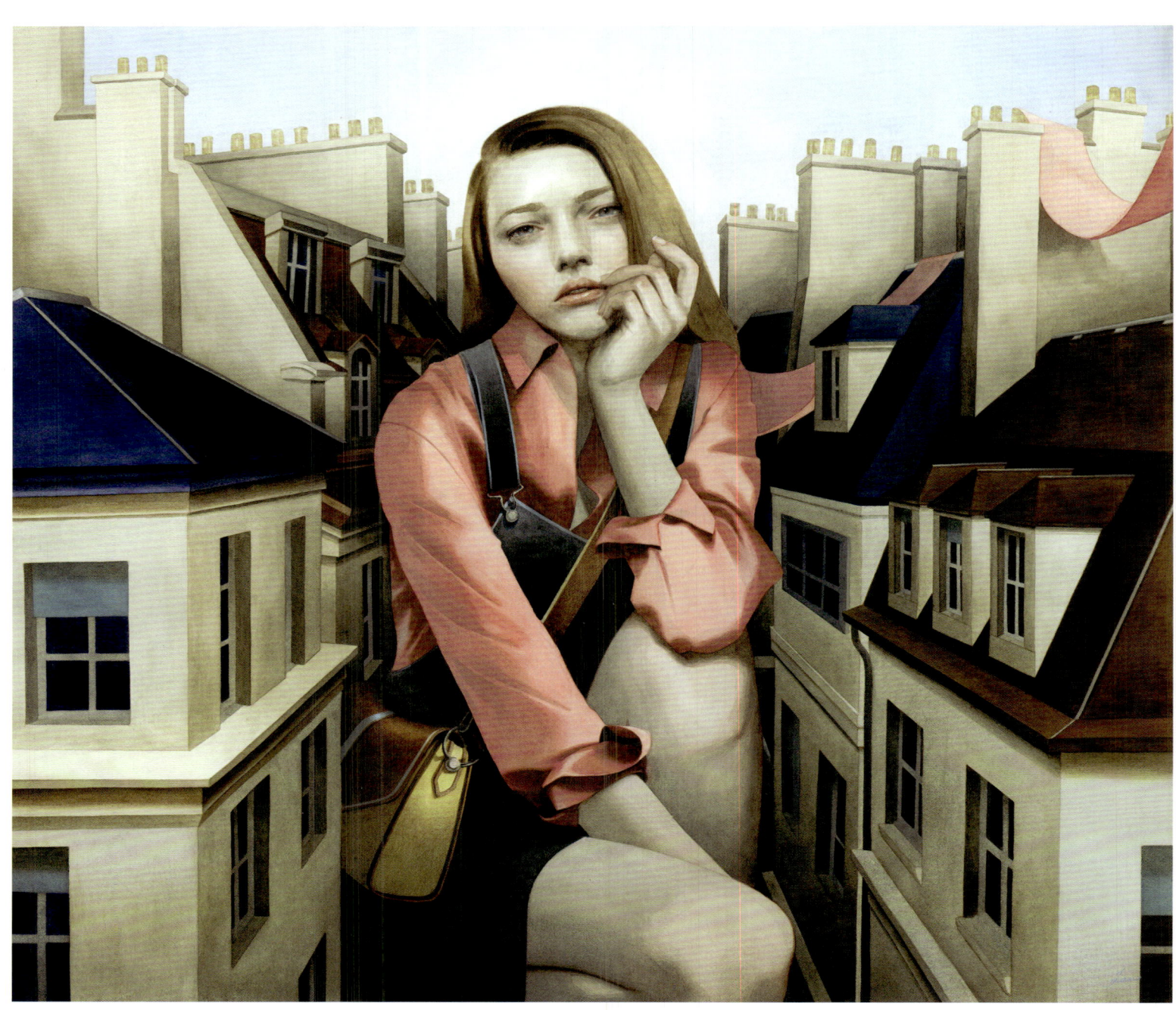

above
A SENTIMENTAL SWALLOW
acrylic & colored pencil on paper, 20" x 24", 2013

right
A CORNERED KEEPSAKE
acrylic & colored pencil on paper, 16" x 20", 2013

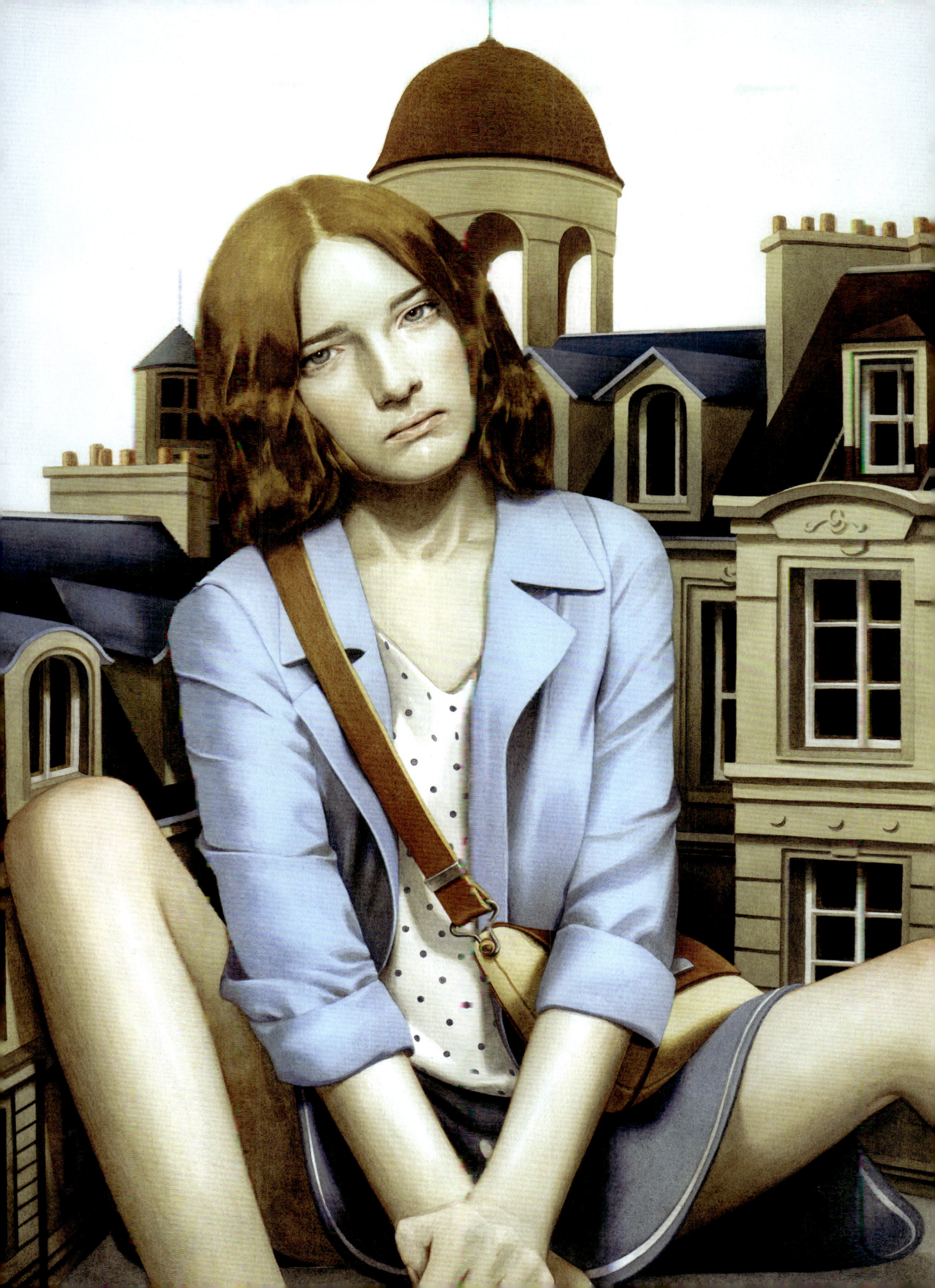

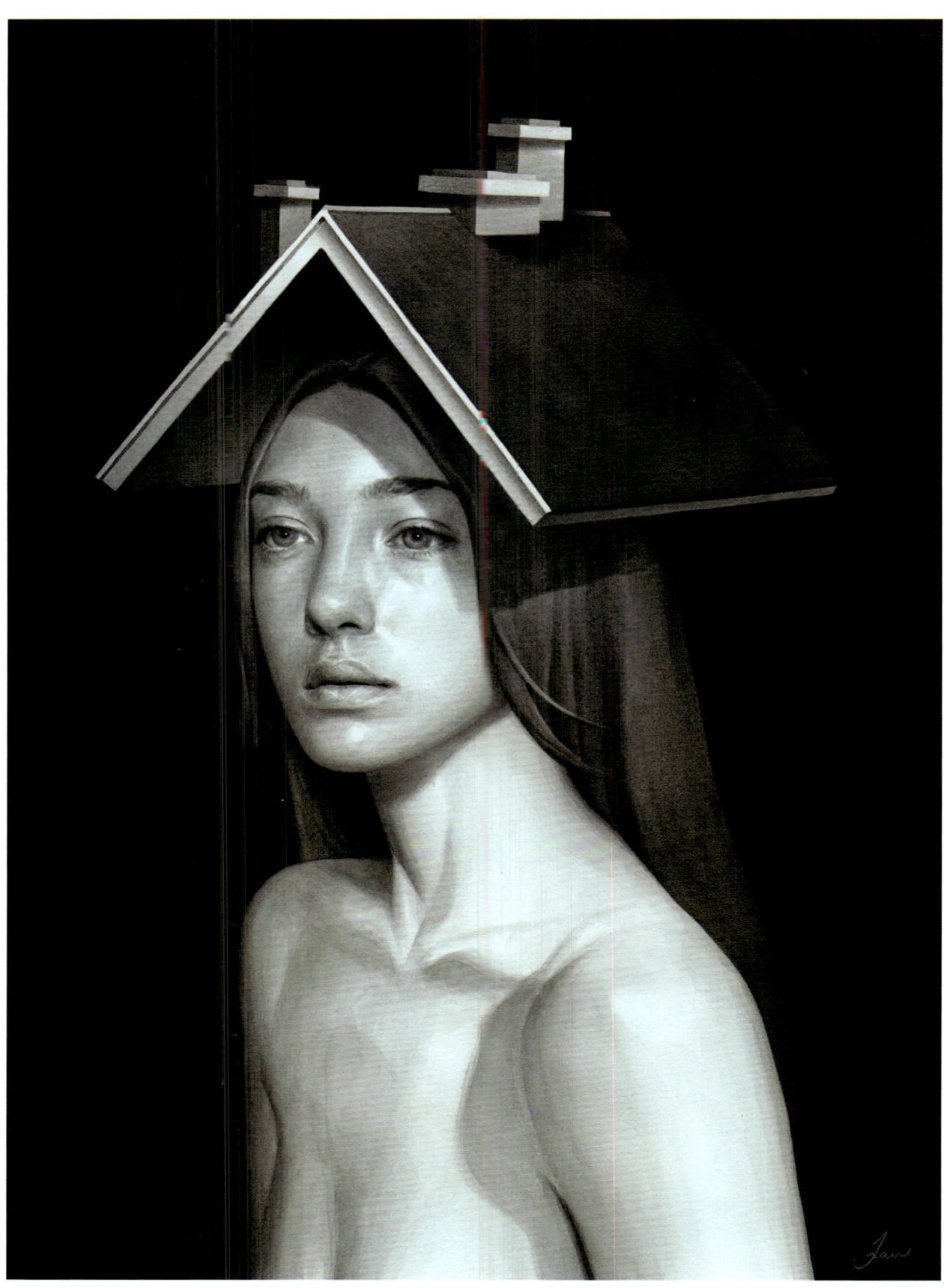

above
A PLACE WE ONCE HOMED I
acrylic & colored pencil on paper, 12" x 6", 2013

right
A PLACE WE ONCE HOMED II
acrylic & colored pencil on paper, 12" x 6", 2013

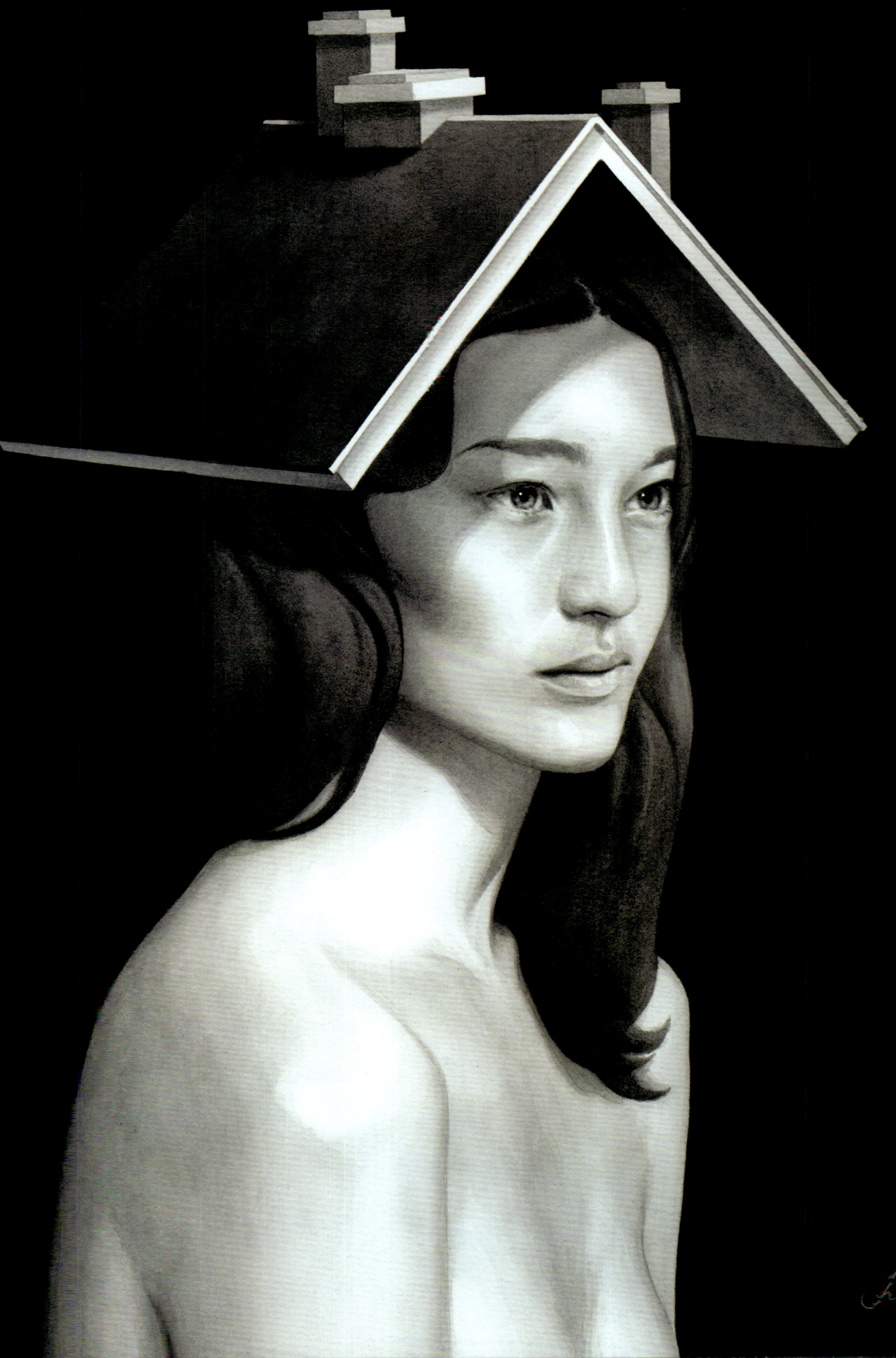

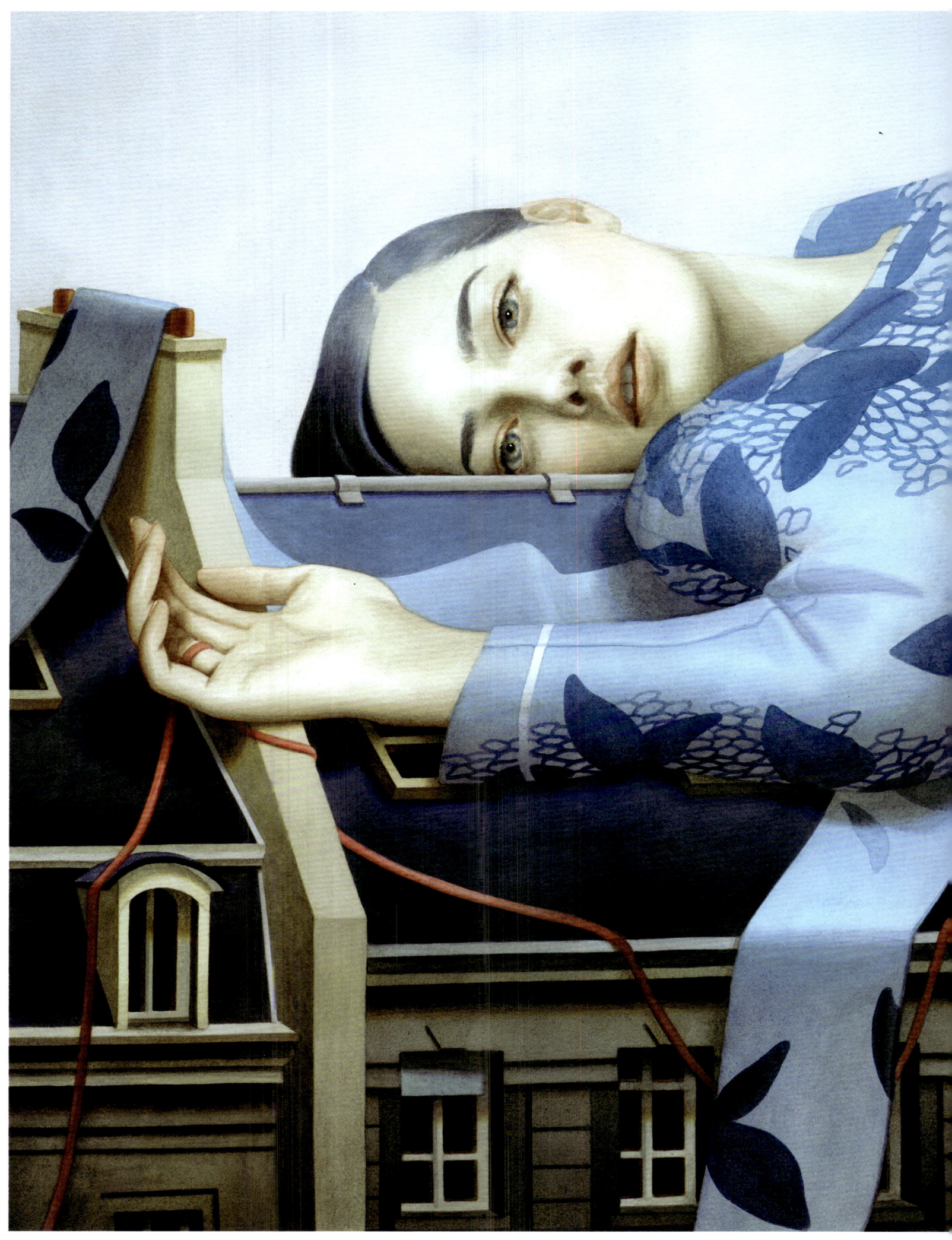

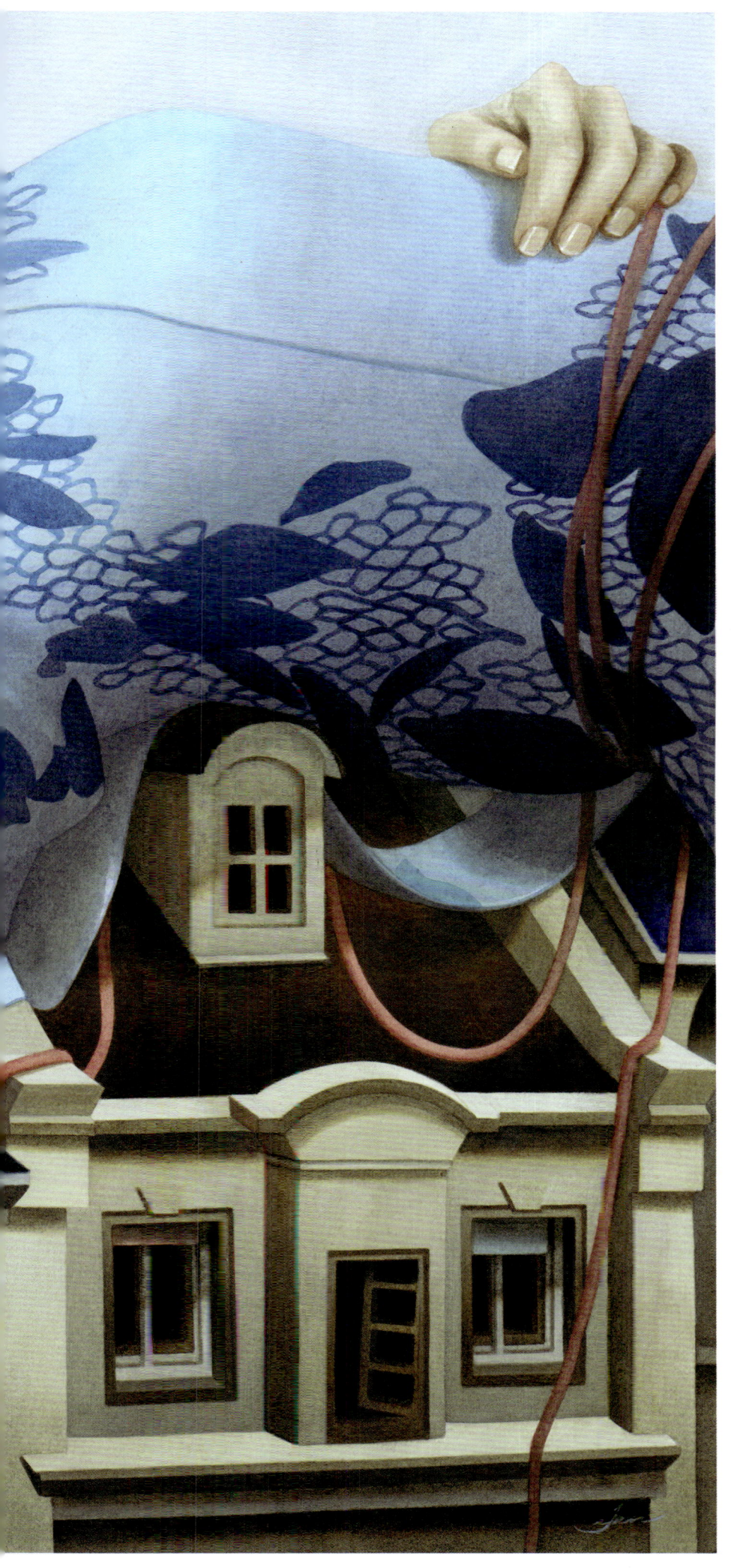

BEDRIDDEN MEMENTOS
acrylic & colored pencil on paper, 14" x 8, 2013

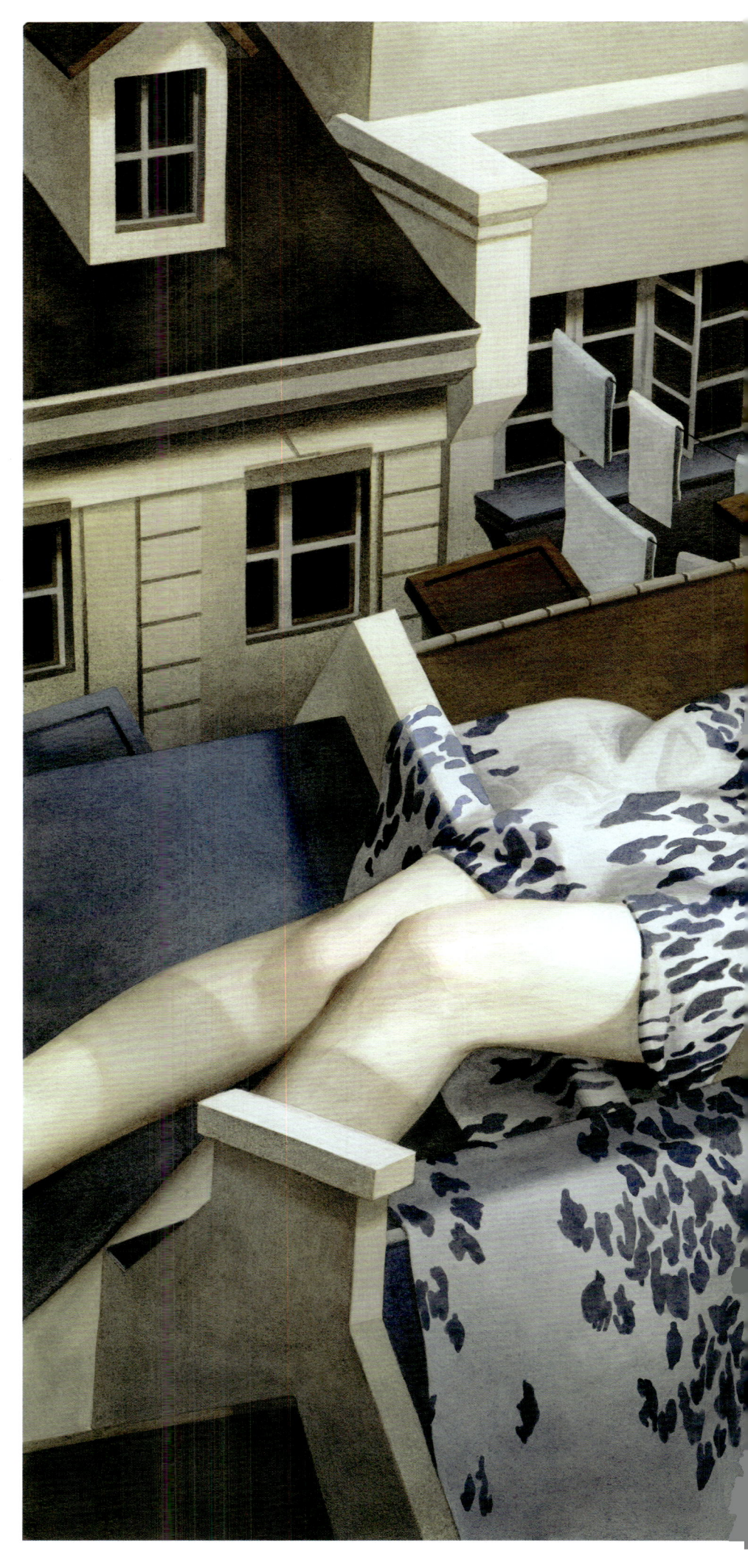

SLEEPING WITH NOSTALGIA
acrylic & colored pencil on paper, 20" x 26", 2013

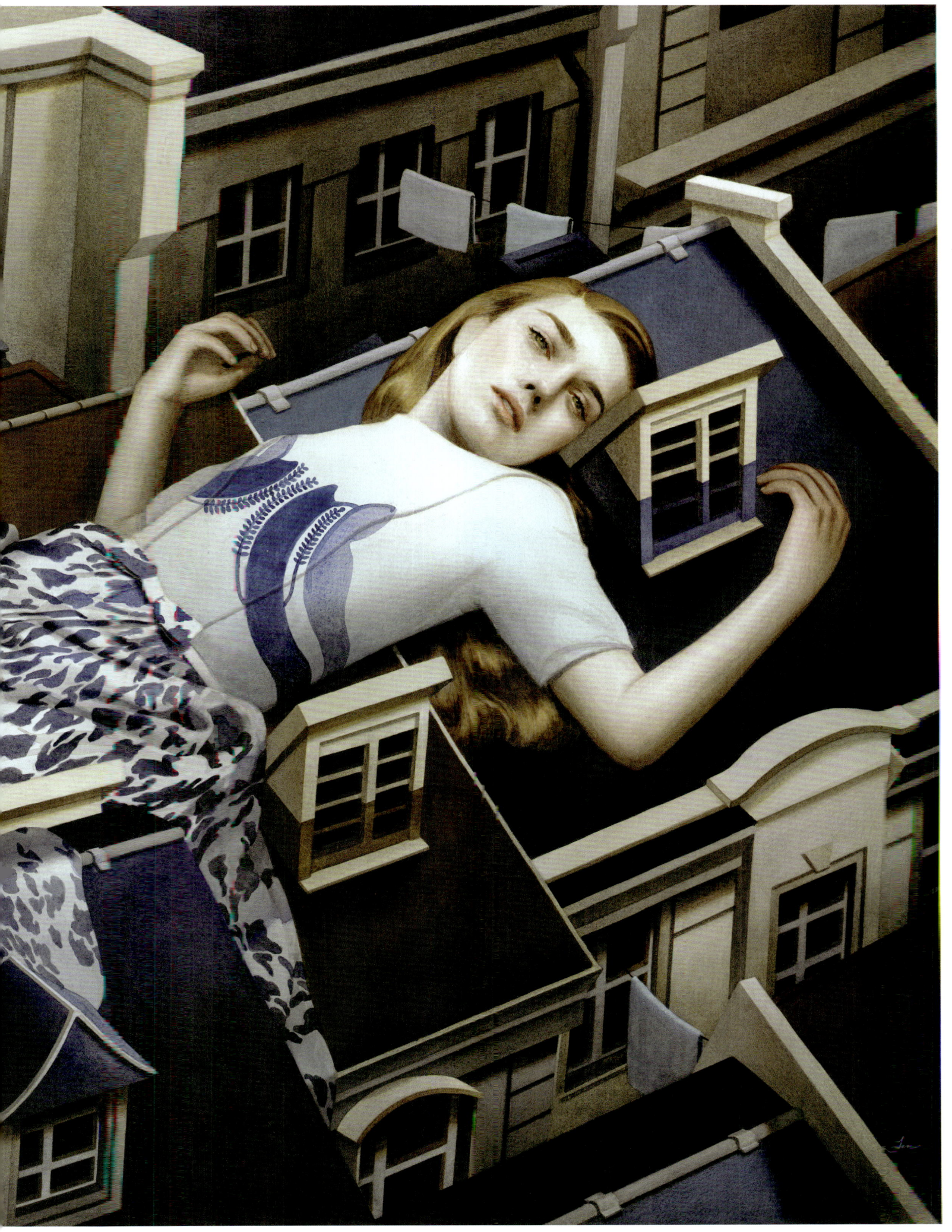

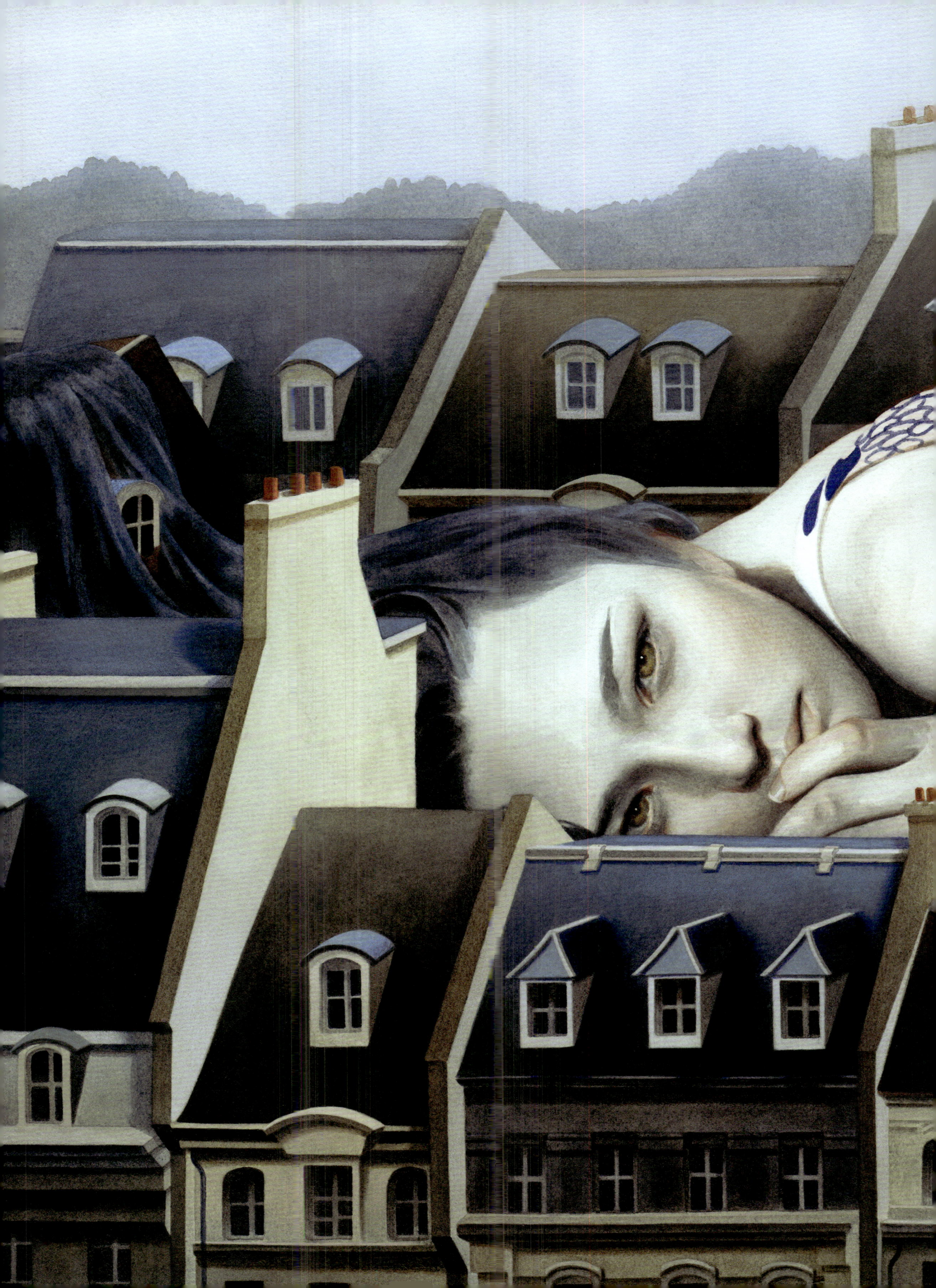

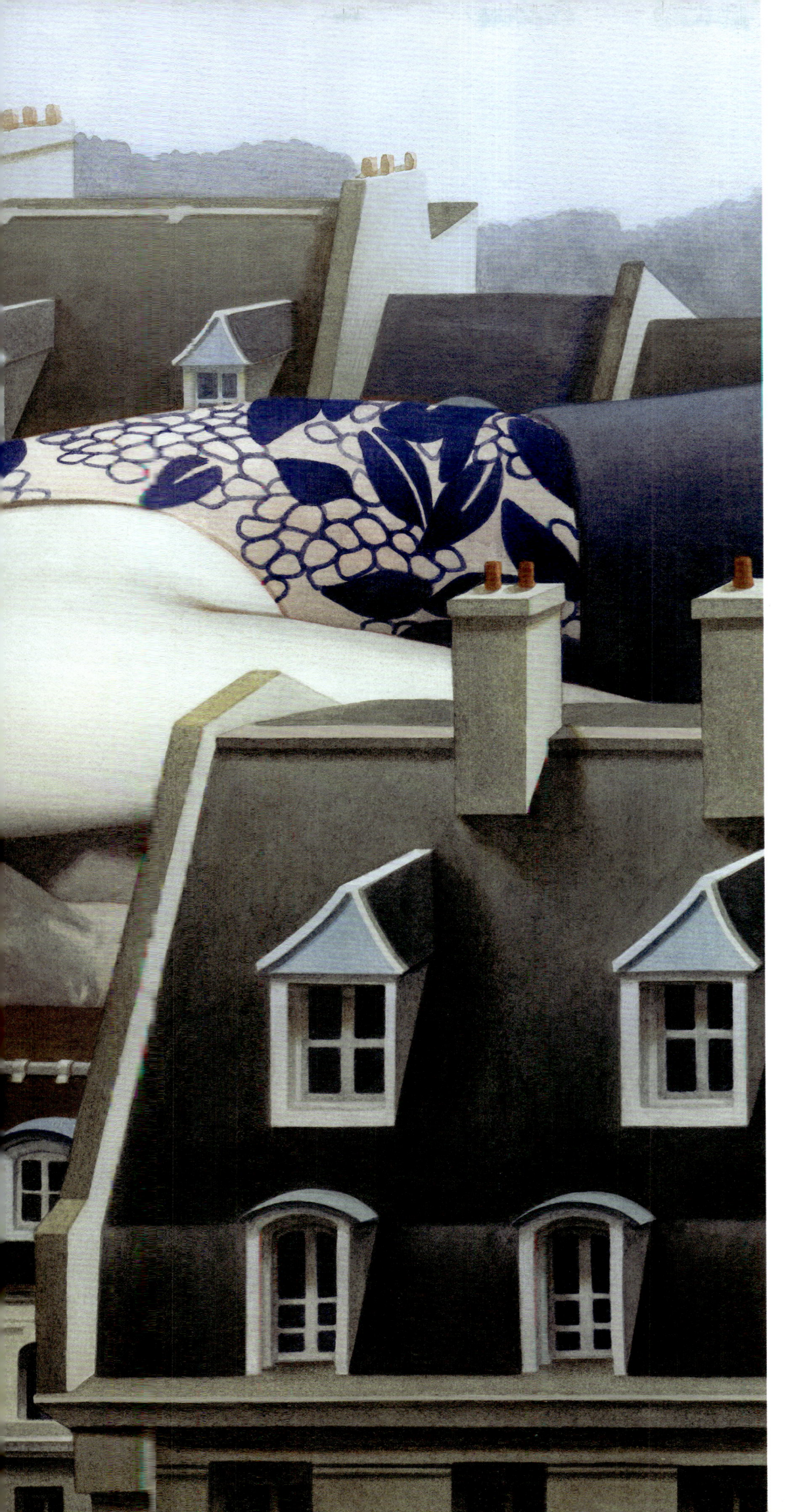

TASTE FOR BITTERSWEET WEEDS
acrylic & colored pencil on paper,
13" x 16", 2013

FORGOTTEN
FISSURE

2014

A fissure is often found in the dark, subconscious corners of the psyche. It offers no definite ends or beginnings, and within it are lost sentiments that are tucked away.

Forgotten Fissure is my visual interpretation of the human brain, embodied as pleated patterns. It's meant to highlight the hidden treasures that can be found when searching inward. By exploring these long, narrow openings between the sulcus and gyrus, visceral stimulation can be procured. What I find populating this space is a pure sense of self.

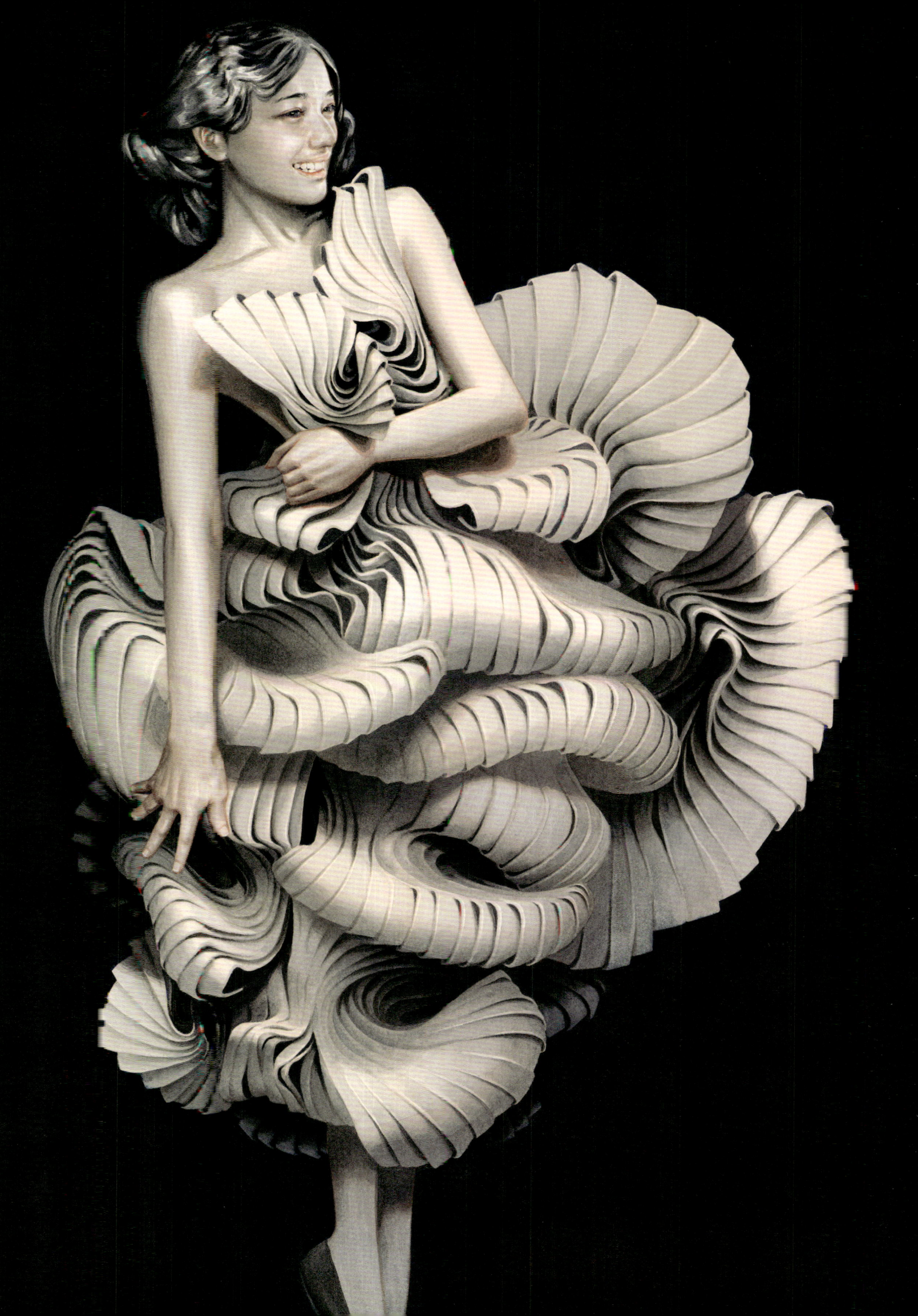

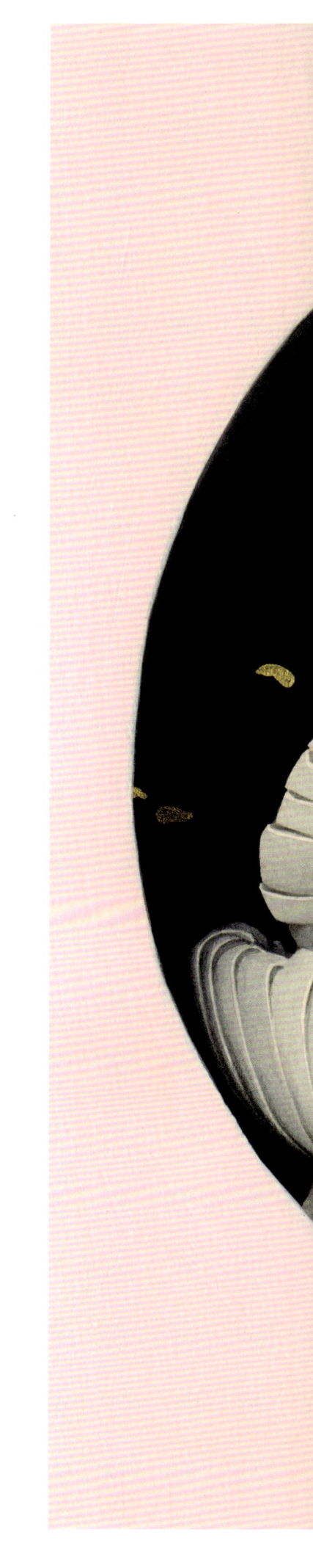

LIVING IN A FORGOTTEN FISSURE I
acrylic & colored pencil on paper, 15" x 15", 2014

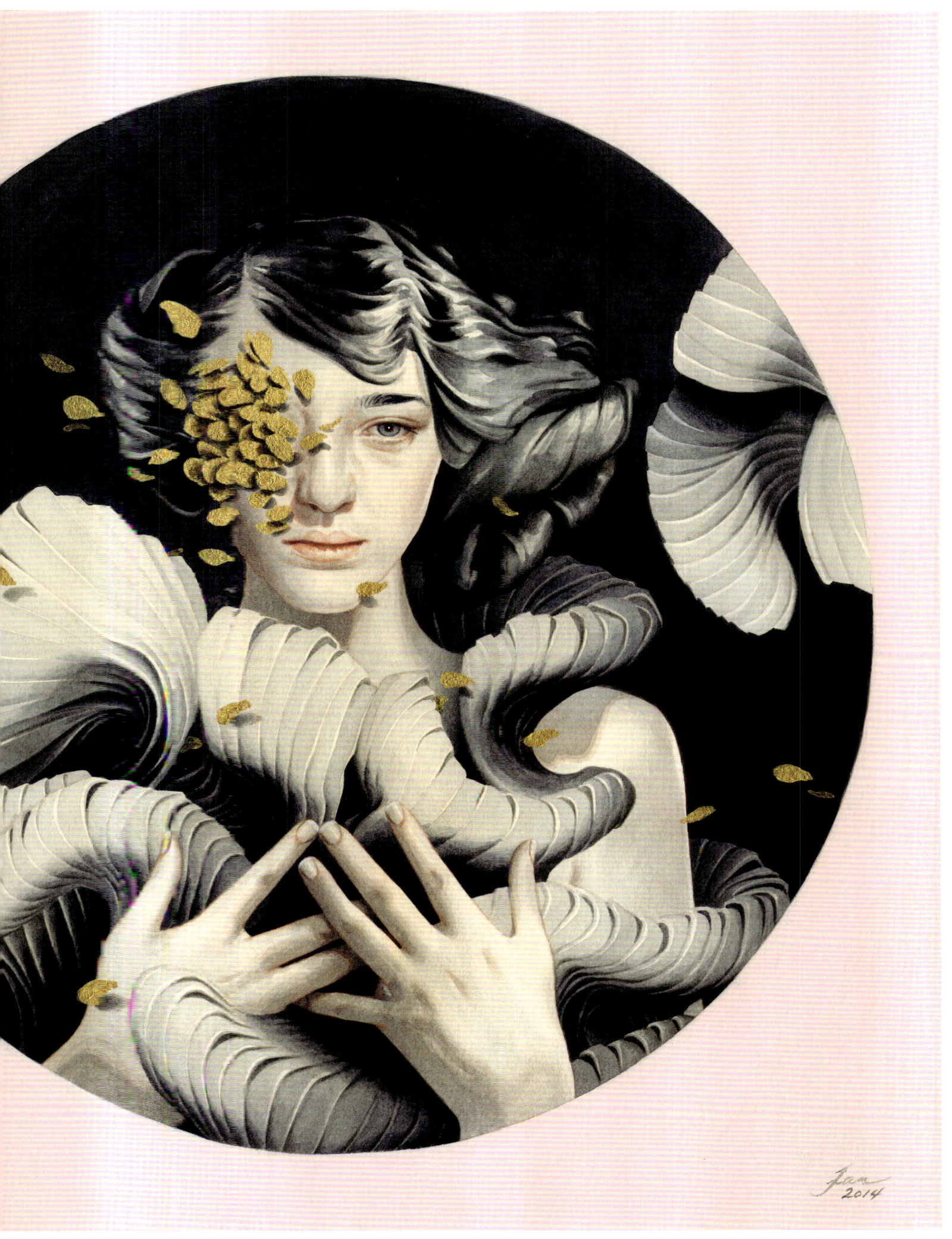

2014

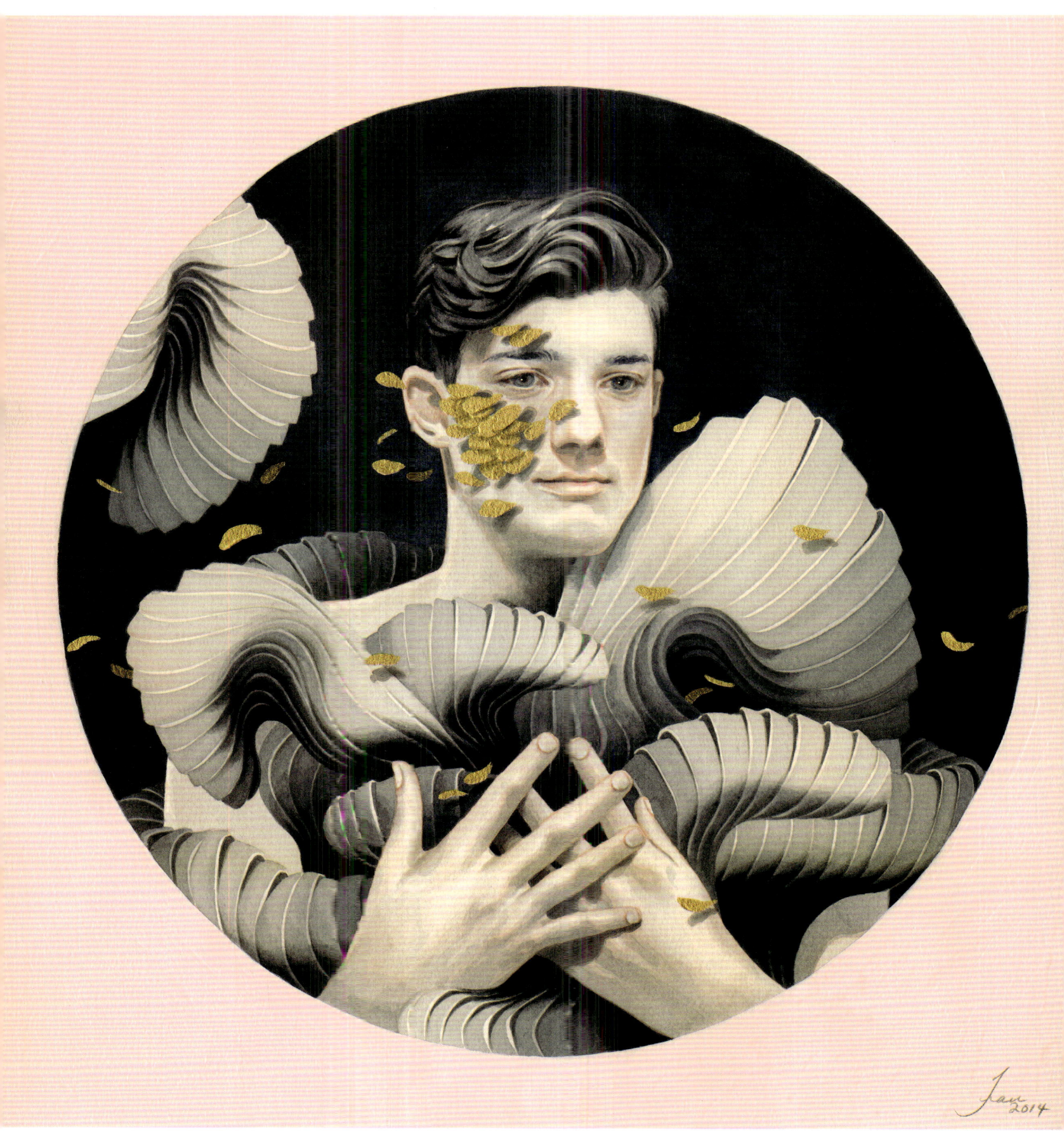

LIVING IN A FORGOTTEN FISSURE II
acrylic & colored pencil on paper, 15" x 15", 2014

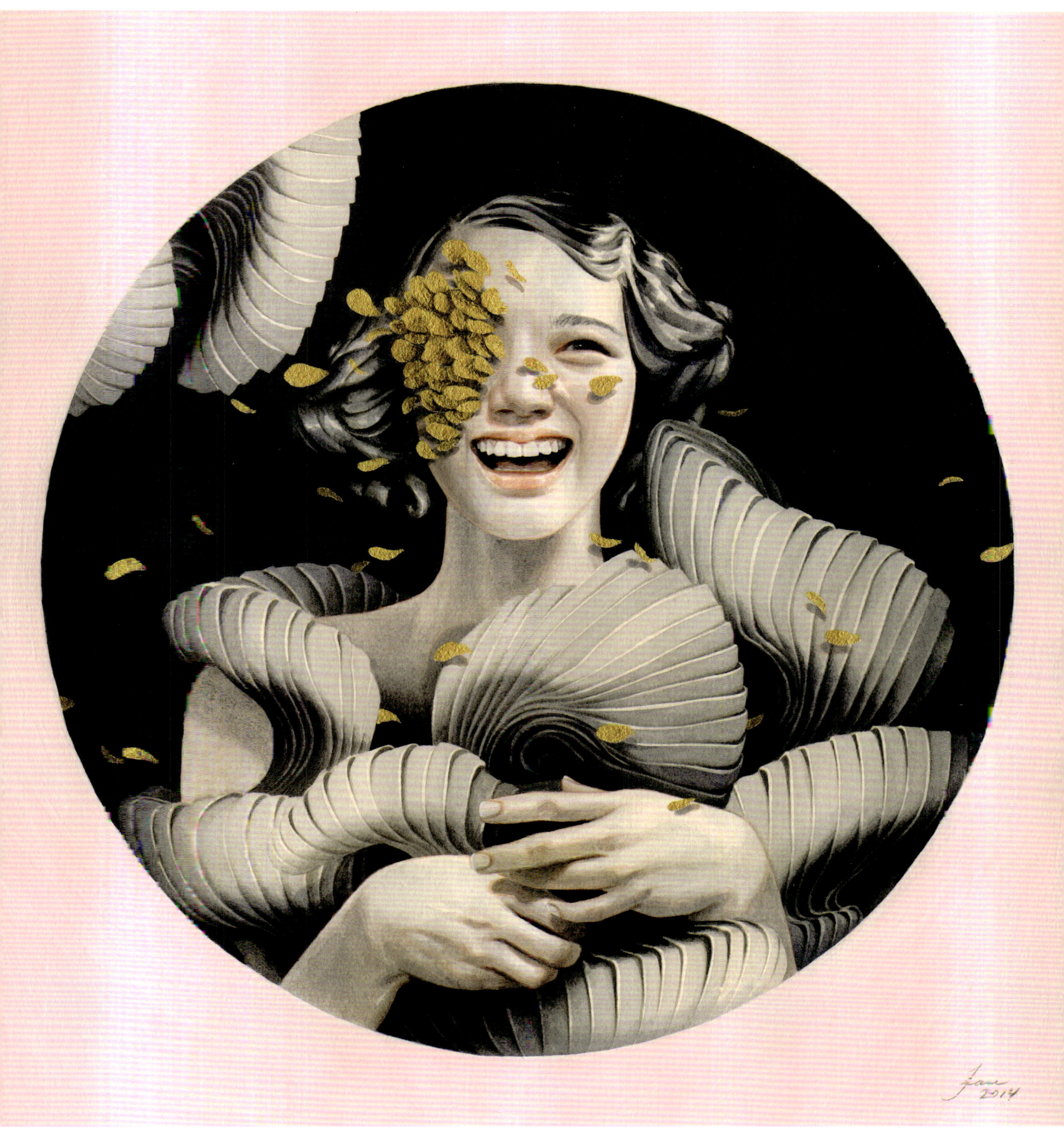

LIVING IN A FORGOTTEN FISSURE III
acrylic & colored pencil on paper, 15" x 15", 2014

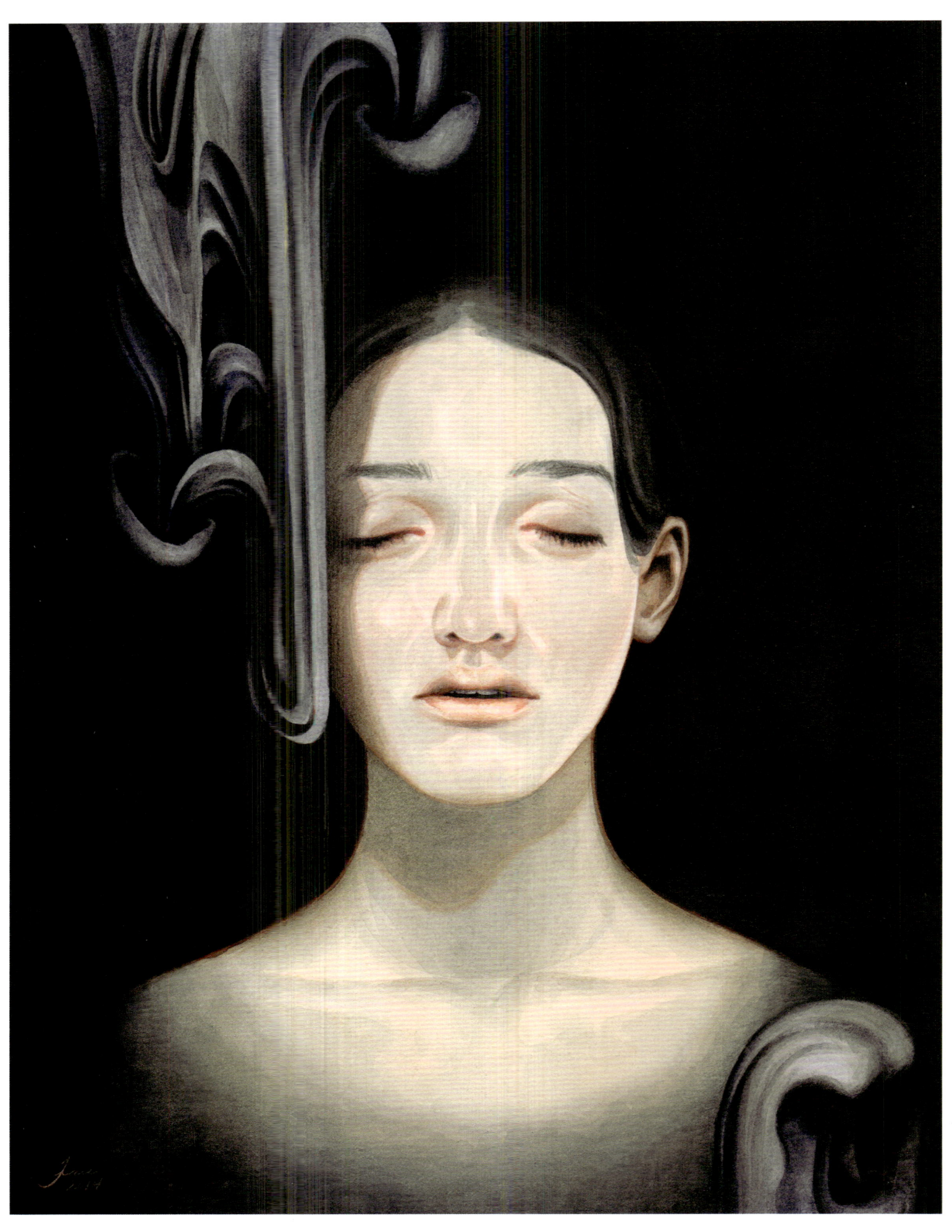

TO MY DEEP-SEATED ABYSS I
acrylic & colored pencil on paper, 11" x 14", 2014

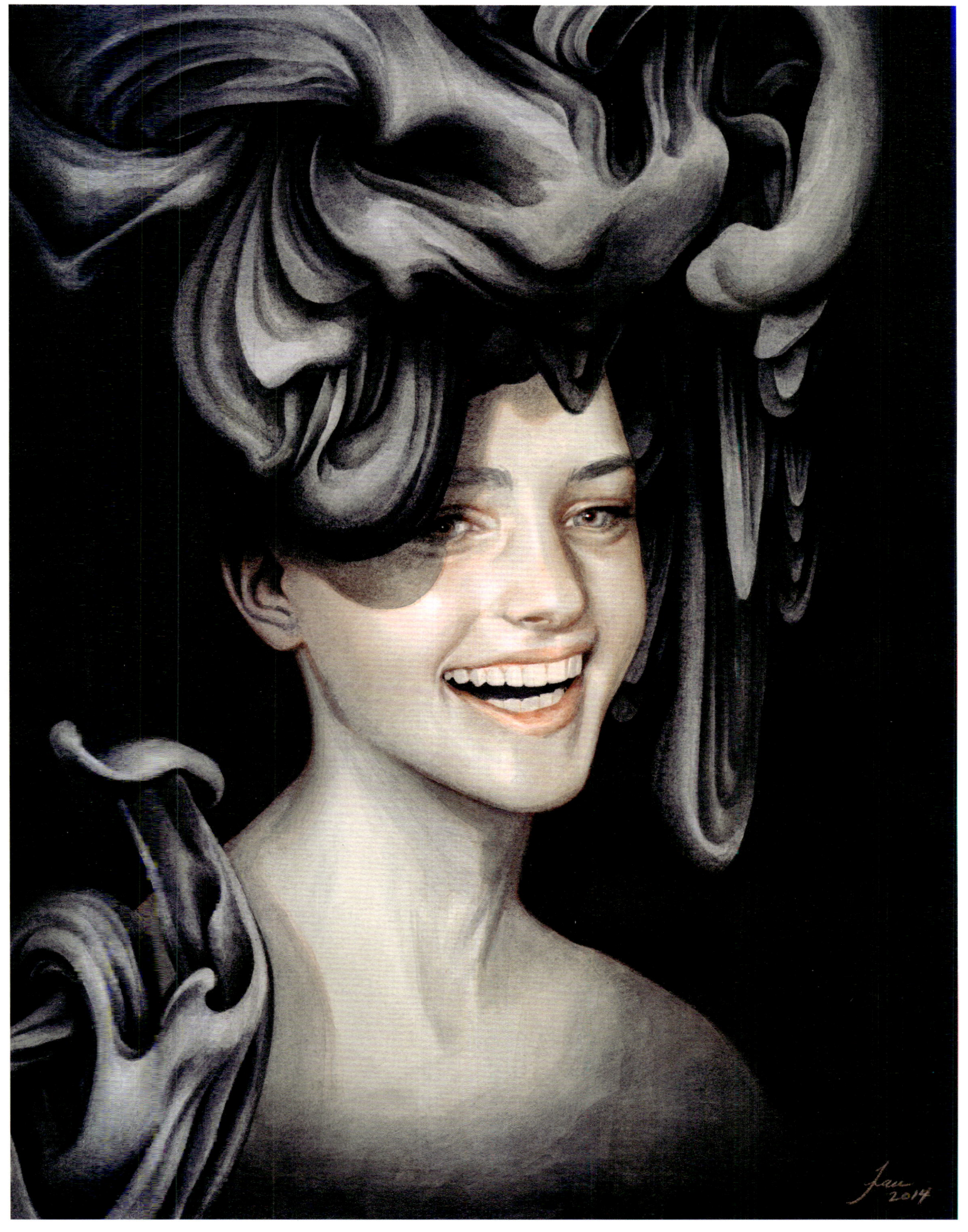

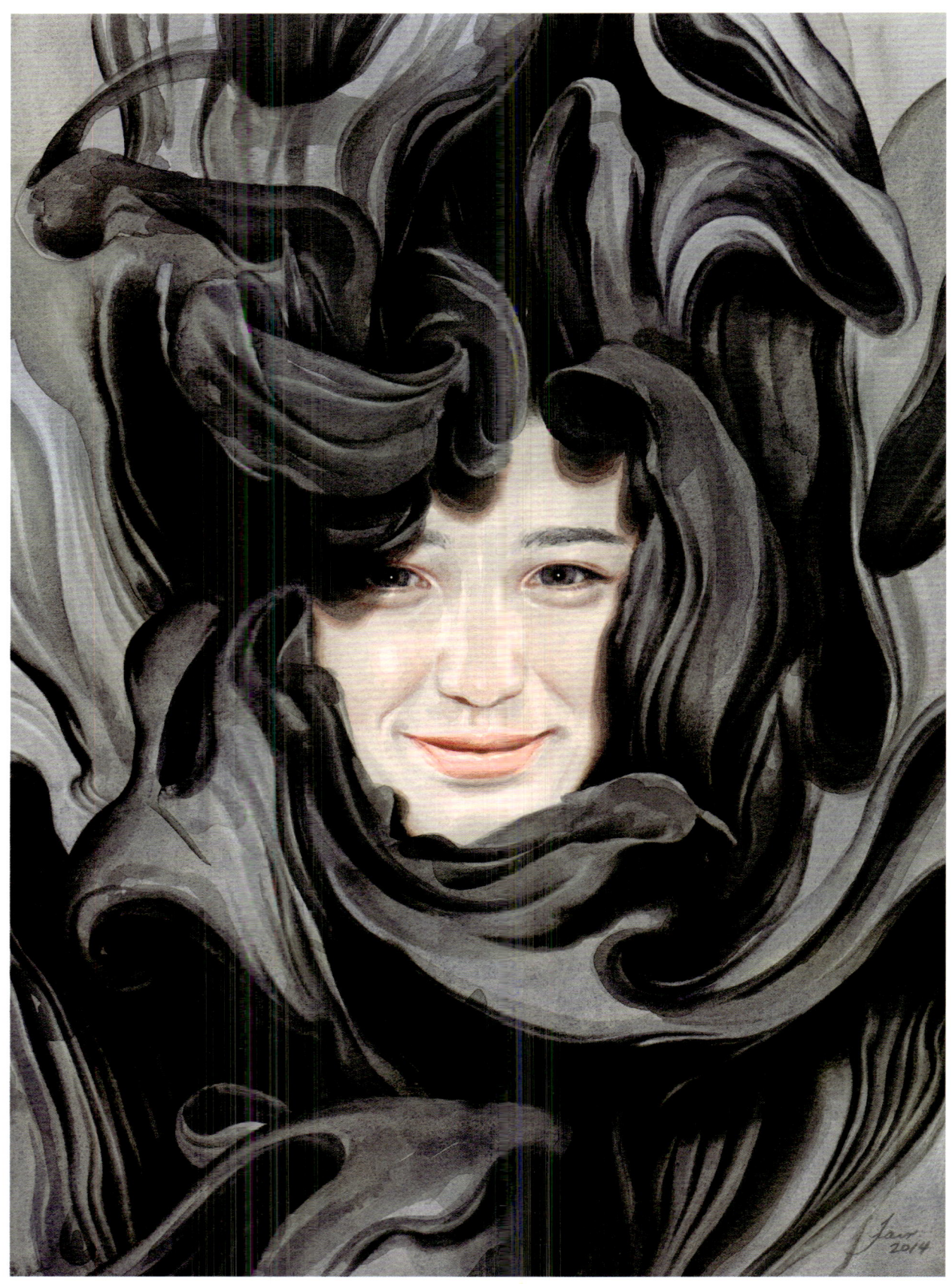

above
TO MY DEEP-SEATED ABYSS IV
acrylic & colored pencil on paper, 11" x 14", 2014

right
TO MY DEEP-SEATED ABYSS III
acrylic & colored pencil on paper, 11" x 14", 2014

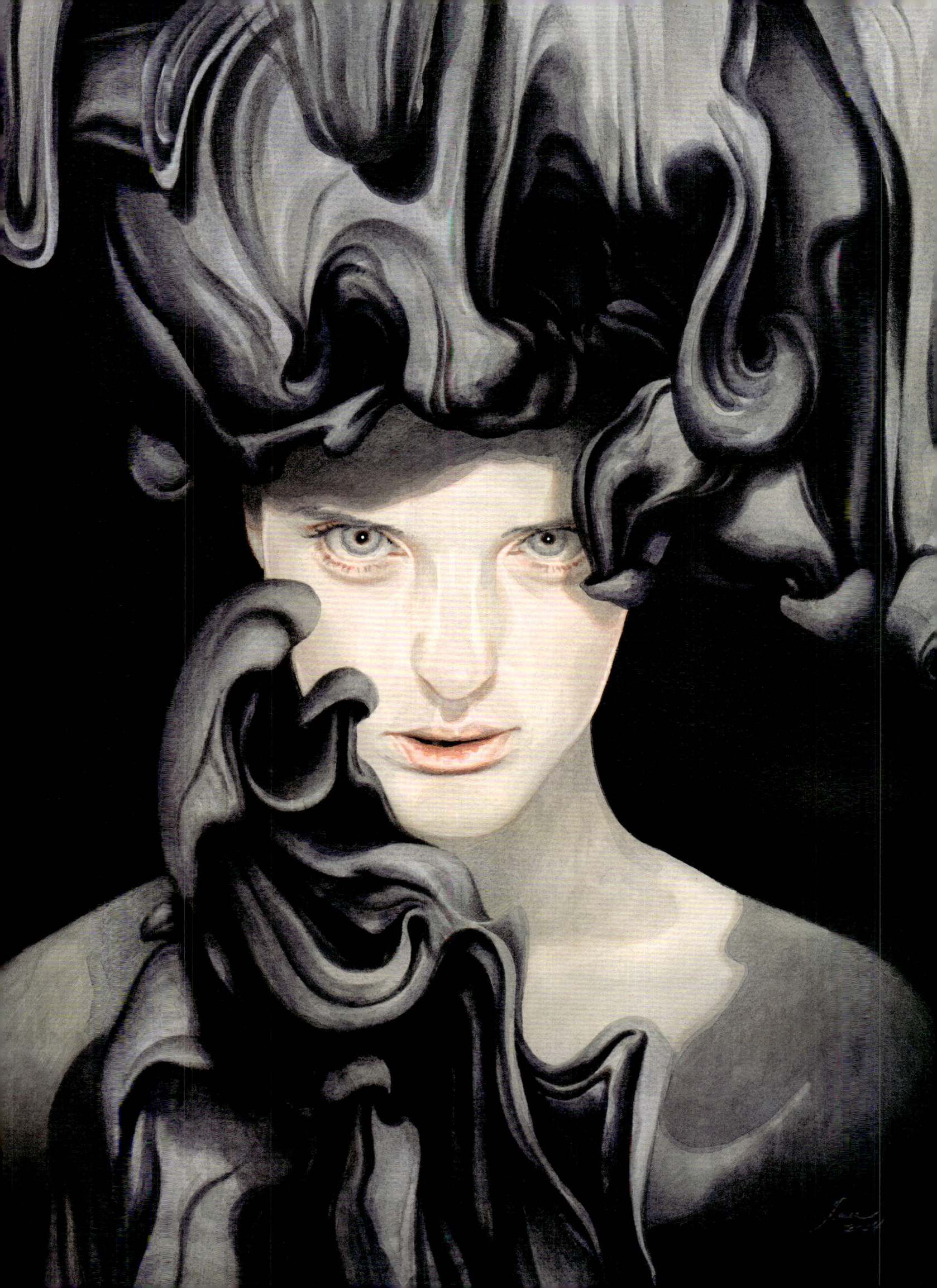

THE FLOODED HOUR

2016

With the continuous reoccurrence of the large-than-life theme over the years, I decided to dedicate an entire show based on it, titled *The Flooded Hour*. Personally, the *flooded hour* represents the period of time that follows distress and the mind's desperate attempt to make sense of things. It's an obscure state of limbo where one finds oneself searching for shelter from a storm. When dealing with extreme stress, I often feel like I'm drowning, and all I can do is try to stay afloat. Sometimes, to keep above the water is to revisit those turbulent memories and find solace in them.

This group of paintings is a mixture of my reoccurring themes of nostalgia and melancholy. It's my attempt to give form to obscure sorrows and how to cope with them.

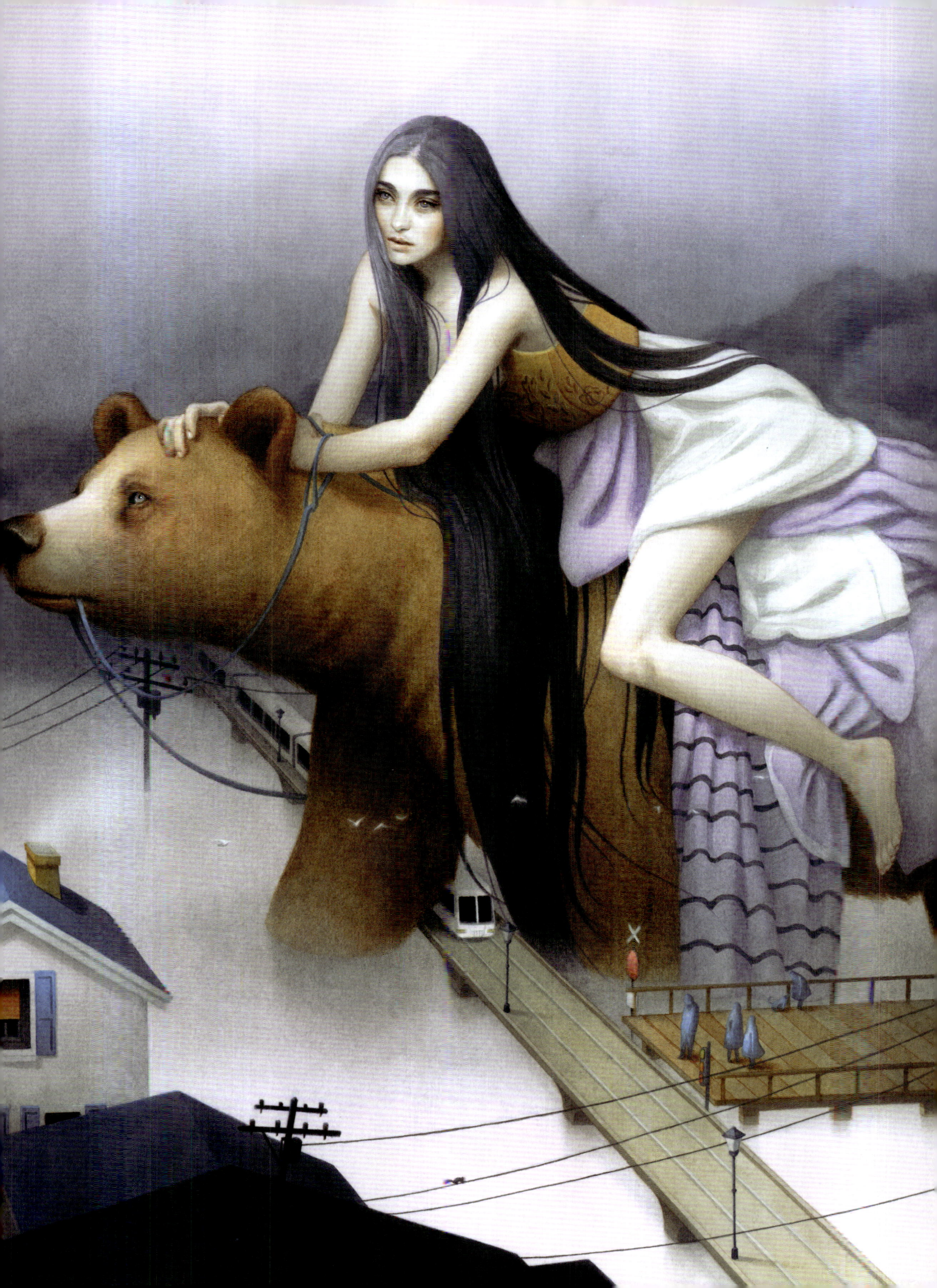

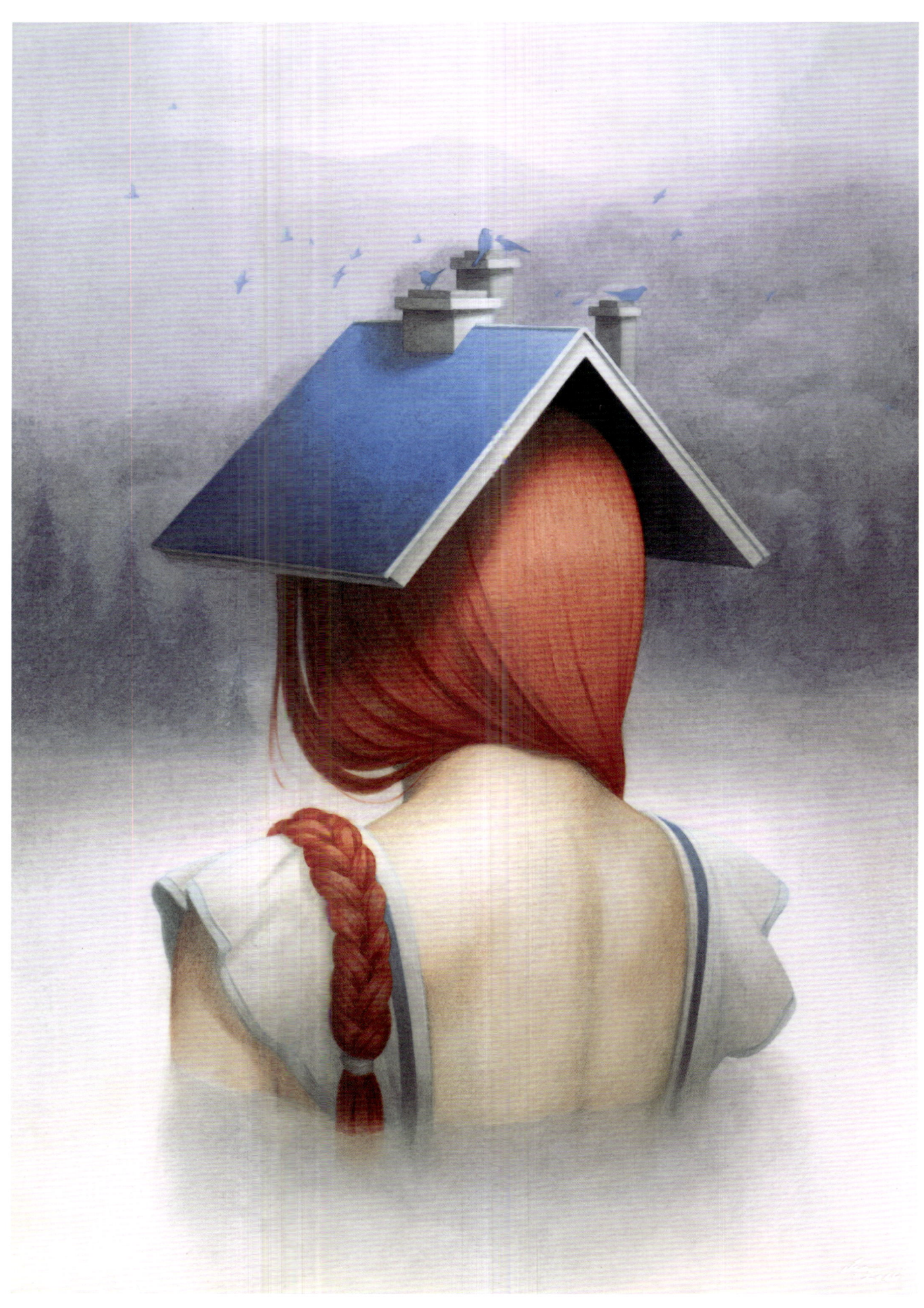

BLUE CARCASSES OF THE DEAD NIGHT
acrylic & colored pencil on paper, 10" x 14" 2016

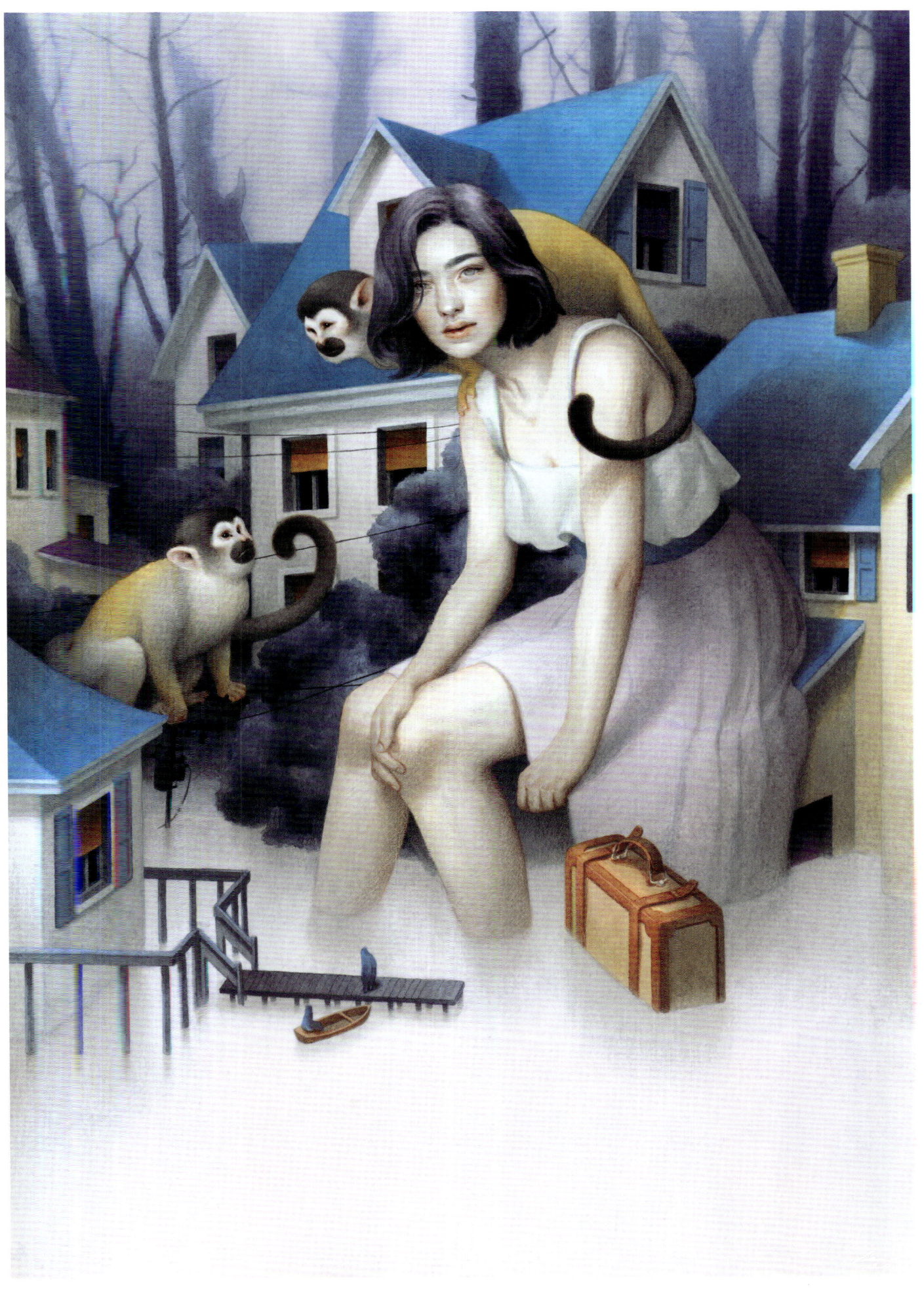

BY THE WAITING HOUR
acrylic & colored pencil on paper 12" x 16.75", 2016

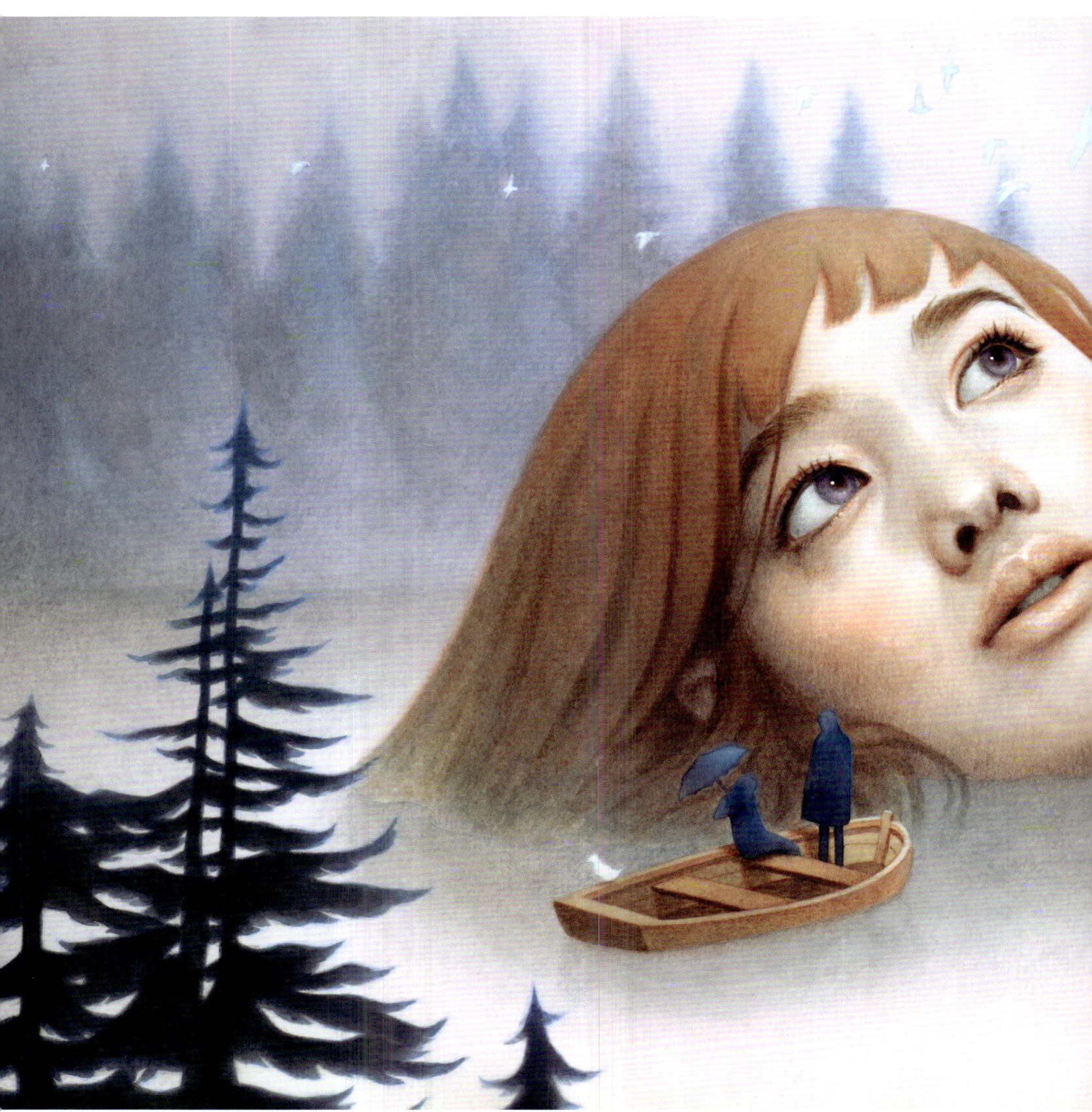

HOMAGE & THE LONE MOON
acrylic & colored pencil on paper, 15.5" x 3.75", 2015

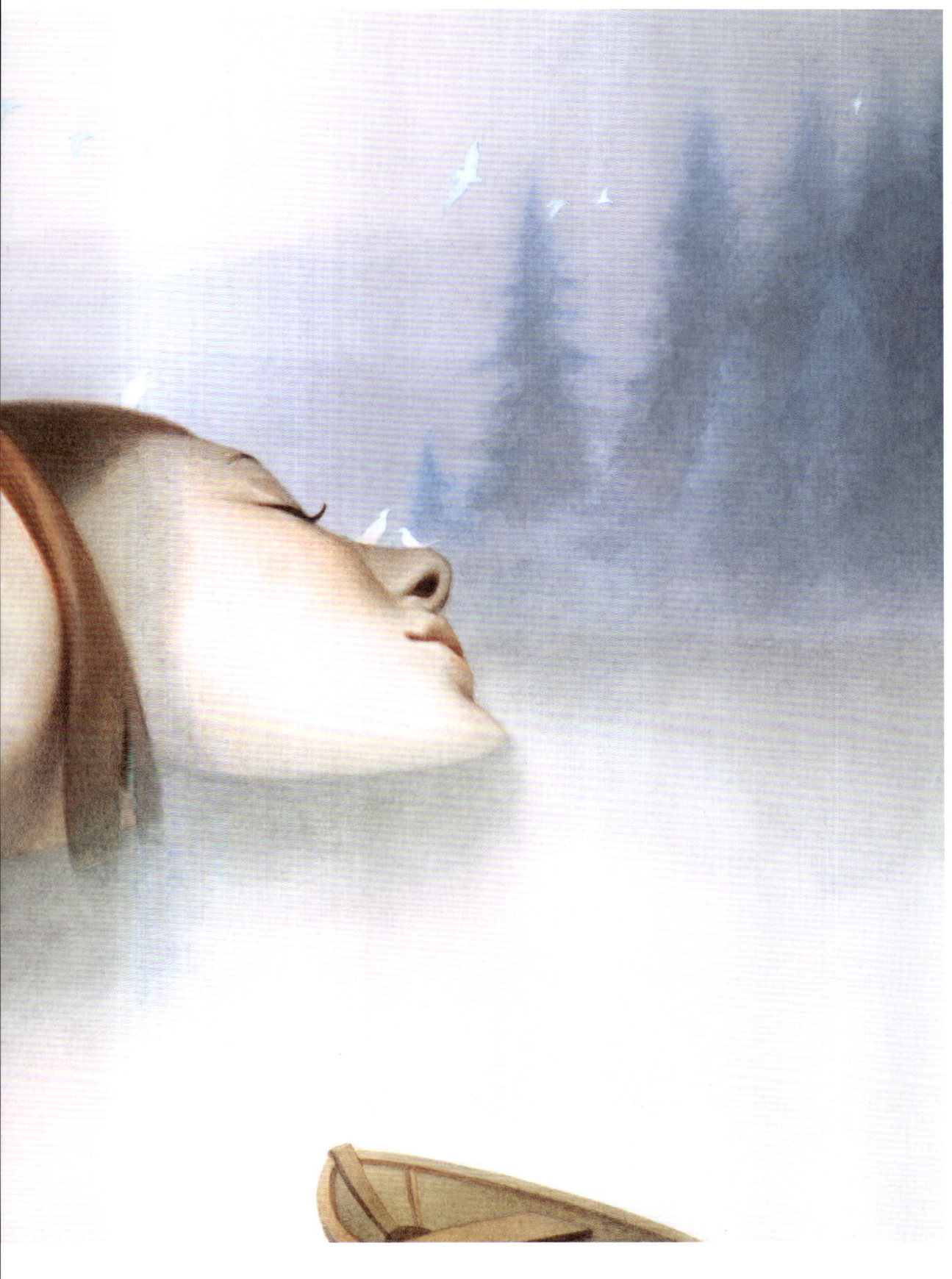

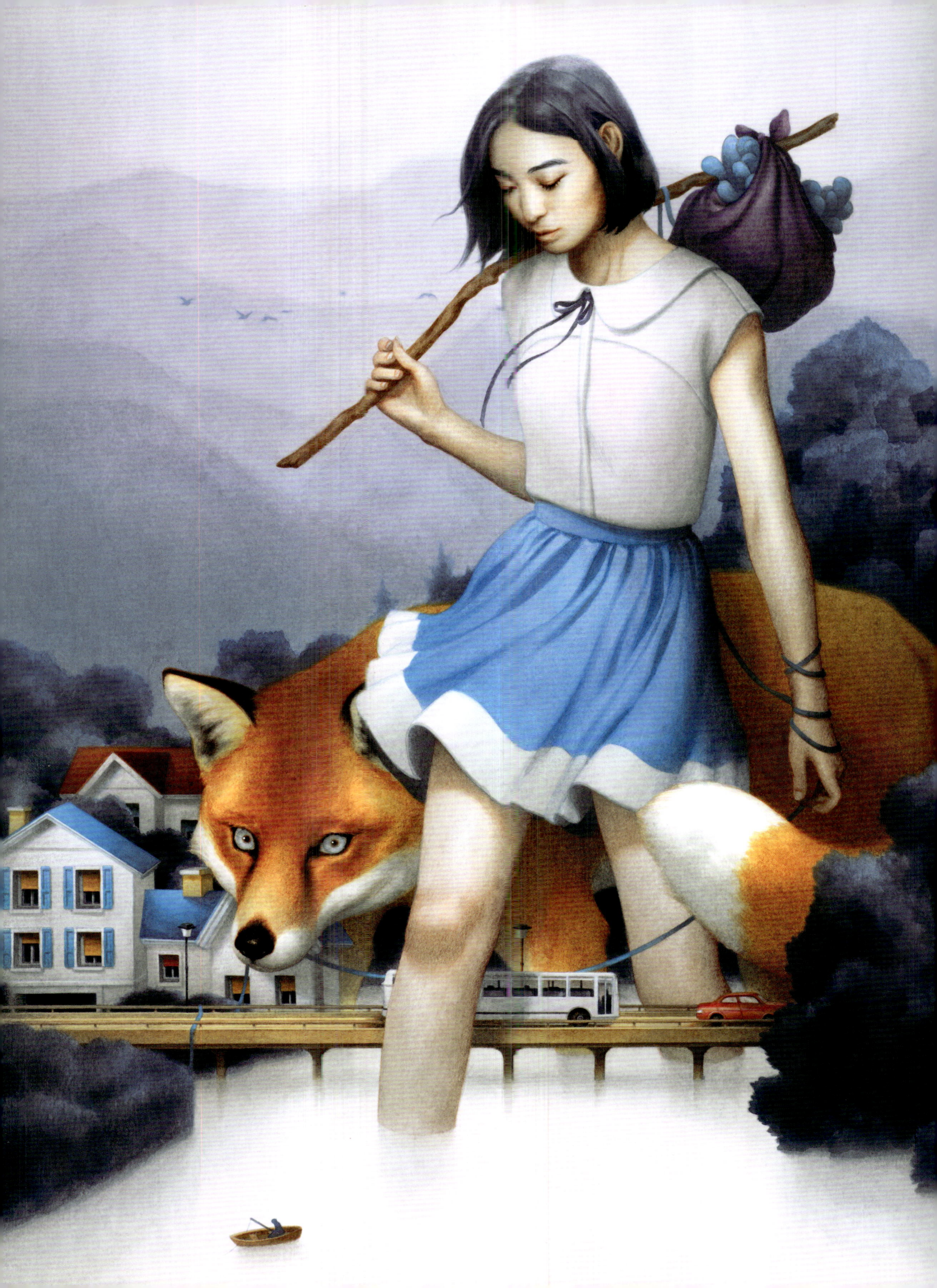

SOMEWHERE BETWEEN NOW & THEN
acrylic & colored pencil on paper, 15" x 19", 2016

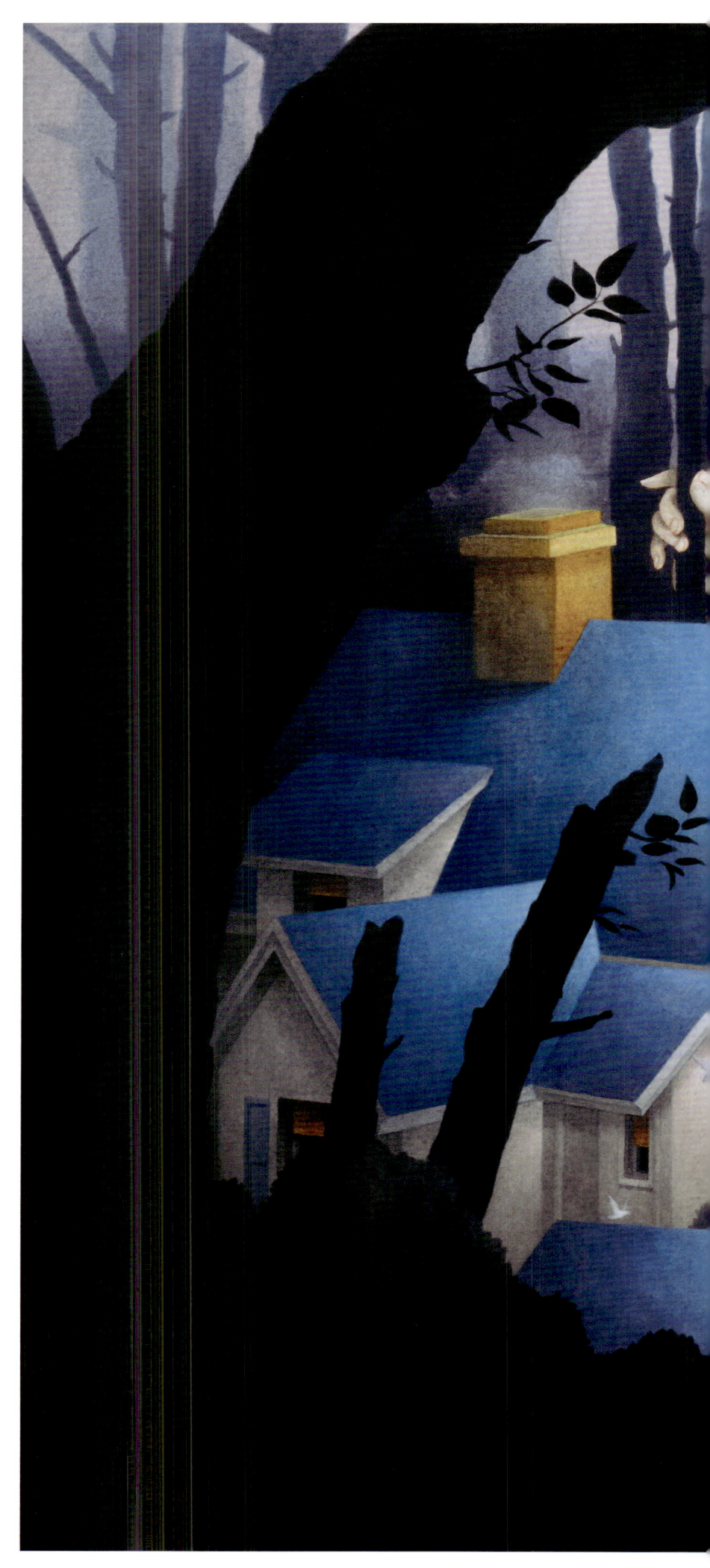

THE RIVERBED NIGHTINGALE
acrylic & colored pencil on paper, 20" x 16", 2016

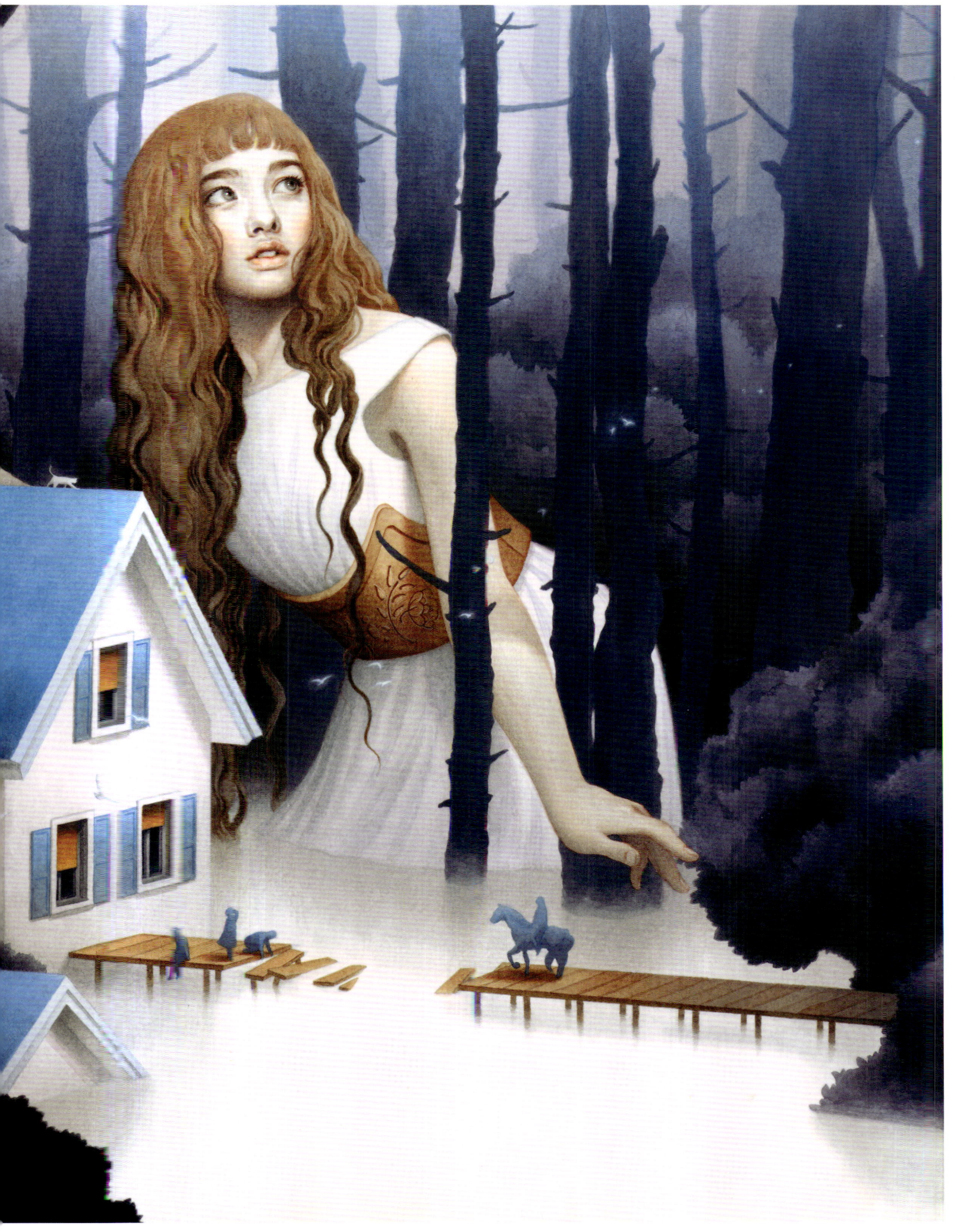

THE FLOODED HOUR II

2017

The following is a continuation of the previous series with the same name. For this five-piece collection, I wanted to expand on the theme of the *flooded hour* during the darker stage of twilight, when the sun sets and roads are lit by street lamps.

A tiny passersby commute to their destinations on boats and buses, they come across a wandering giantess. But they are oblivious to one another and go about their journeys. The painting's larger-than-life vagabonds find themselves in dimly lit towns as glowing trails of warm light illuminate their path.

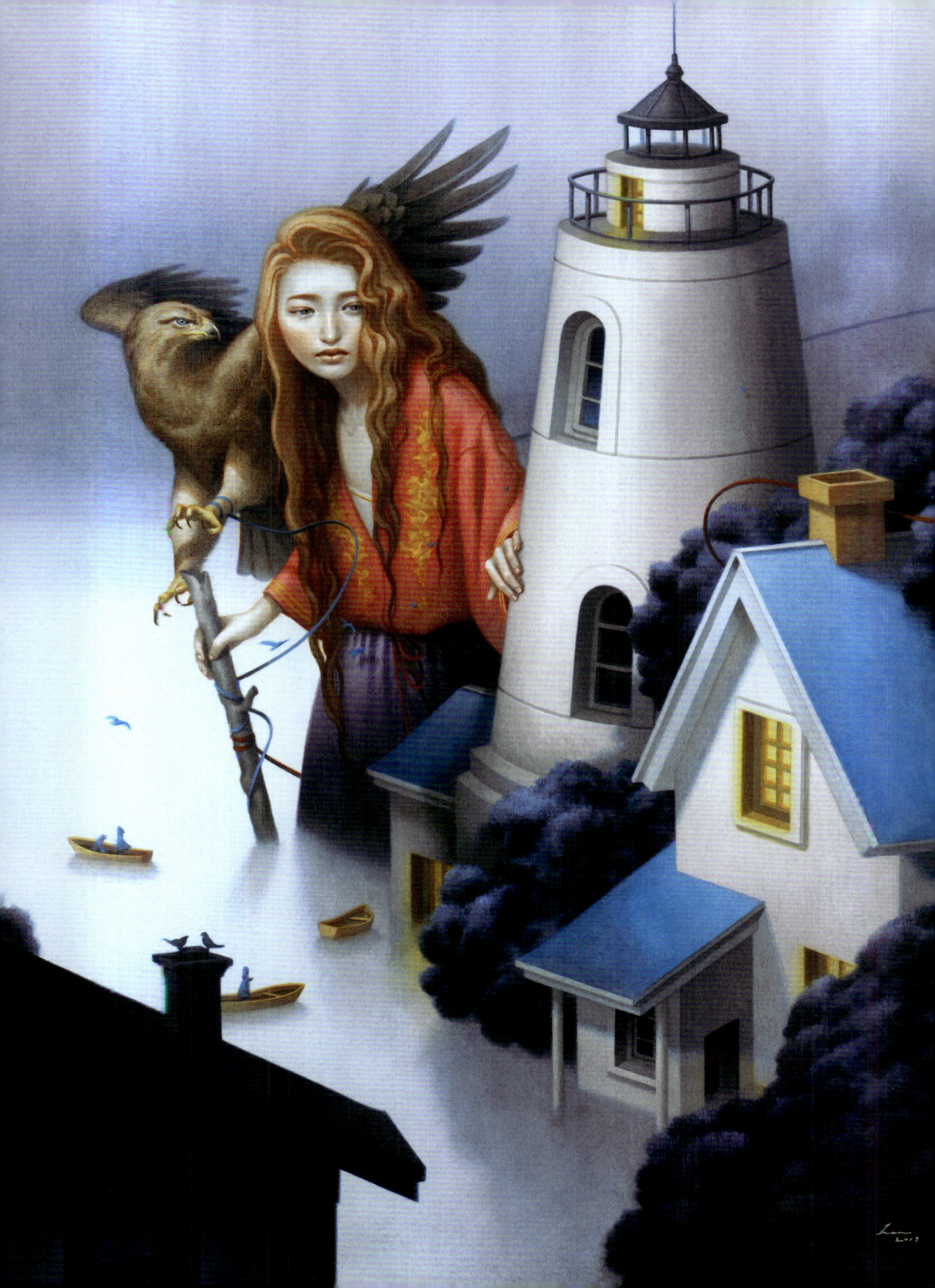

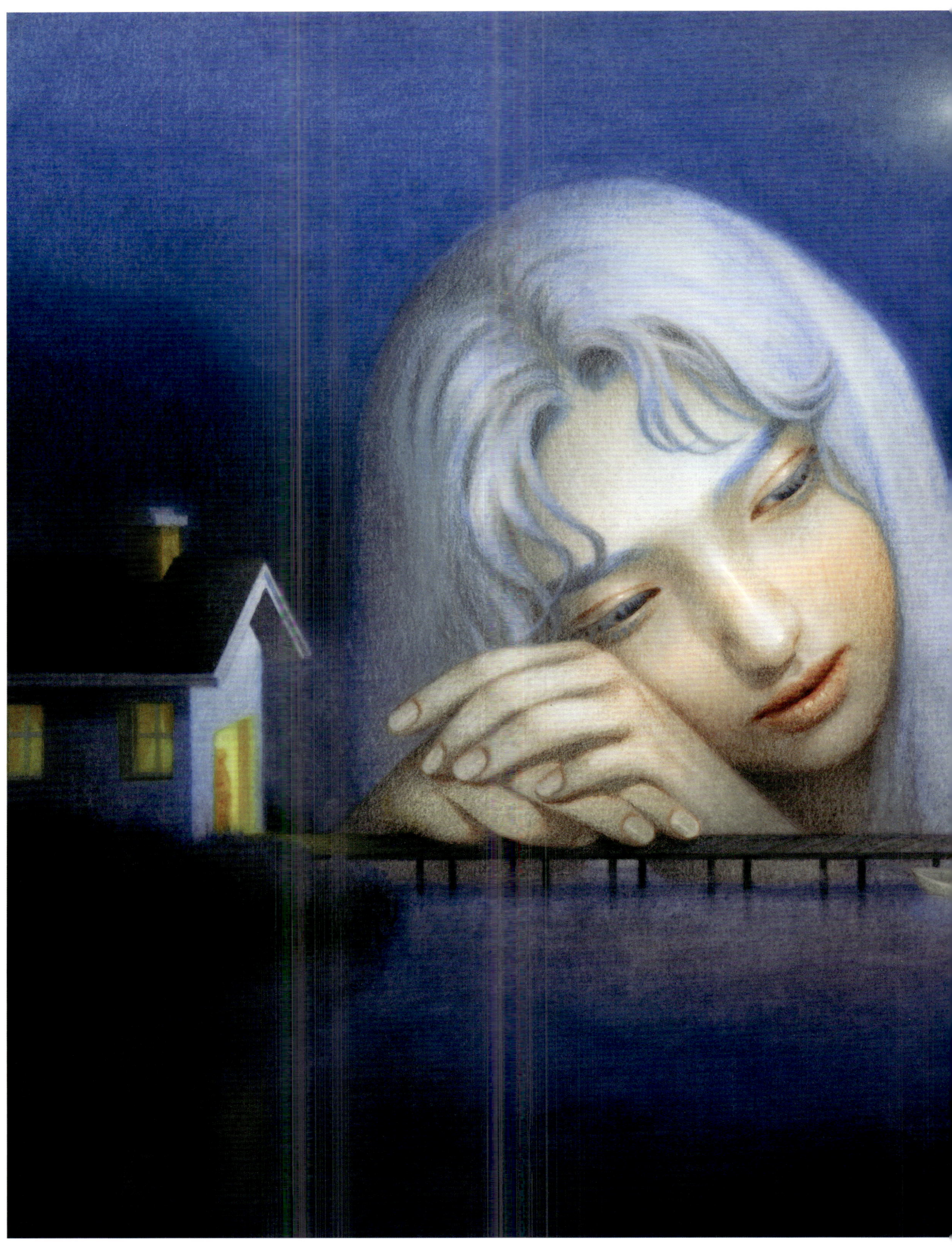

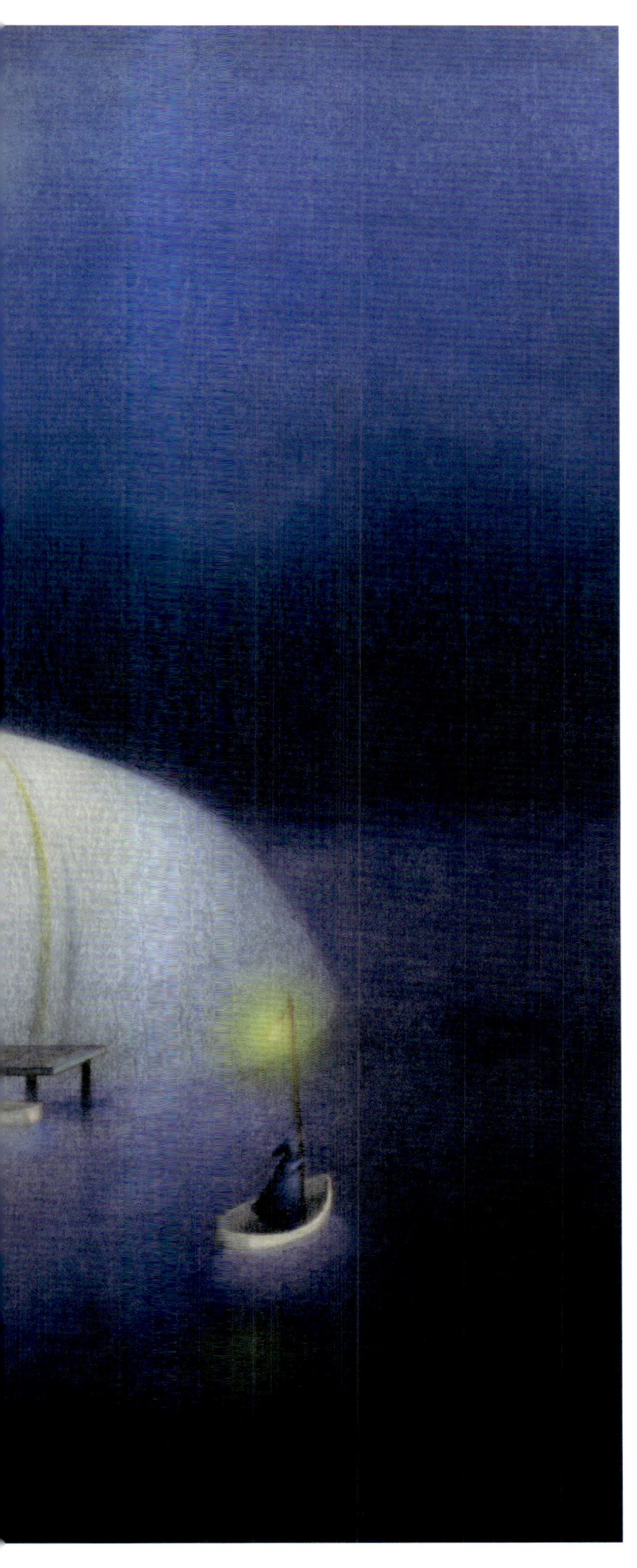

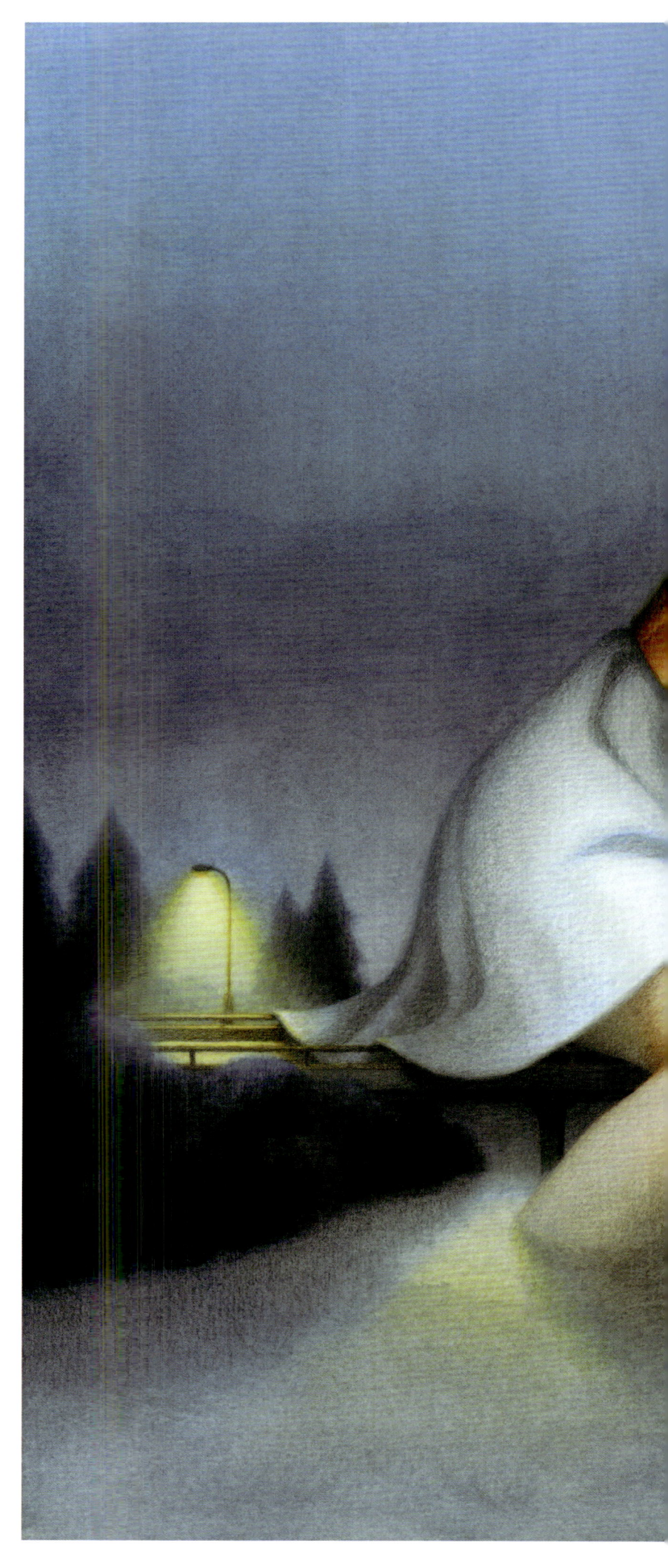

MIDNIGHT PASSERBY
acrylic & colored pencil on paper, 15" x 12", 2017

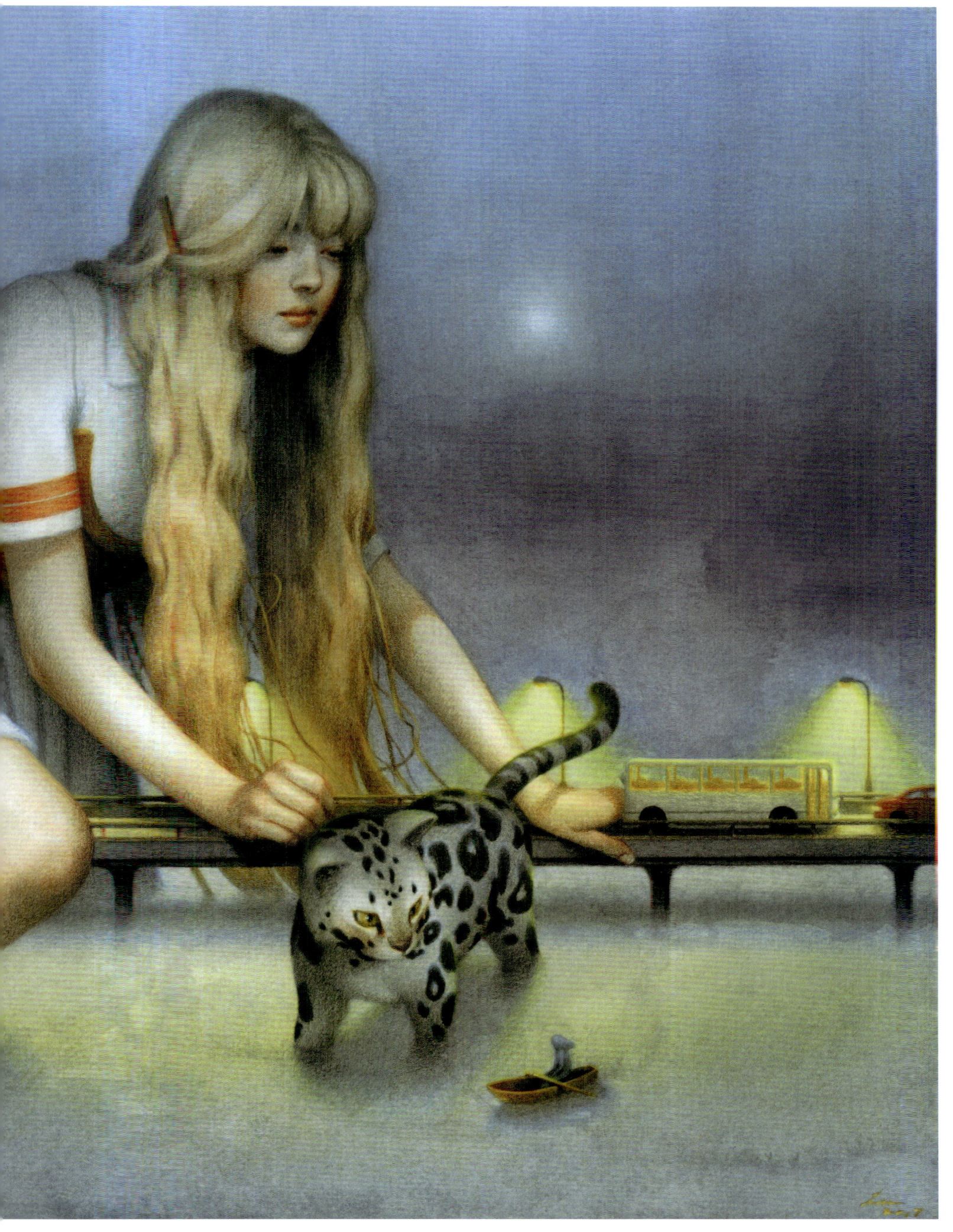

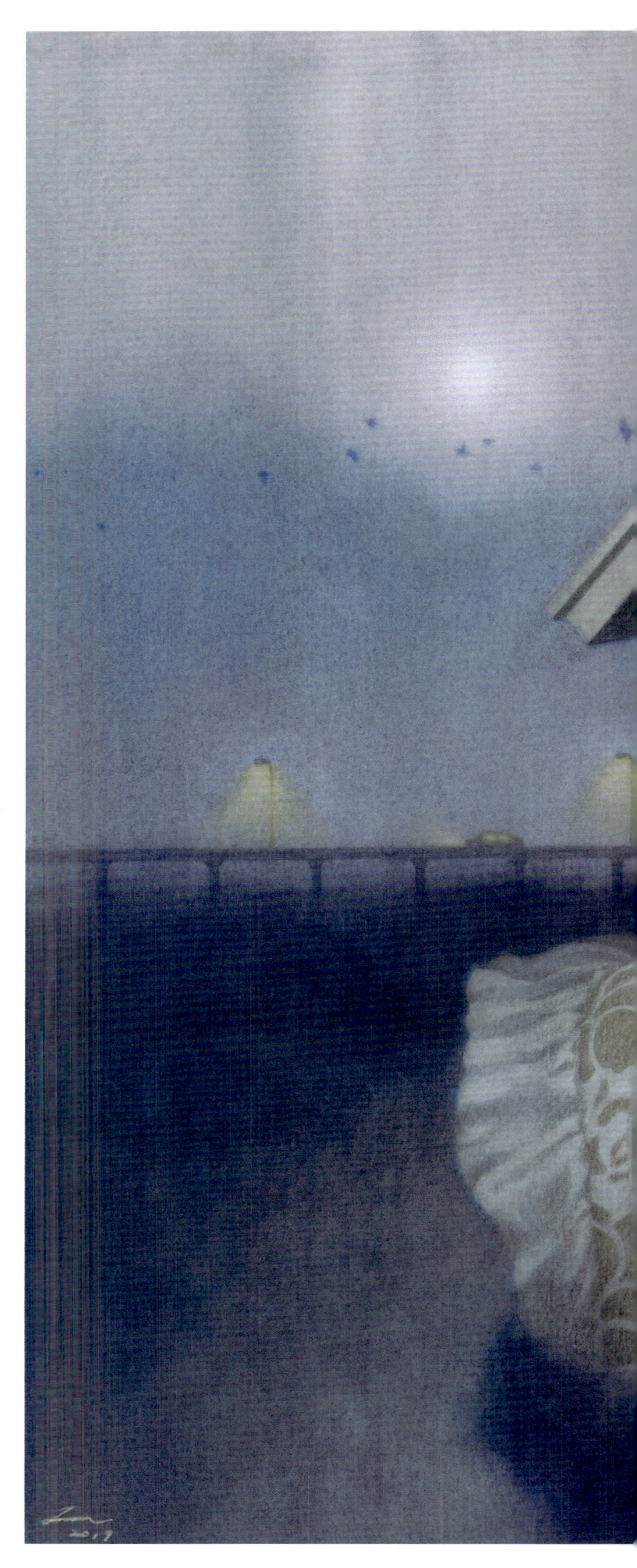

SEE YOU ON THE MORROW
acrylic & colored pencil on paper, 14" x 11", 2017

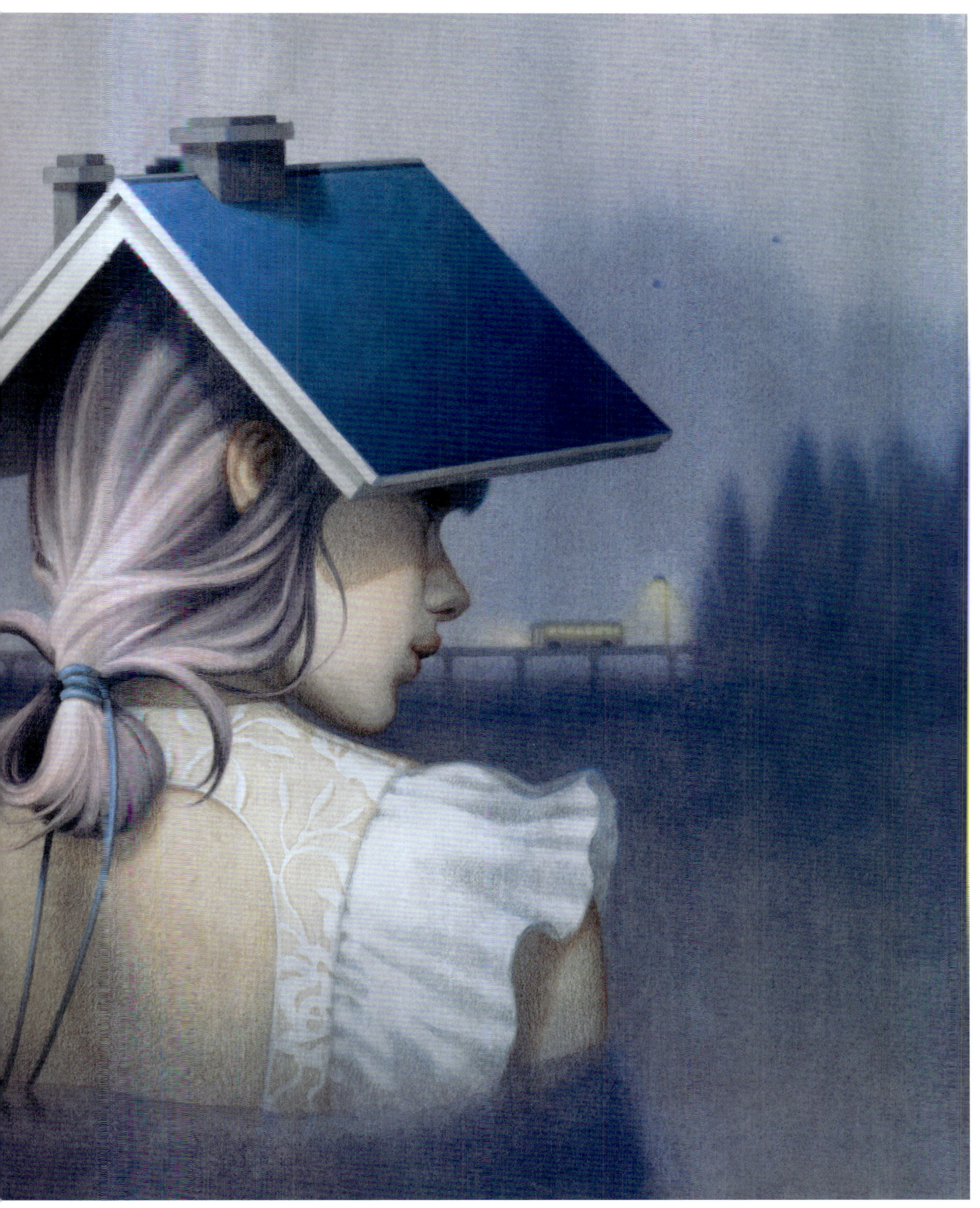

THRICE BY TWILIGHT
acrylic & colored pencil on paper, 16" x 20", 2017

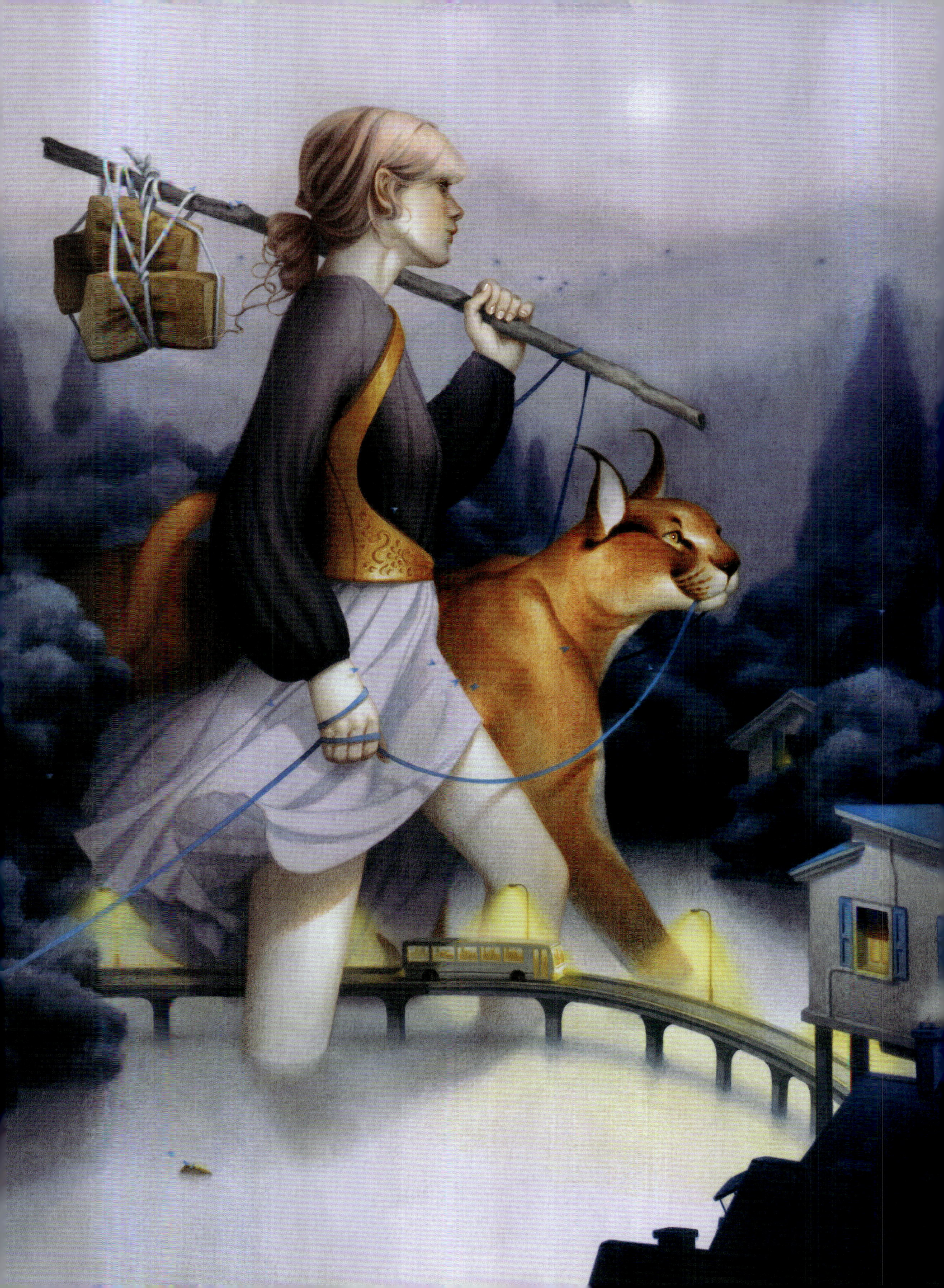

GROUP EXHIBITION

2009-2018

Many of the underlaying themes in my work are inspired by my experiences of having a mentally ill loved one, the loss of my little brother and my memories of growing up. Motifs such as billowing fabric, truncated trees, boats, fog-filled atmospheres, floating shapes and little silhouetted people are reoccurring symbols that I use to convey this melancholy. They work together to tell my part of the story. The paintings are bound by a personal symbology meant to embody emotional nuances that I find difficult to articulate with words.

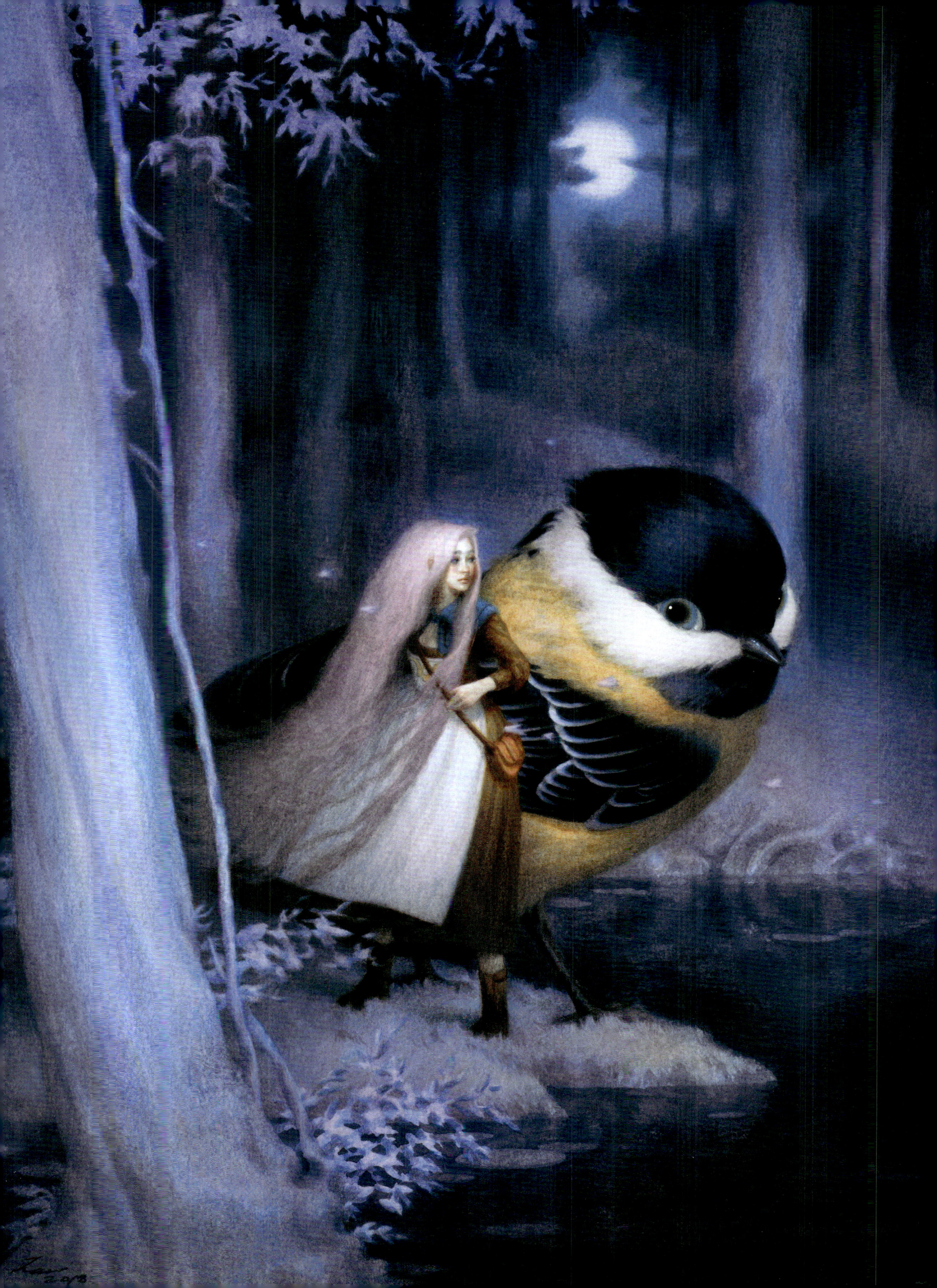

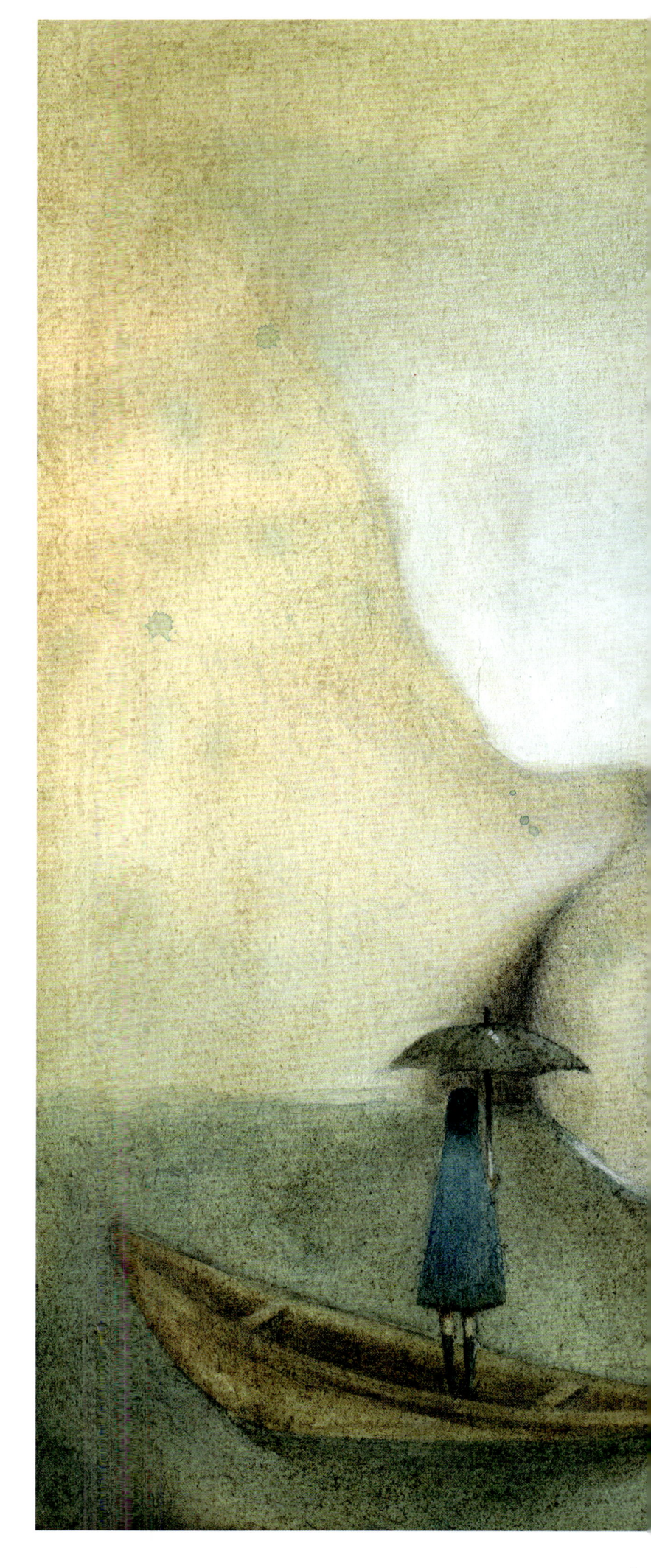

AS I LAY HERE, DYING
acrylic & colored pencil on paper, 10.5" x 3.5", 2009

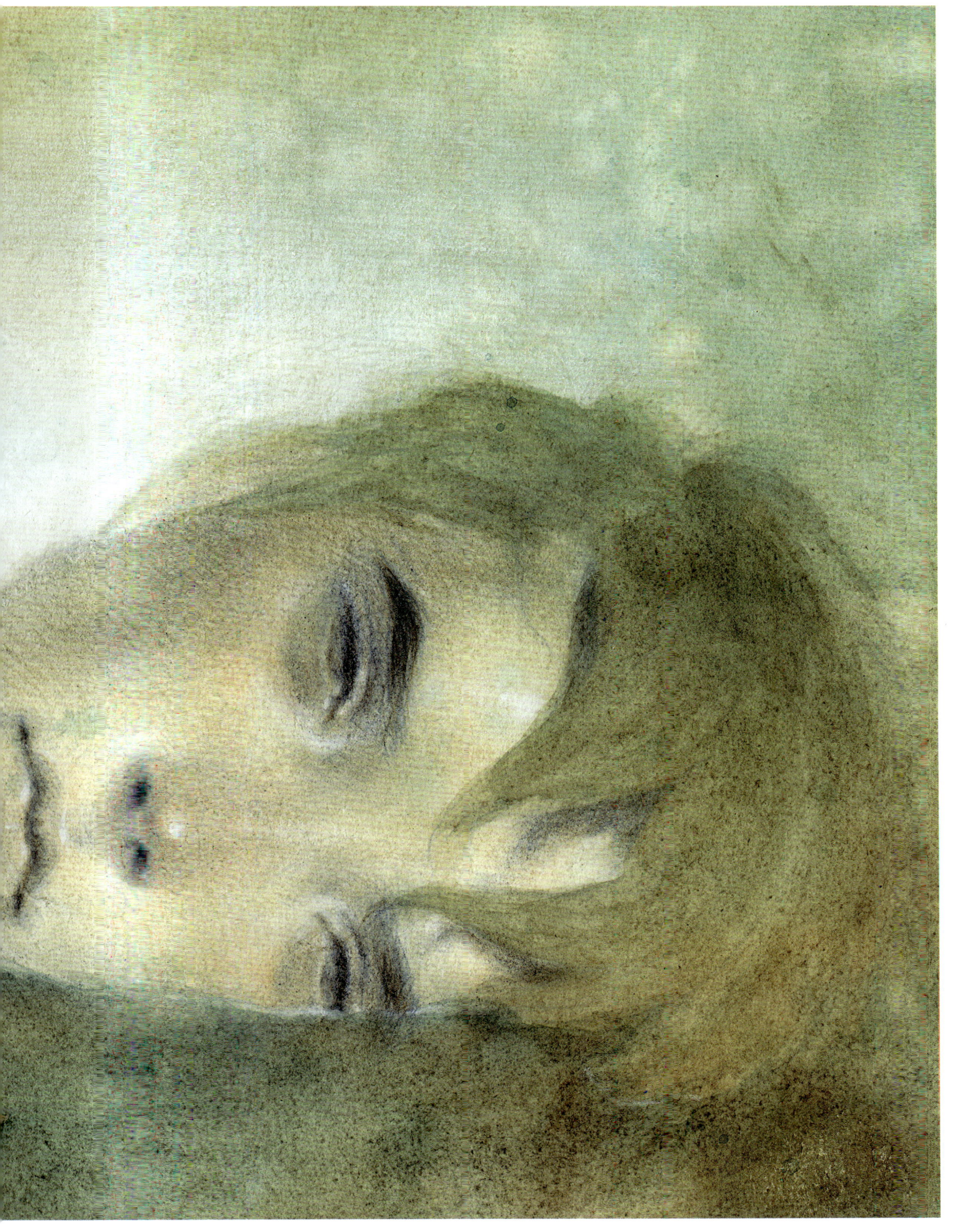

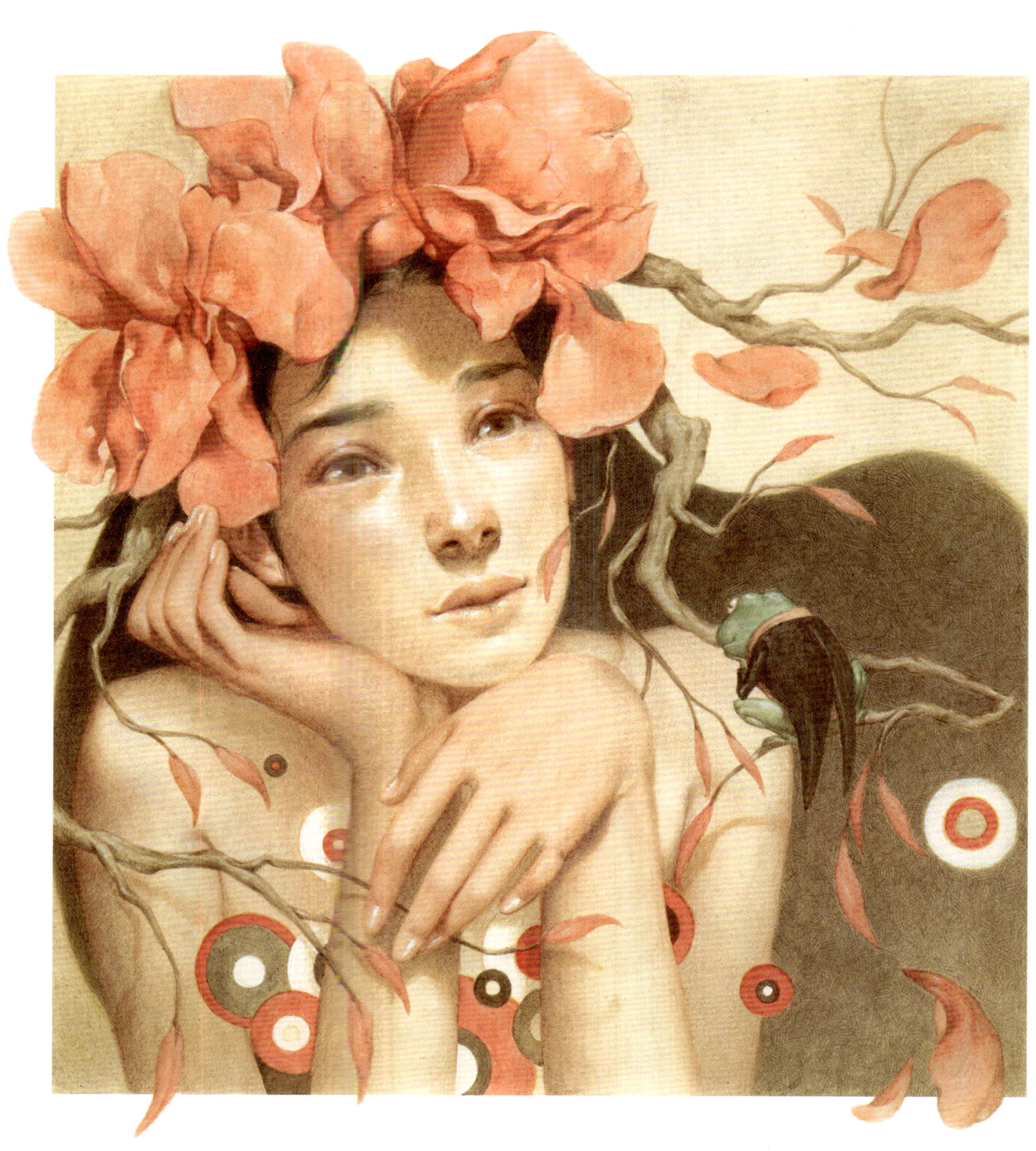

BONJOUR SAID THE PRINCE
acrylic & colored pencil on paper, 13" x 13", 2009

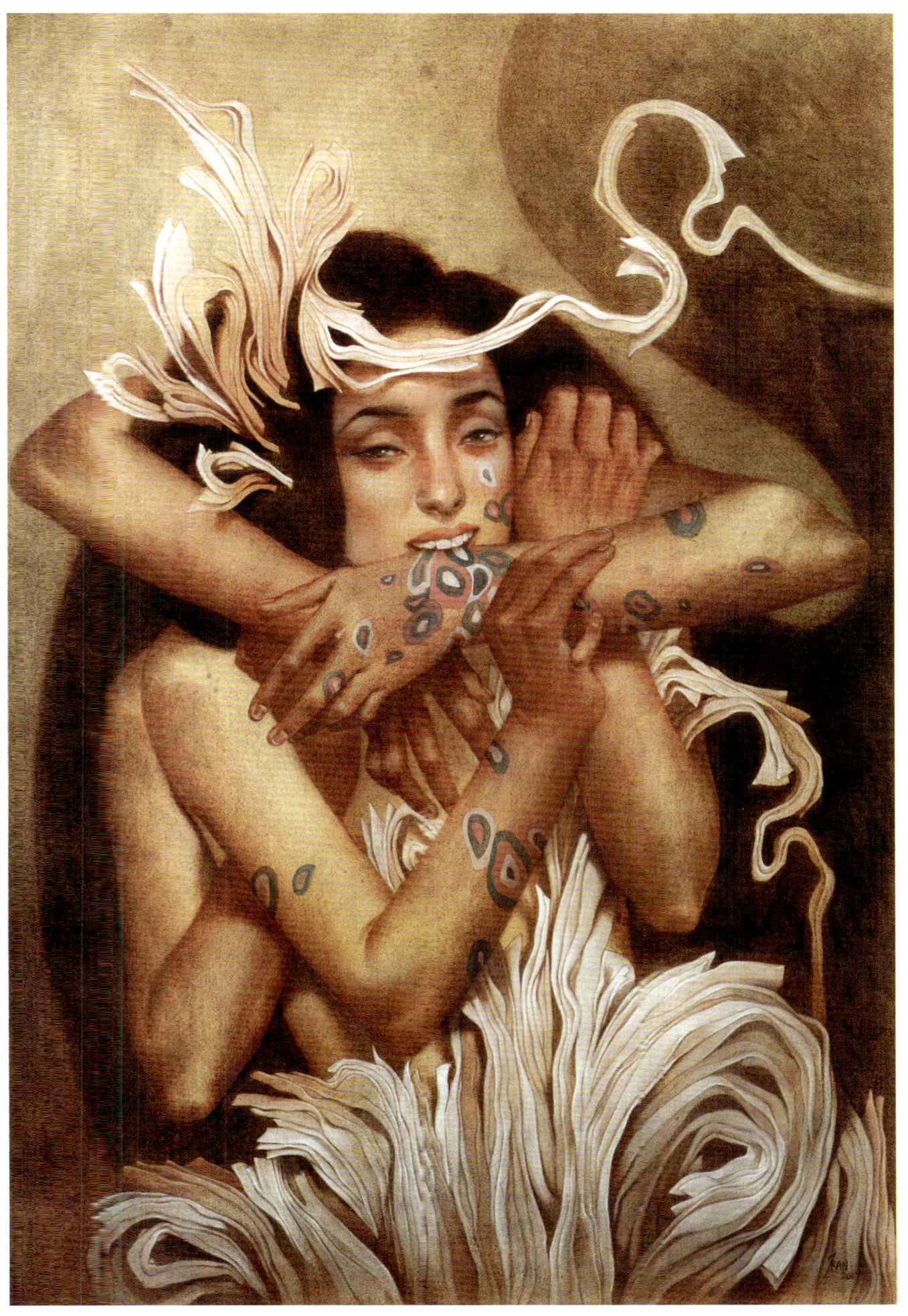

COMING APART BUT FALLING TOGETHER
acrylic & colored pencil on paper, 13.5" x 17.5" 2009

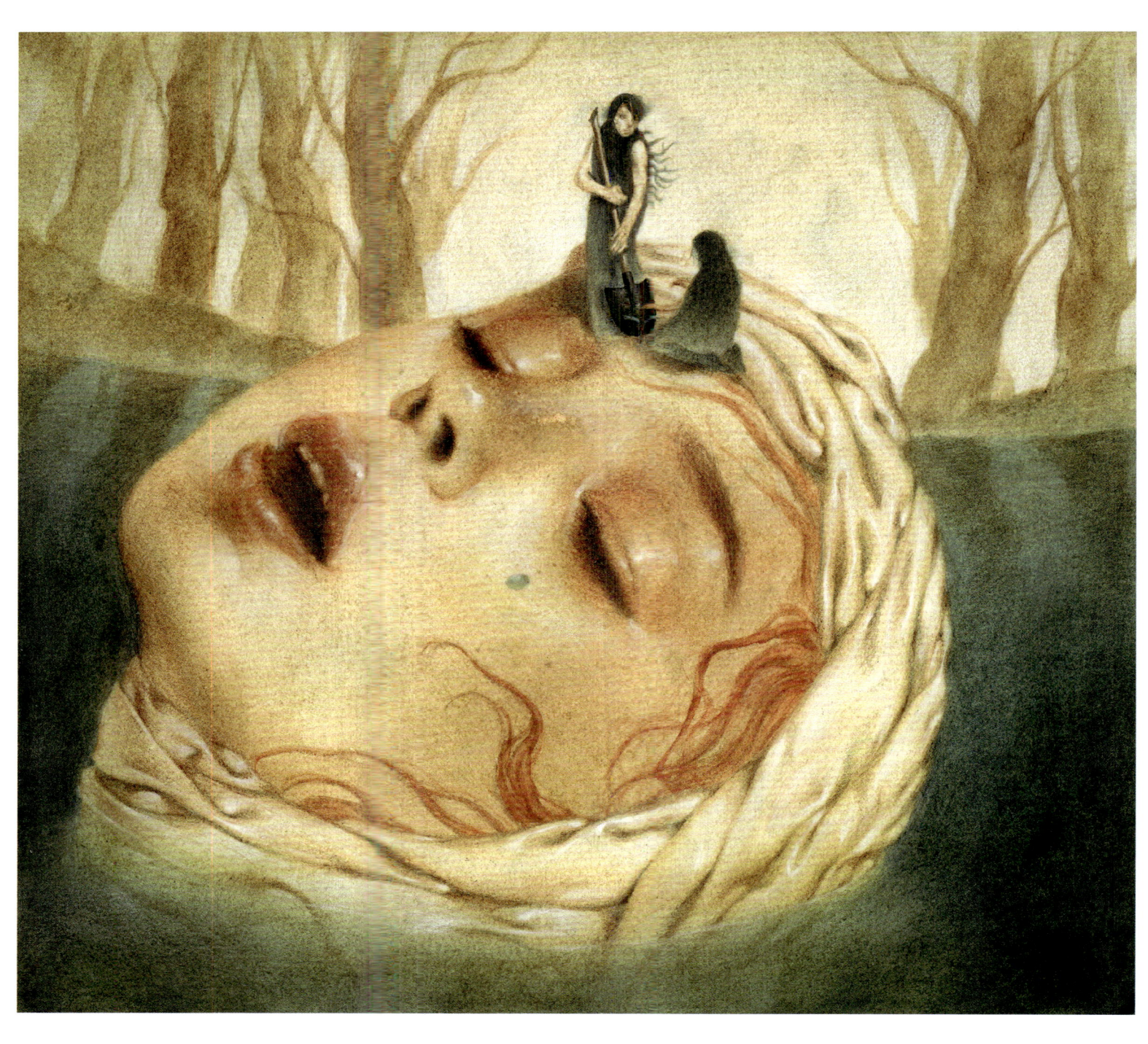

FURIAE
acrylic & colored pencil on paper, 13" x 11", 2009

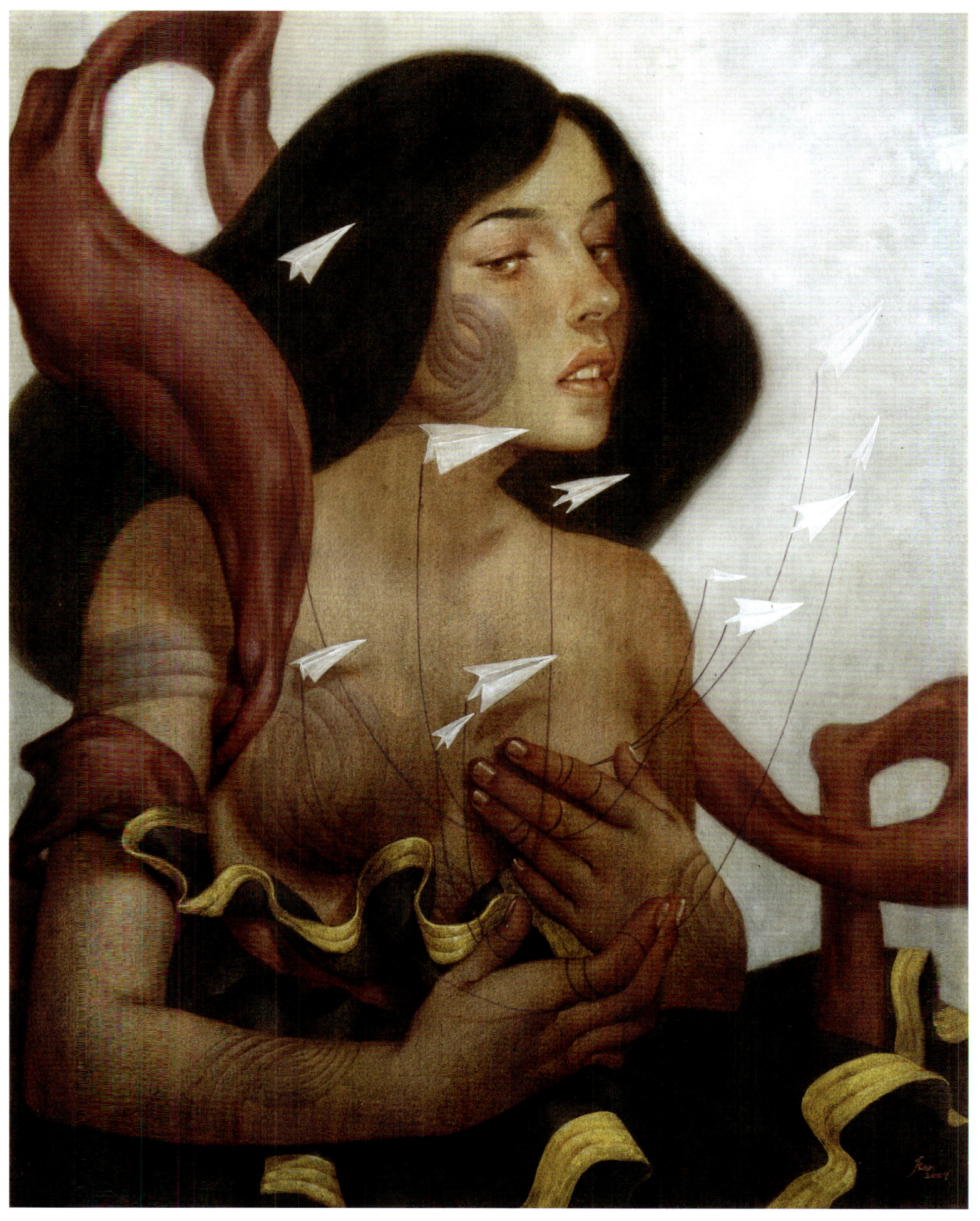

IF ONLY THERE WERE SULPHUR IN DREAMING
acrylic & colored pencil on paper, 16" x 20", 2009

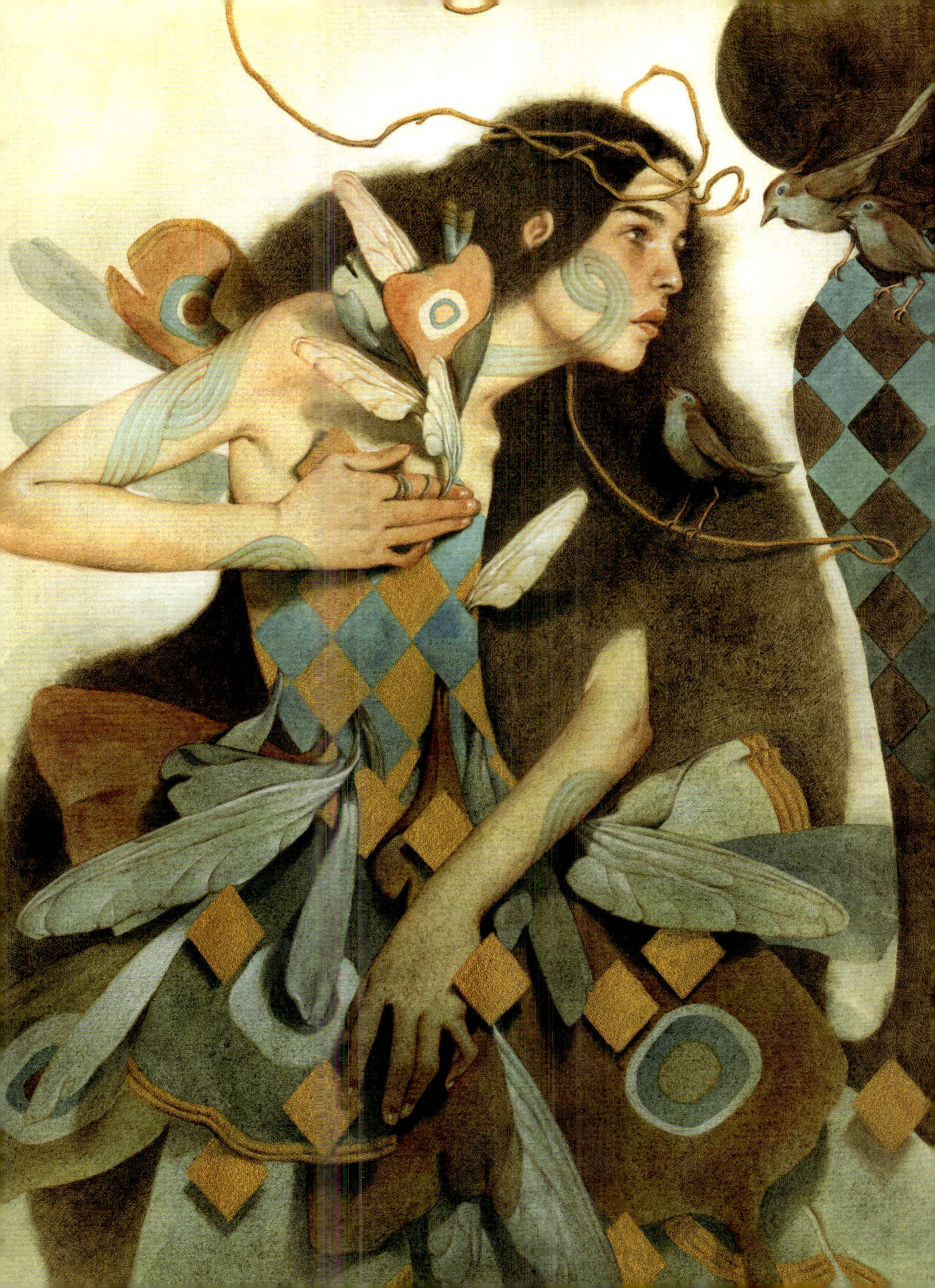

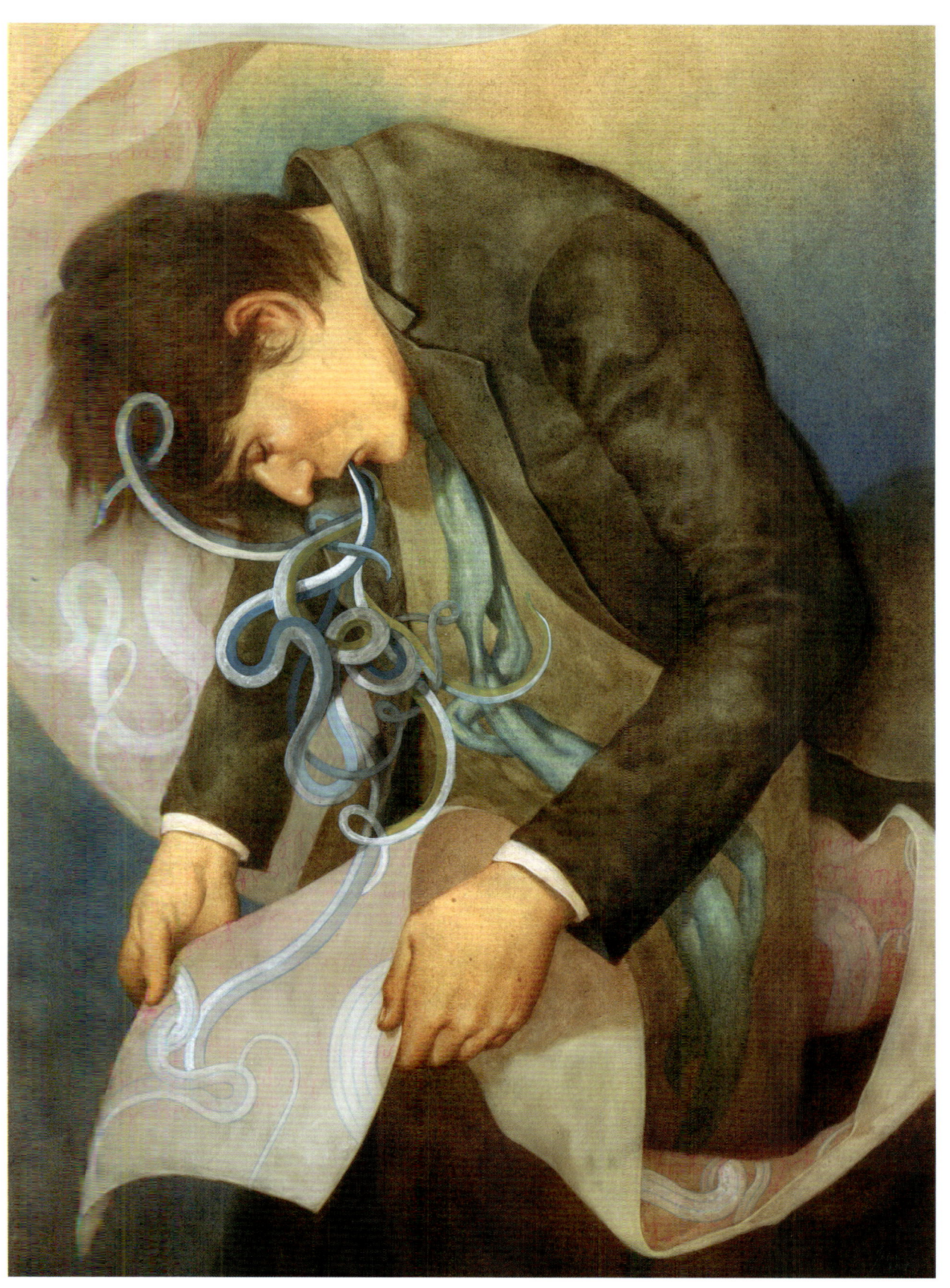

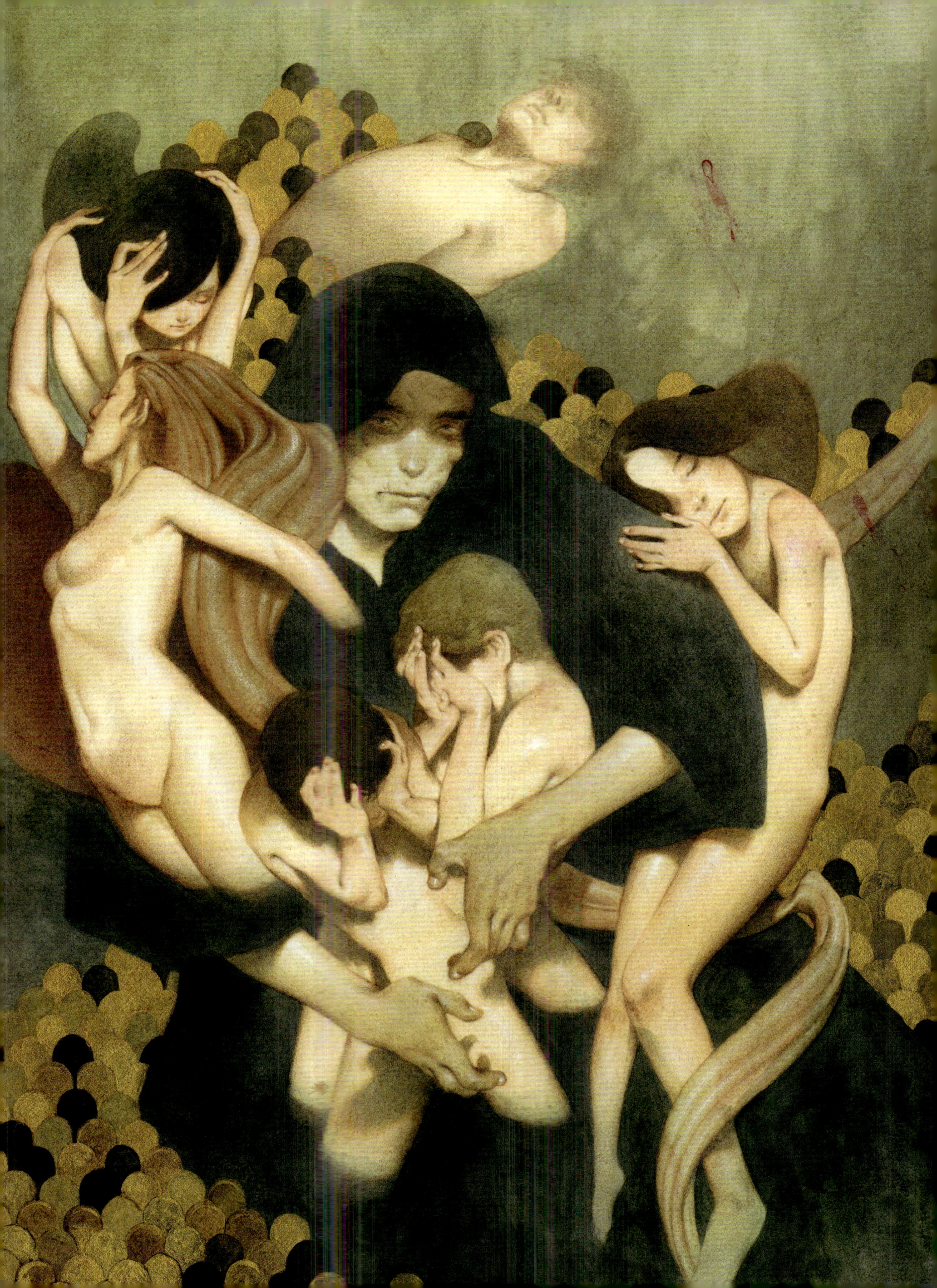

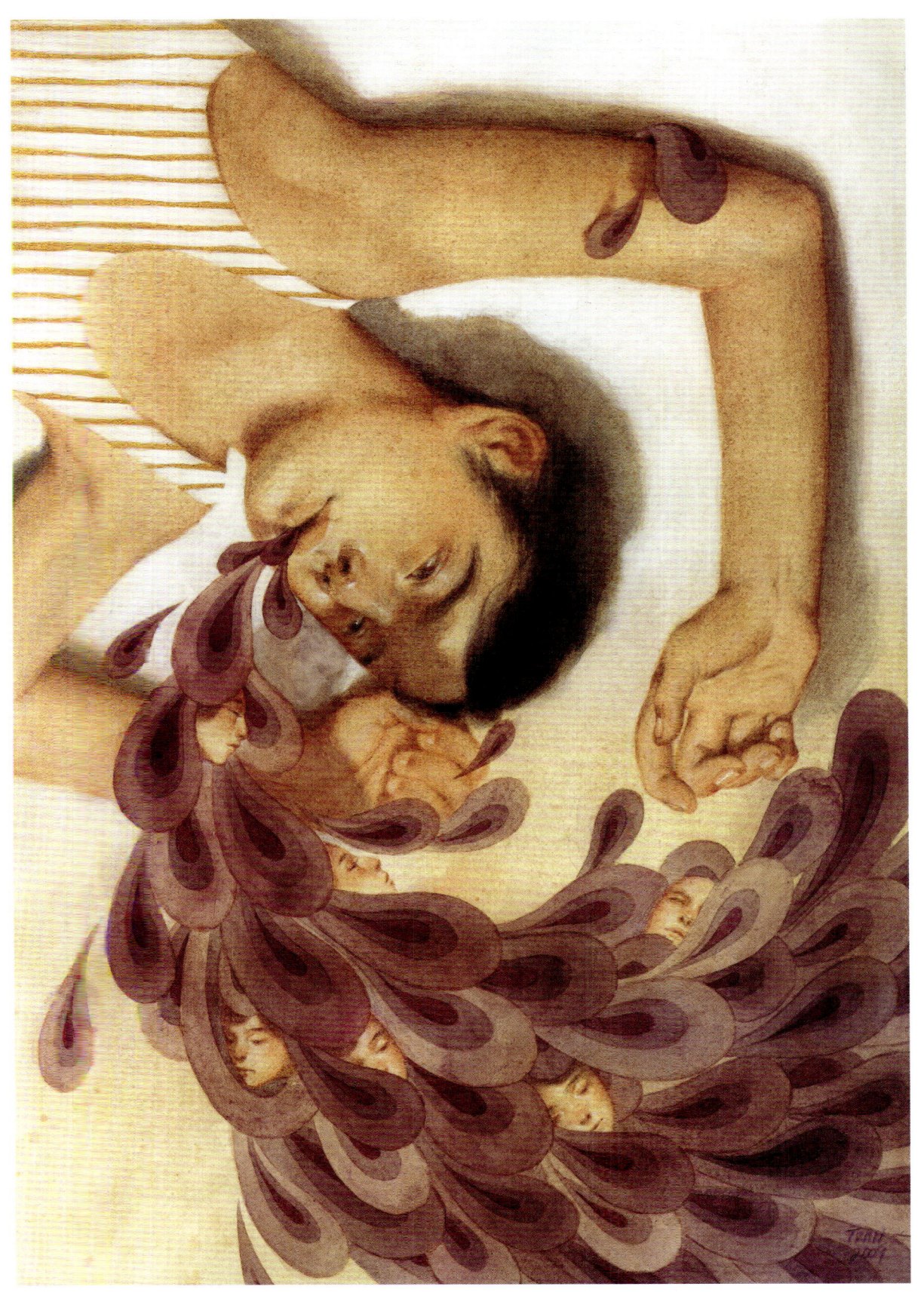

above
TO THE 9, WE GO
acrylic & colored pencil on paper, 11" x 15.5", 2009

left
TO HIS CONTENT & MY DEMISE
acrylic & colored pencil on paper, 12.5" x 17", 2009

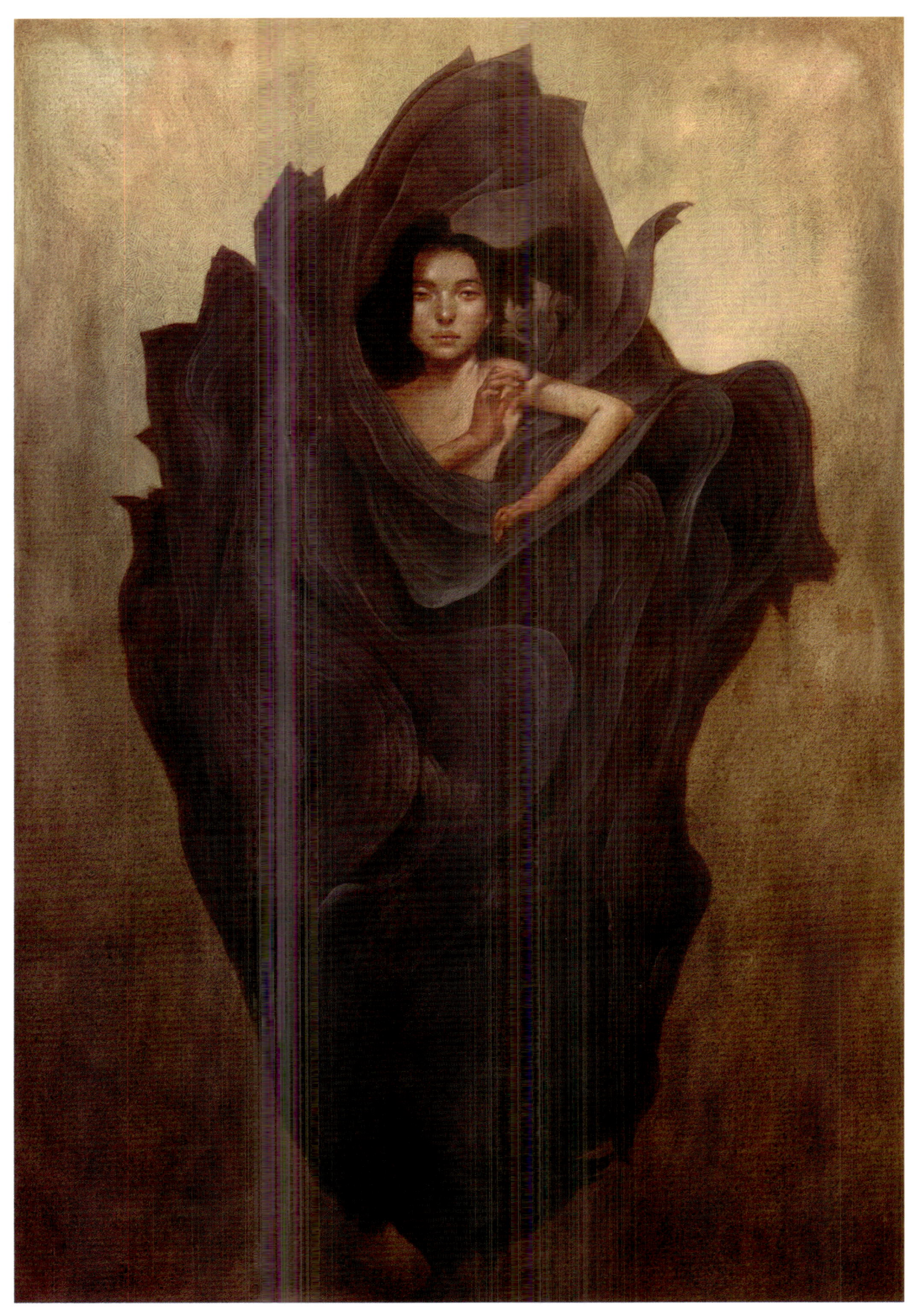

WHEN RED DAYS SETTLE IN BLUE HOURS
acrylic & colored pencil on paper, 14" x 20, 2009

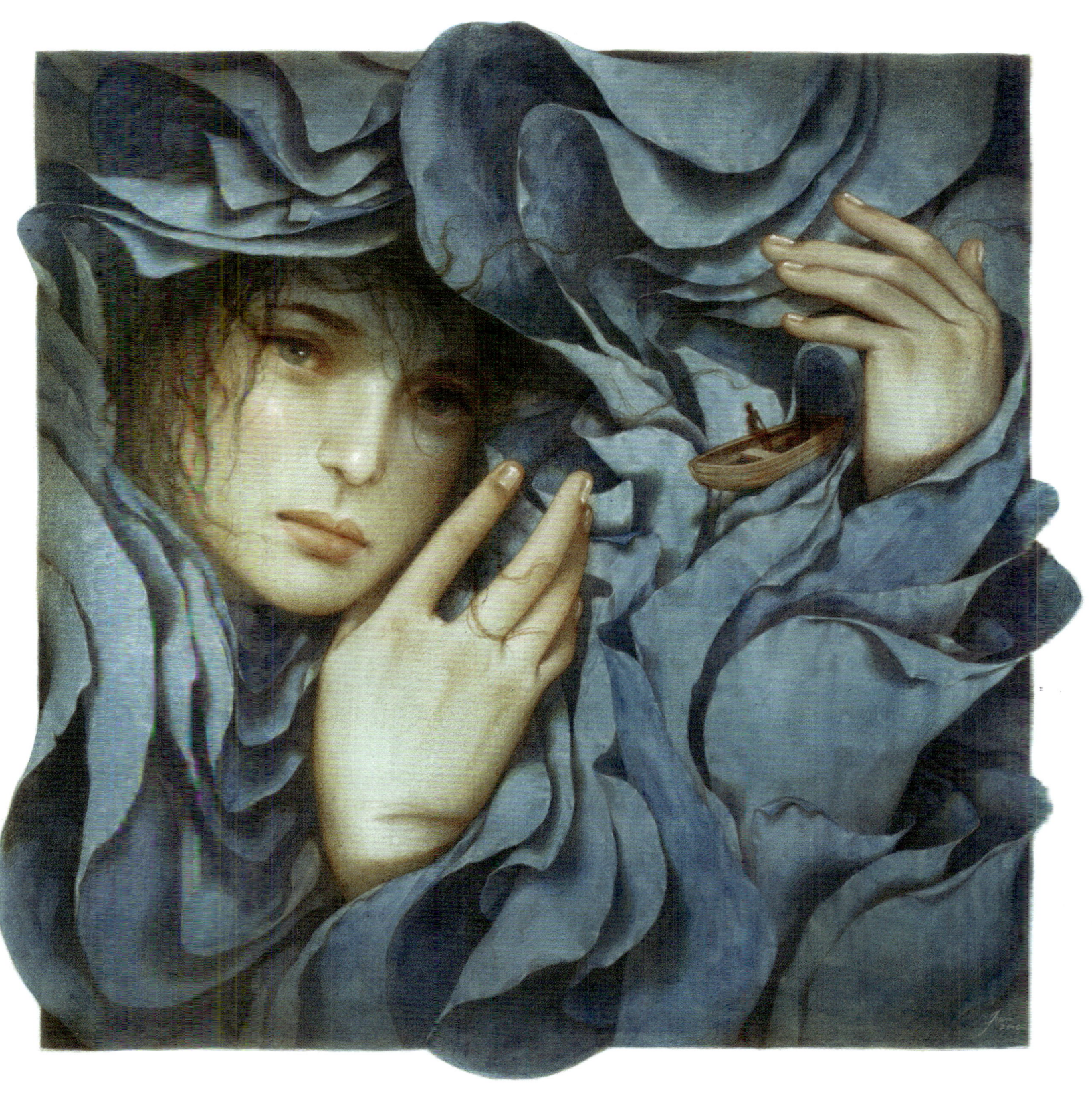

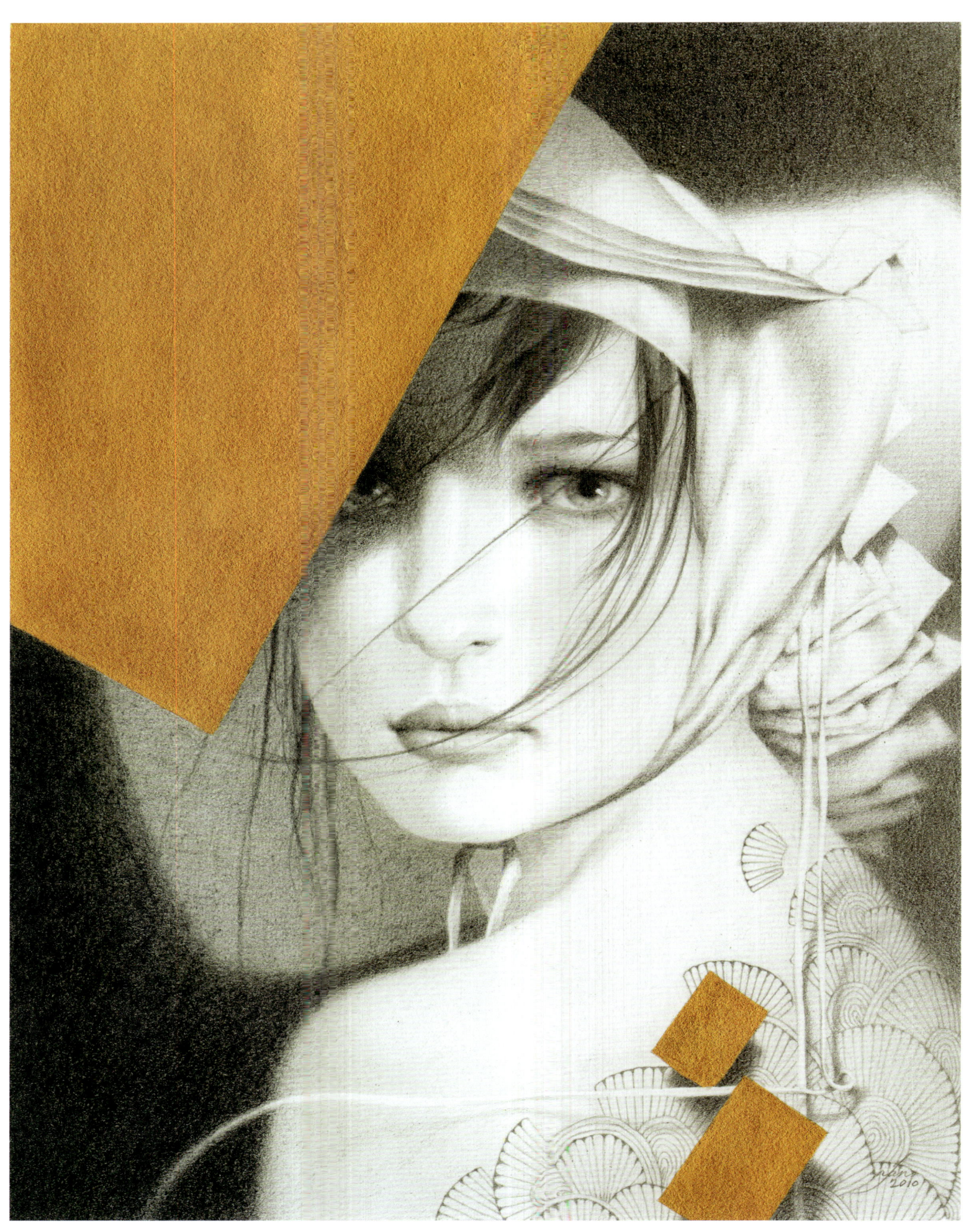

HOW CLOUDY IS AN OVERCASTED PSYCHE
acrylic & graphite on paper, 8" x 10", 2010

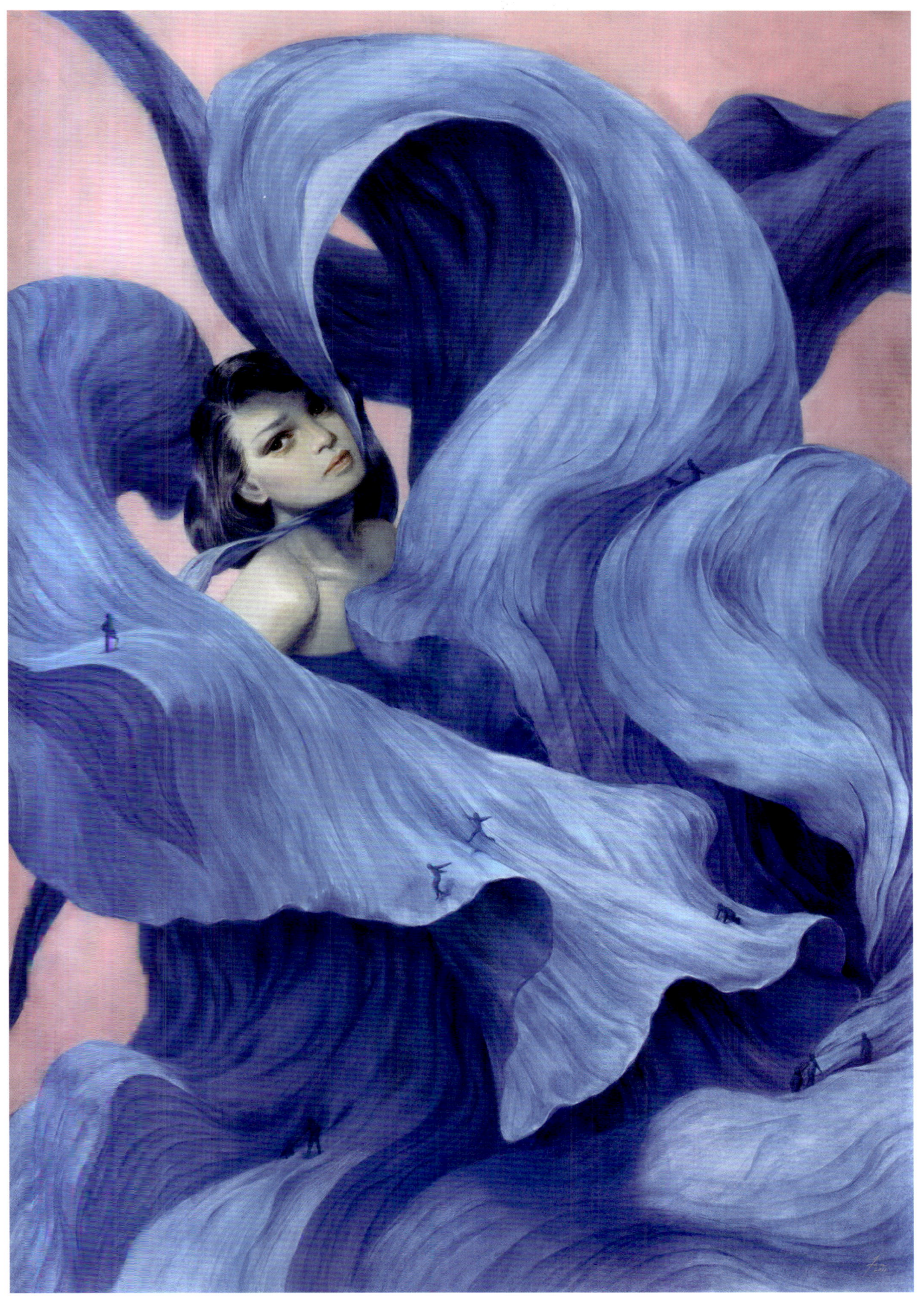

ACROSS THE BLUE-BILLOWED CREVICE
acrylic & colored pencil on paper, 20" x 28", 2

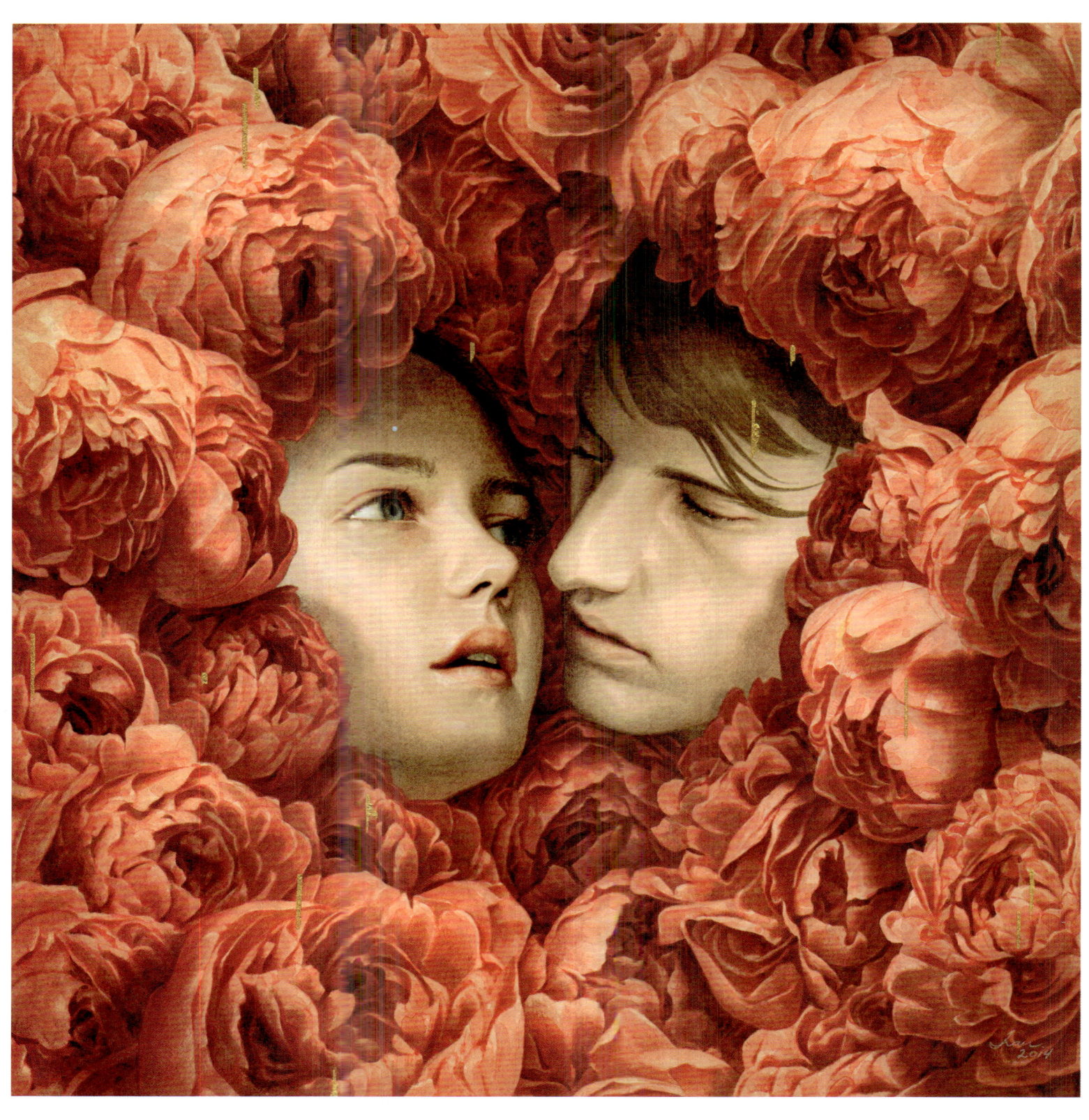

A BORROWED TOMORROW
acrylic & colored pencil on paper, 14" x 14", 2014

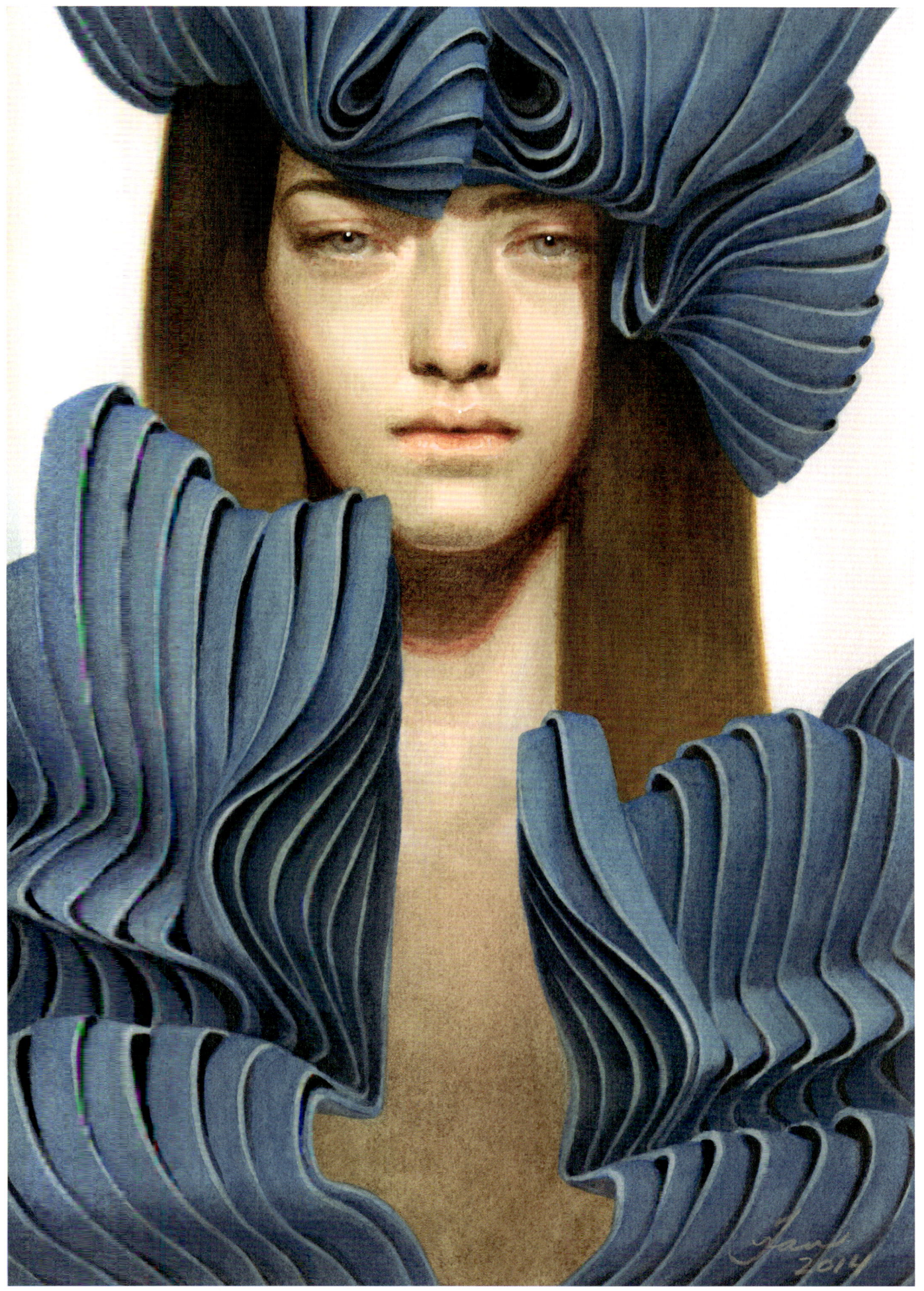

MICROVISION
acrylic & colored pencil on paper, 5" x 7", 2014

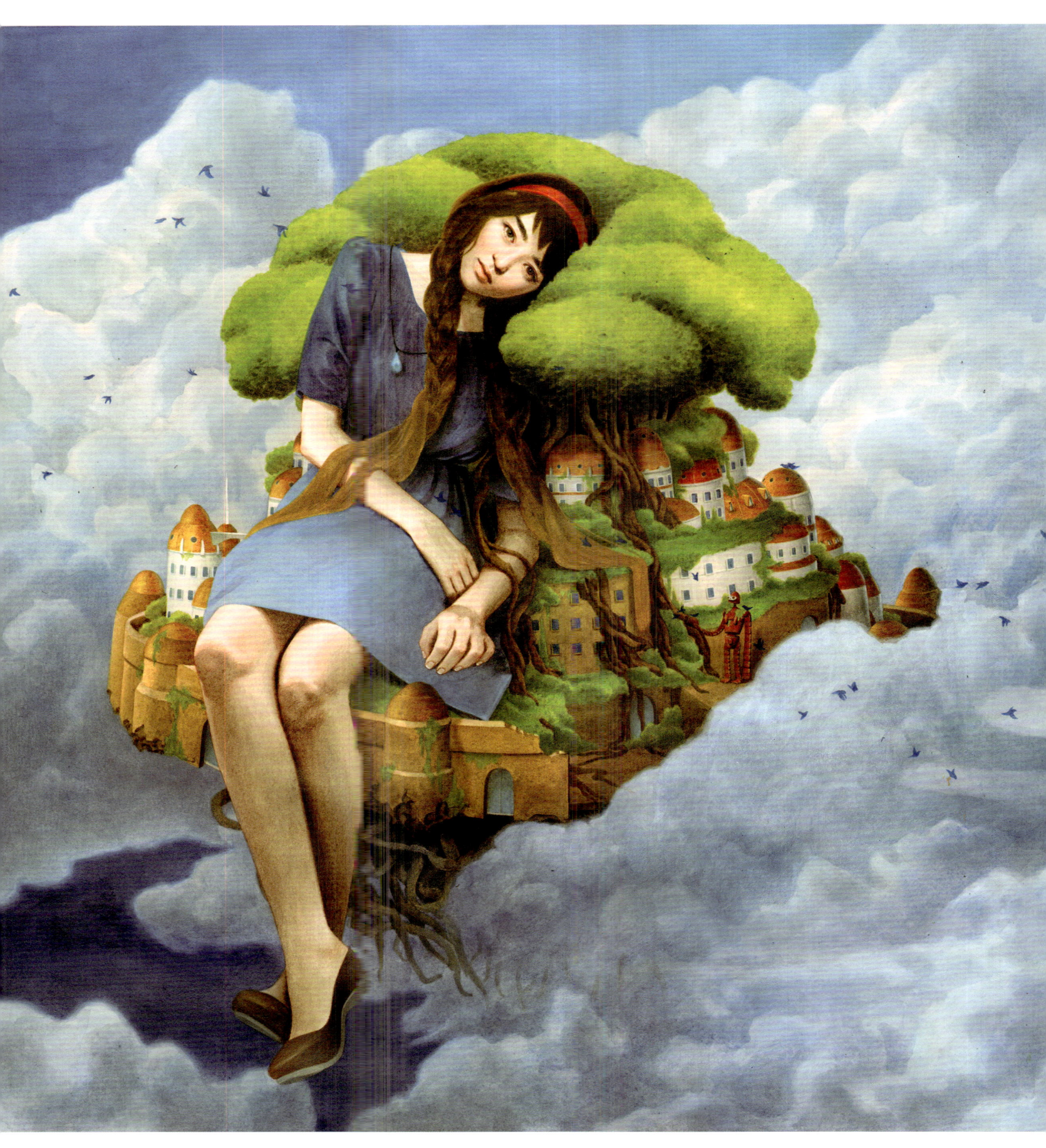

THE CASTLE & I
acrylic & colored pencil on paper, 21.5" x 25", 2014

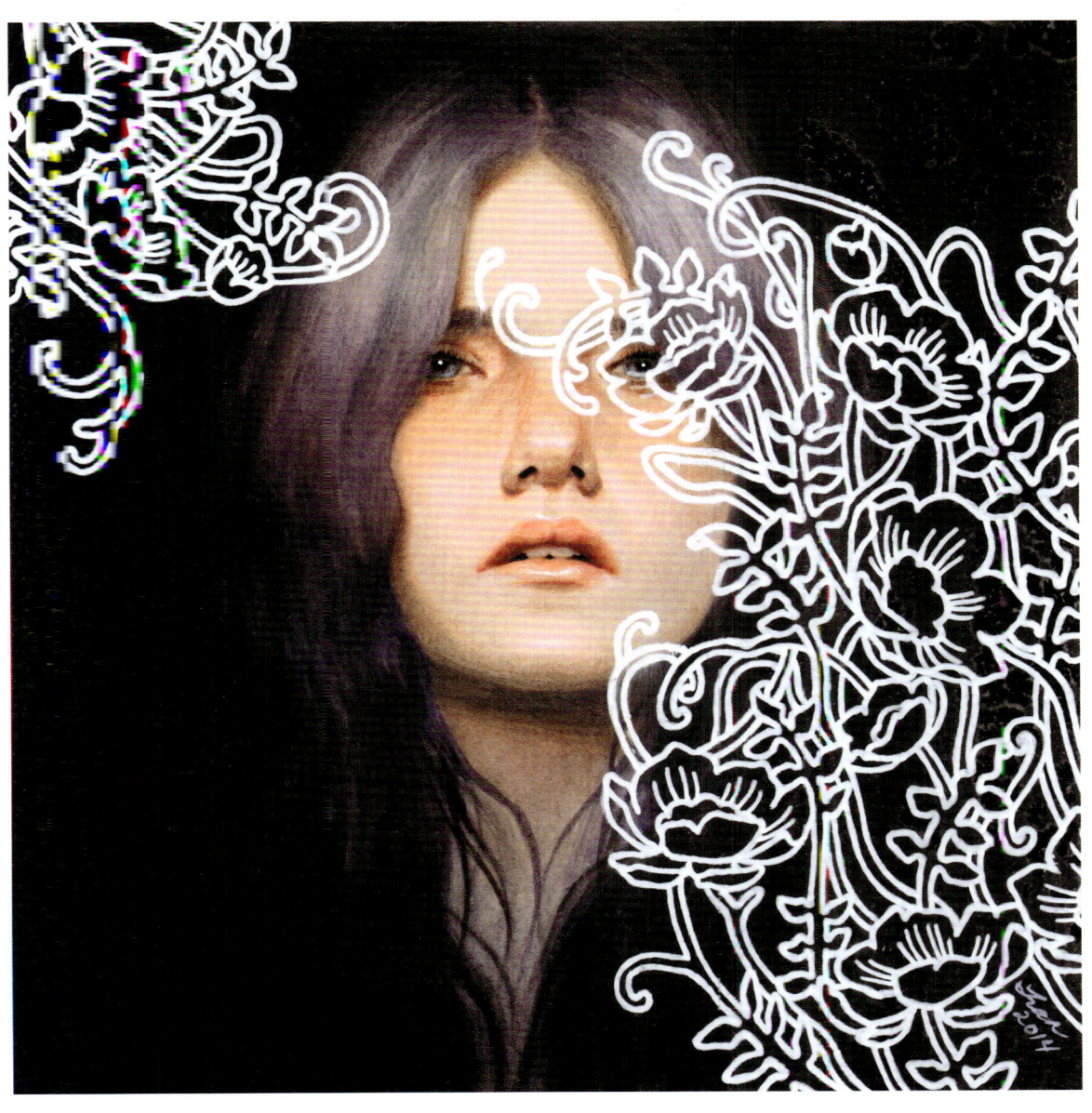

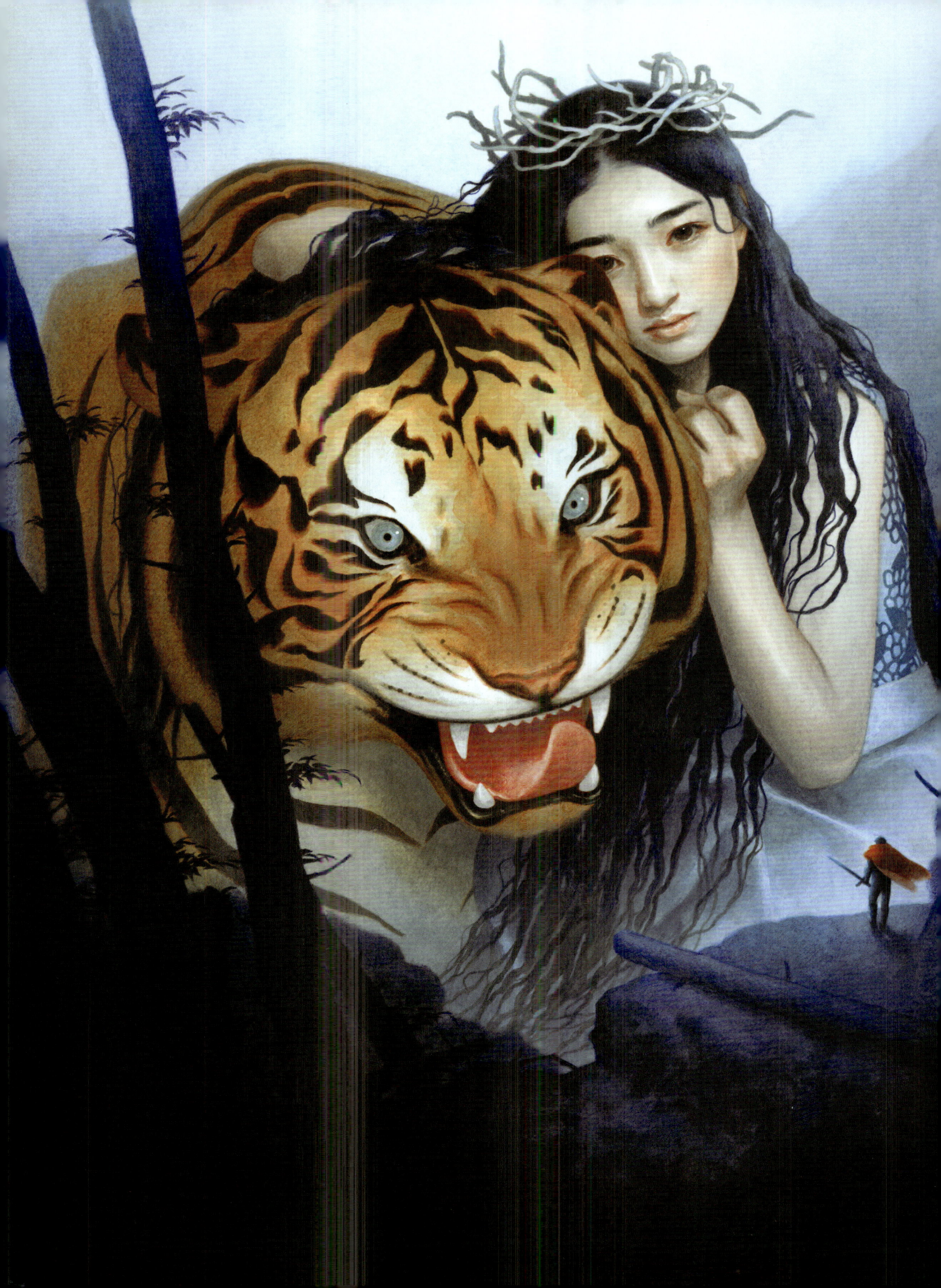

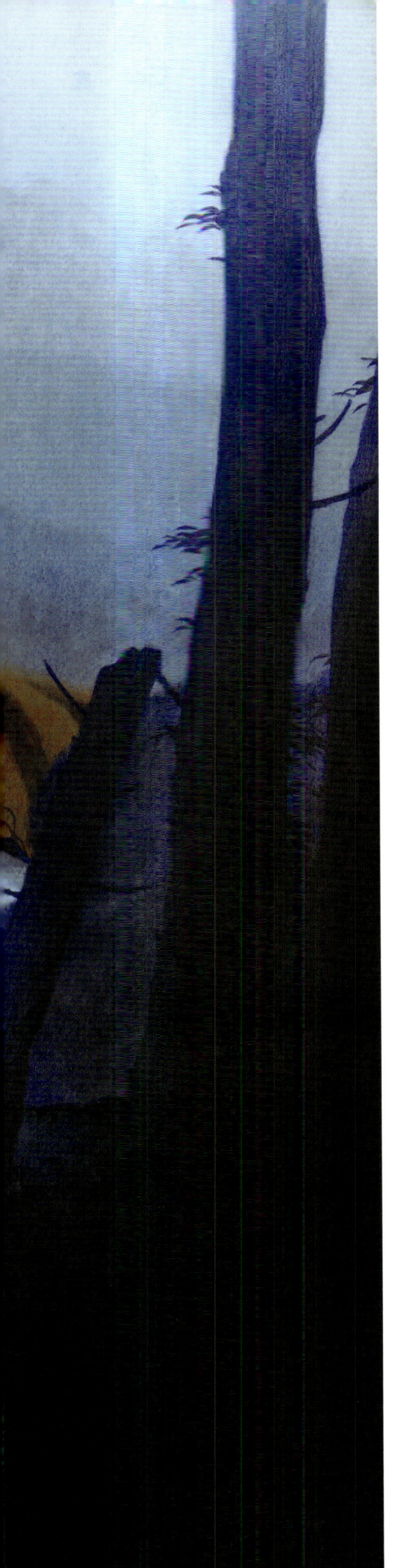

ORANGE IS NOT YOUR COLOR
acrylic & colored pencil on paper, 12" x 12", 2016

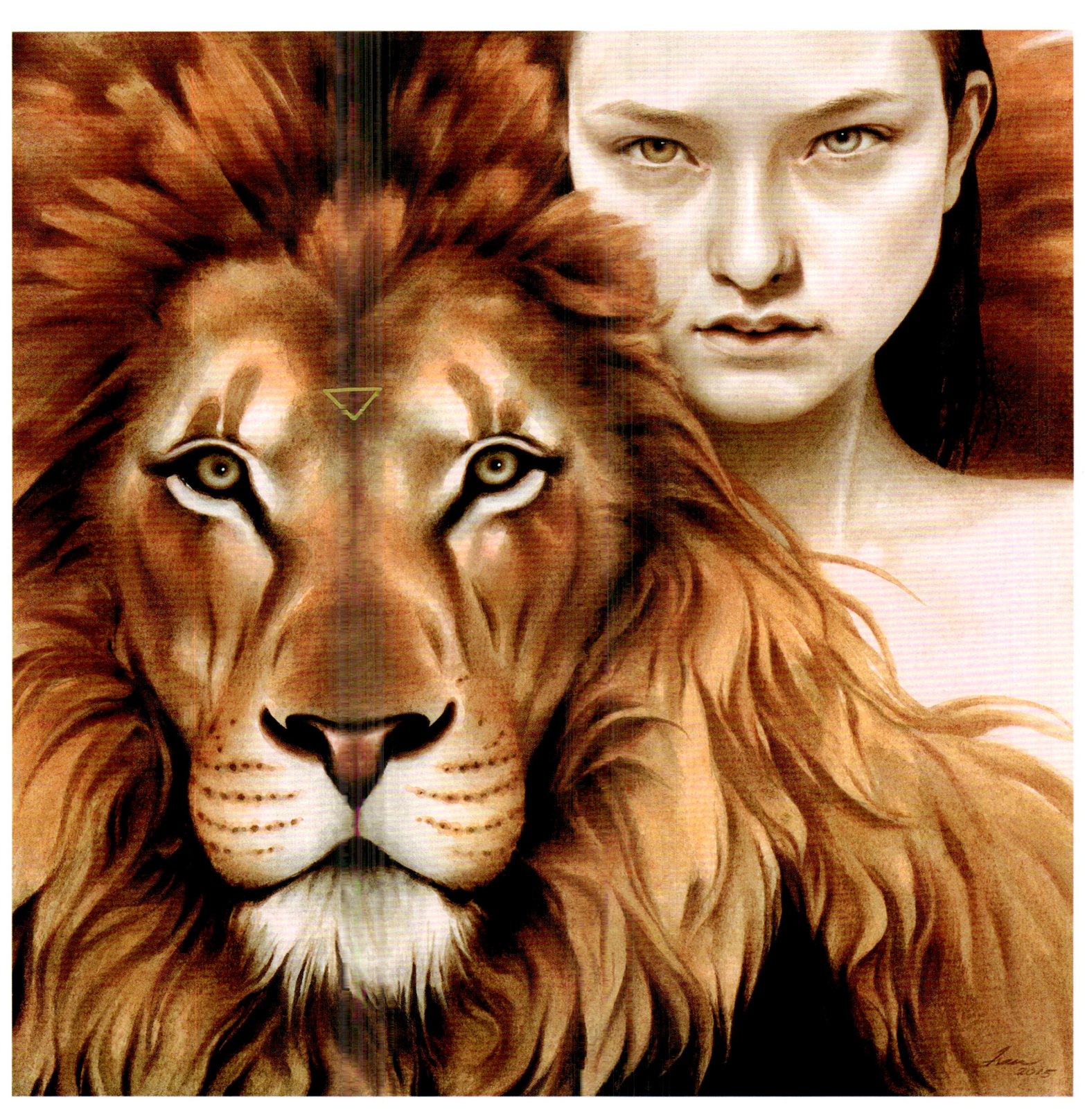

PERPENDICULAR TO PRETTY
acrylic & colored pencil on paper, 12" x 12" 2015

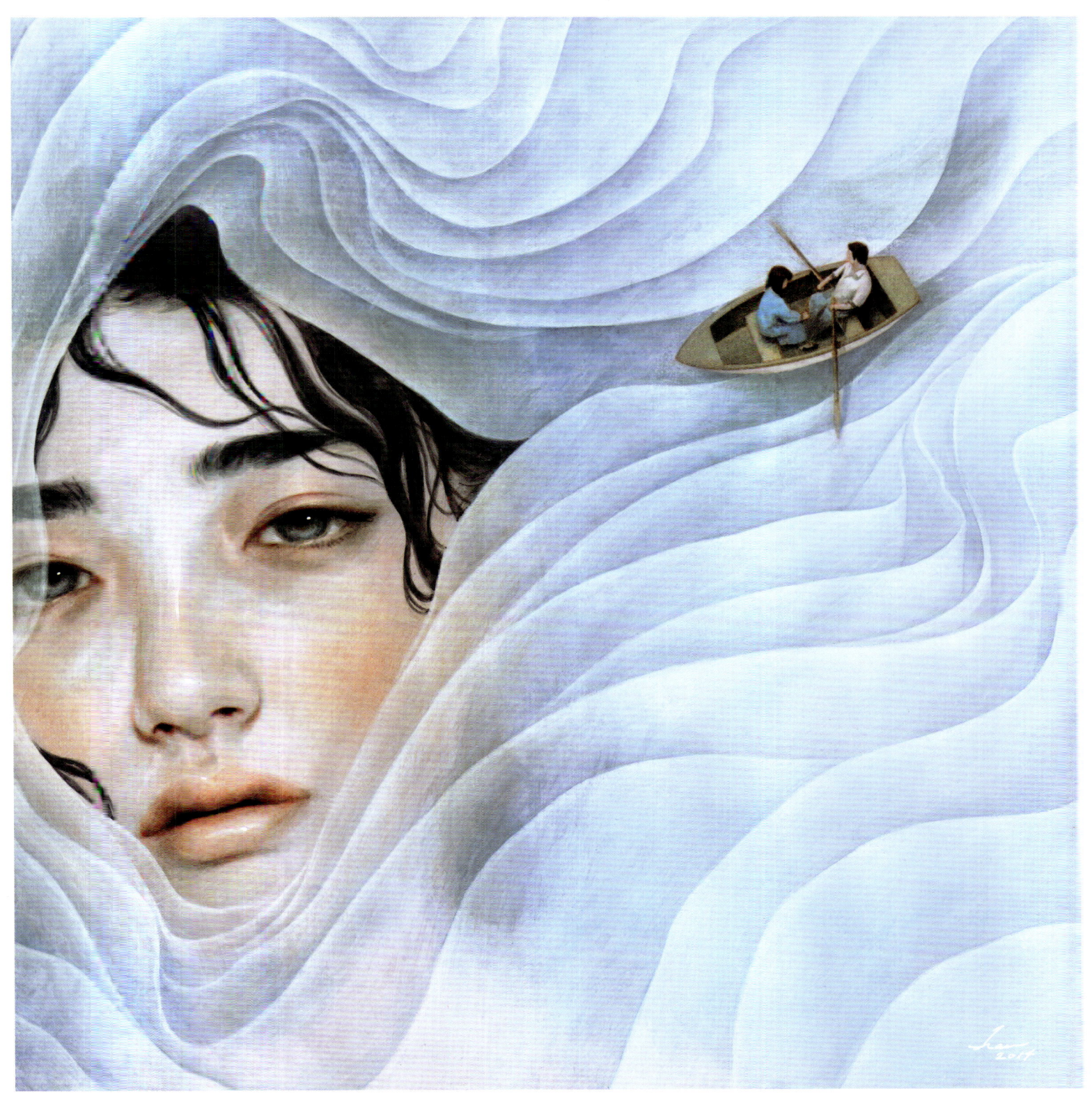

THE LILAC LADY

acrylic & colored pencil on paper, 10" x 10", 2015

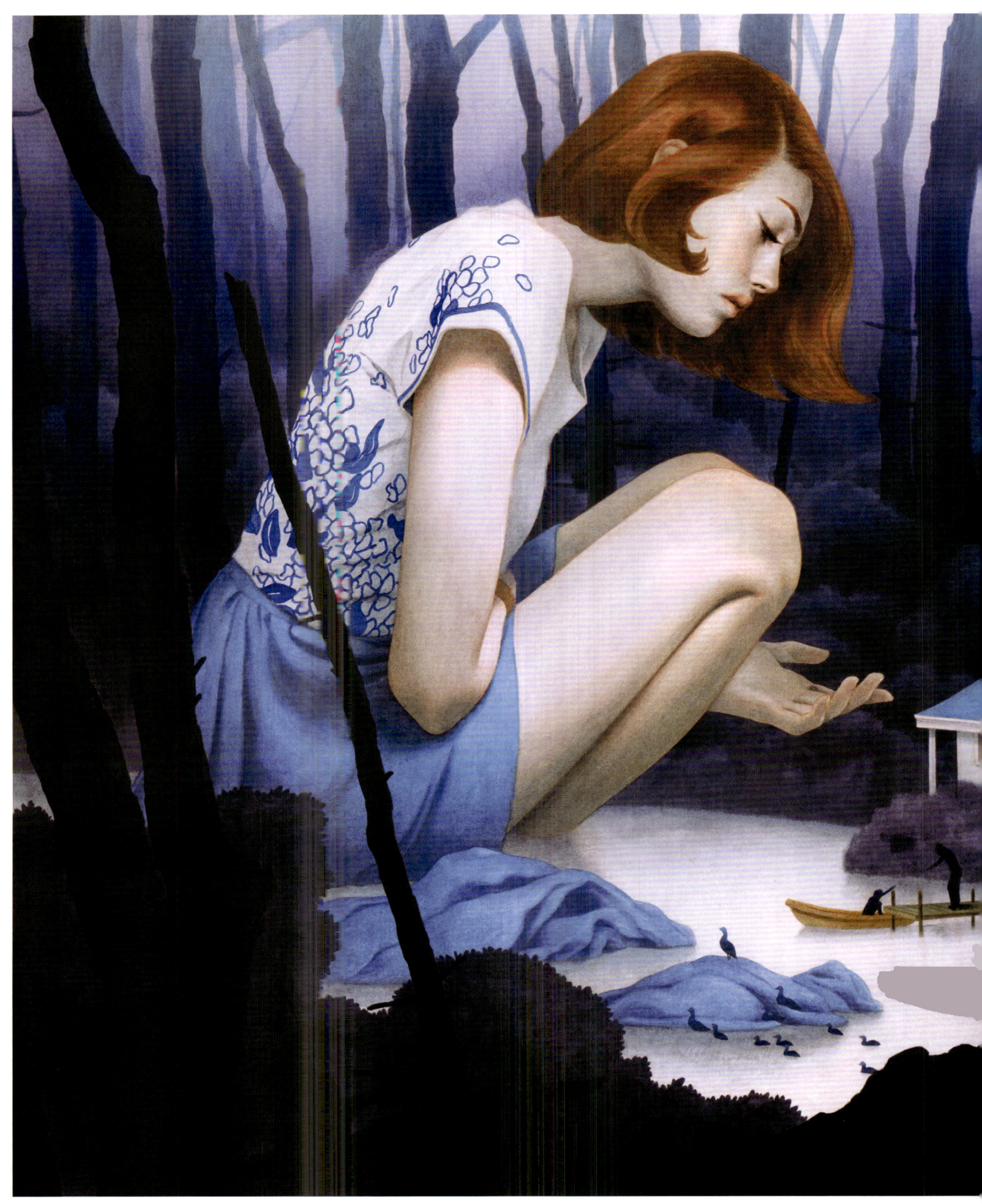

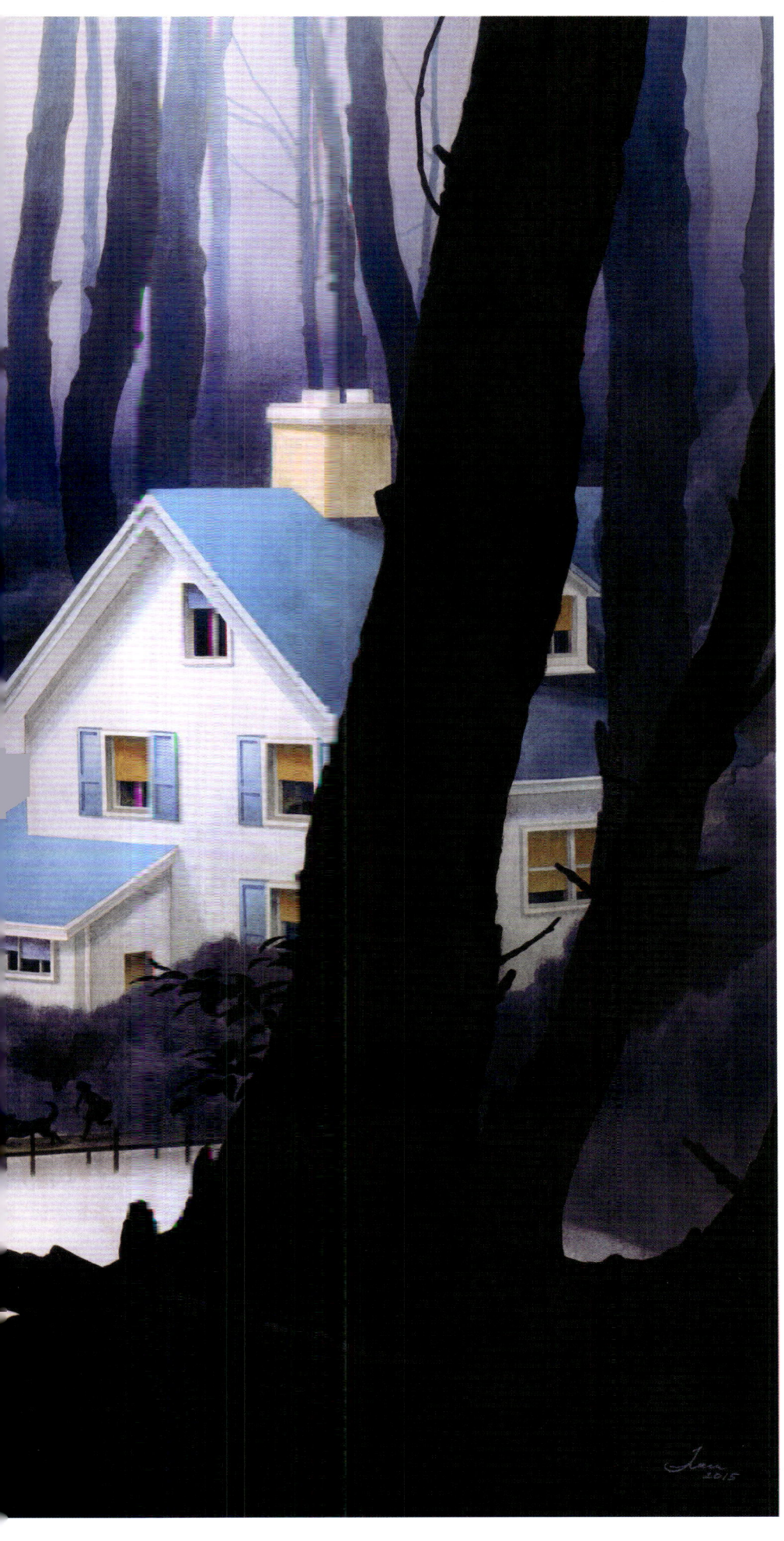

THROUGH A LONE, WINDING ROAD
acrylic & colored pencil on paper, 28" x 28", 2015

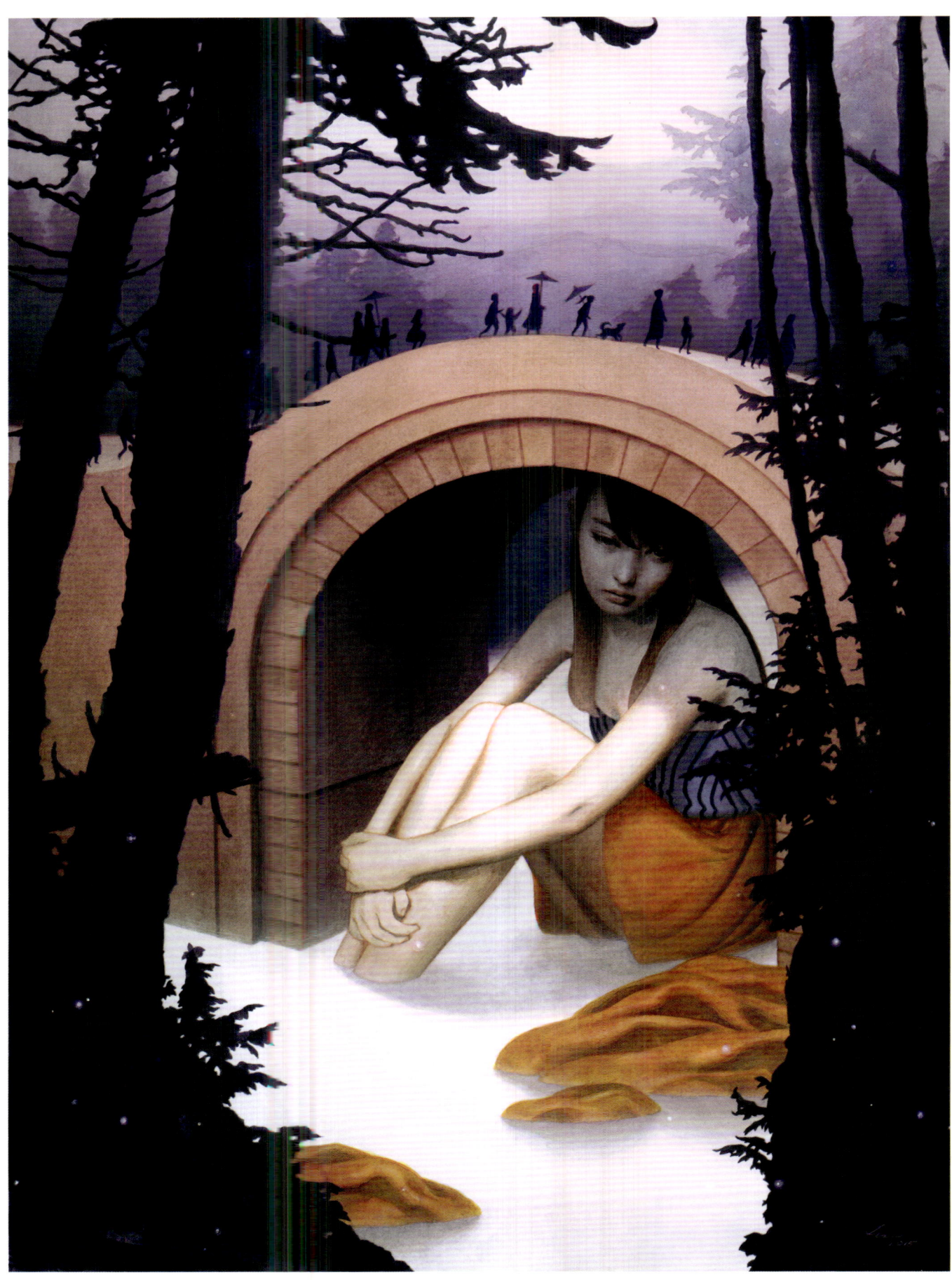

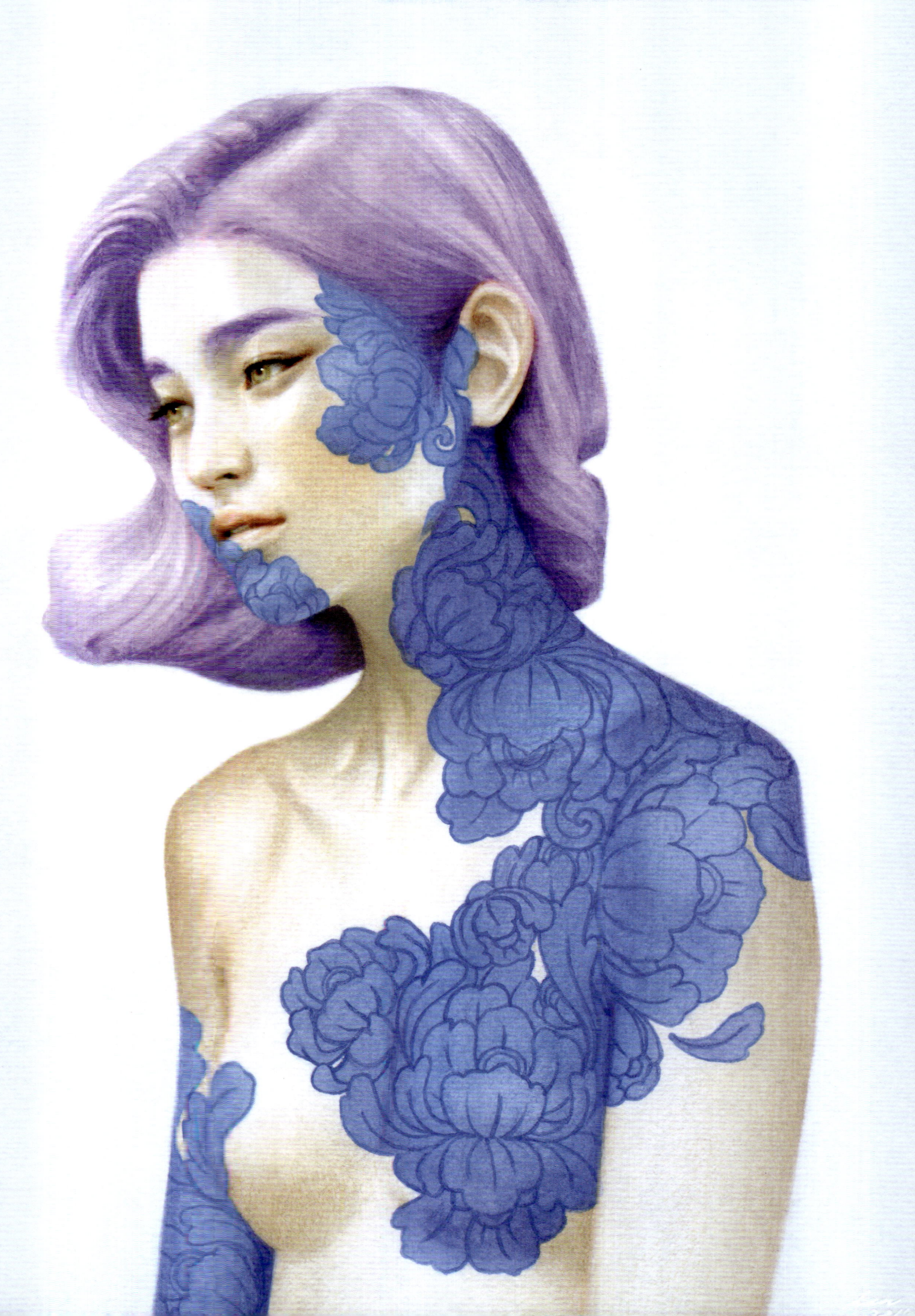

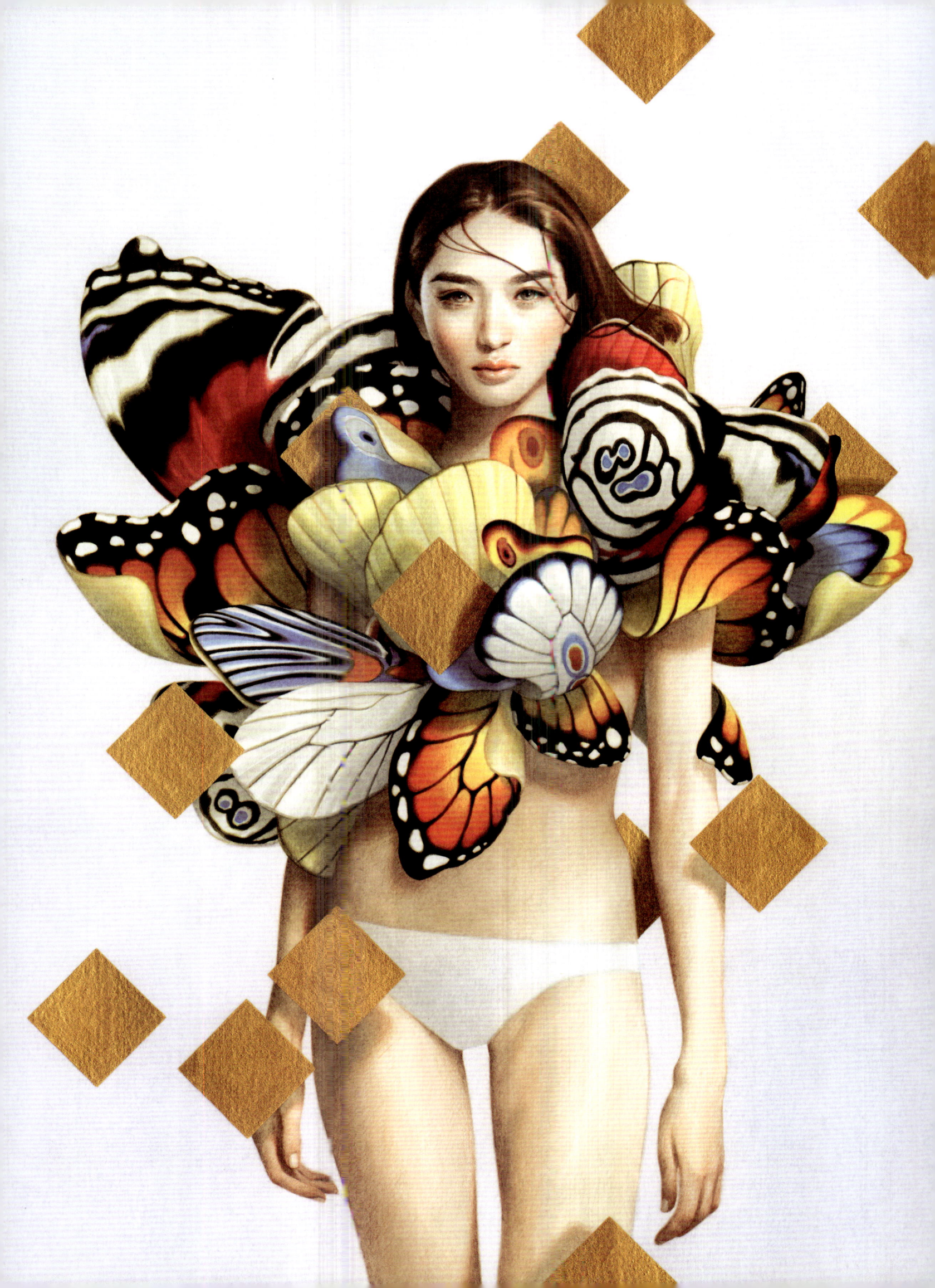

REBIRTH
acrylic & colored pencil on paper, 16" x 20", 2016

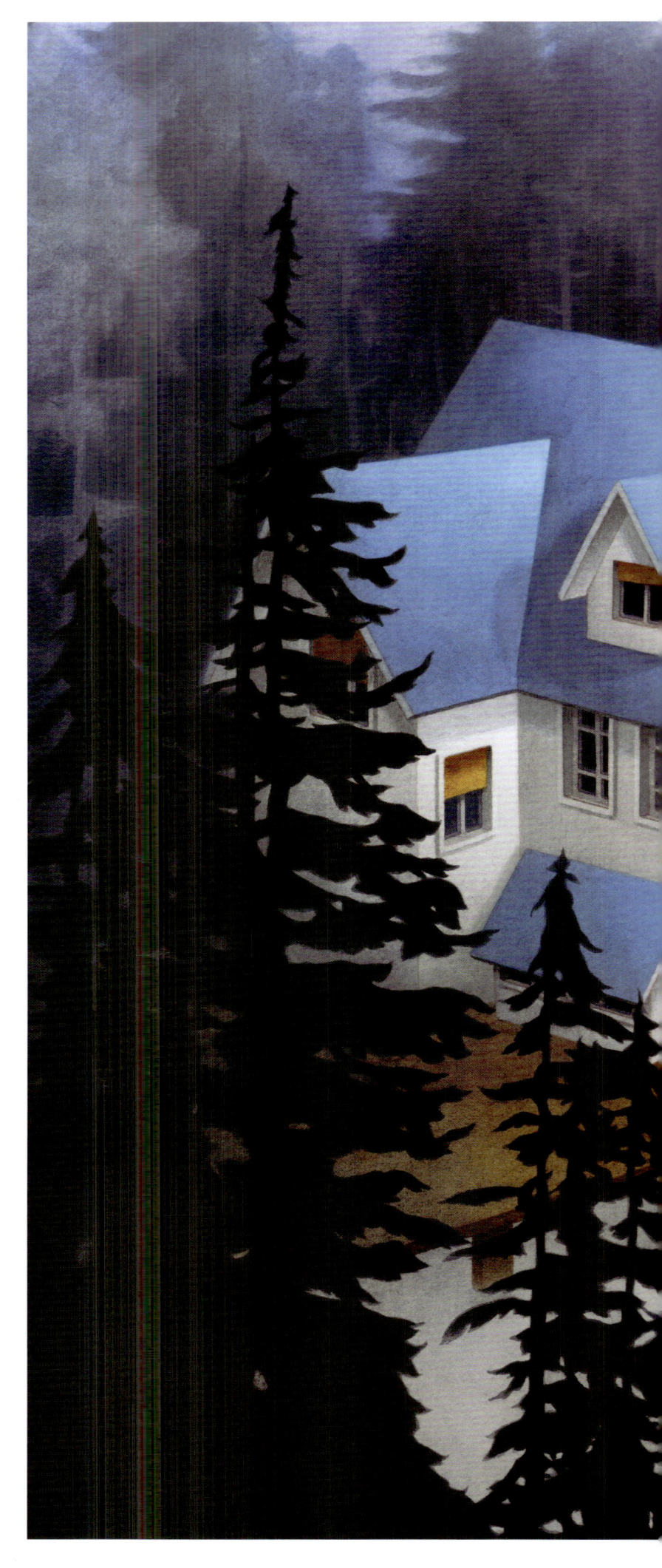

WHERE THE CREEK STOOD STILL
acrylic & colored pencil on paper, 20" x 16", 2016

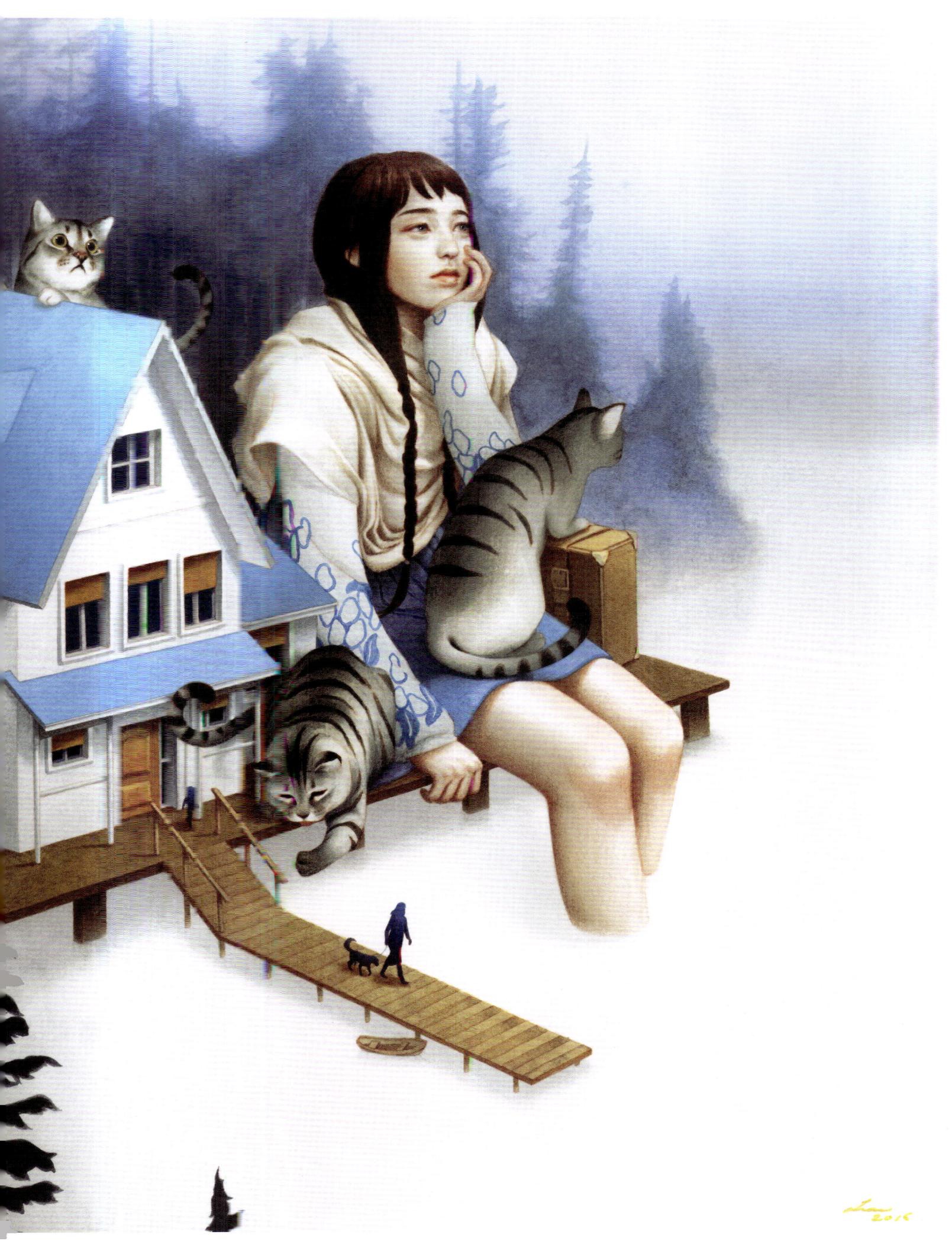

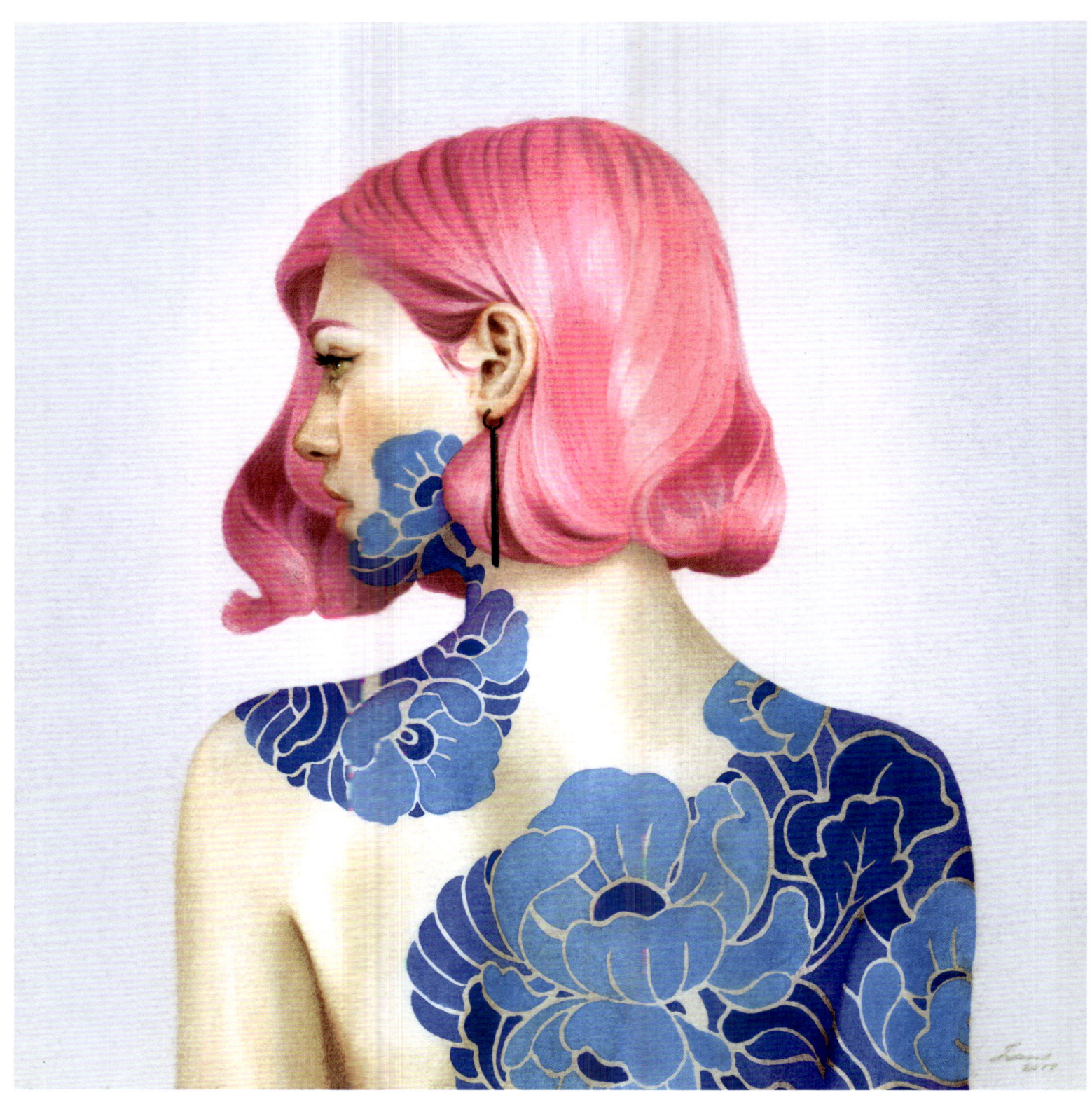

above
A MAGENTA MAIDEN
acrylic & colored pencil on paper, 9" x 9", 2017

right
THE CERULEAN GIRL
acrylic & colored pencil on paper, 9" x 12", 2017

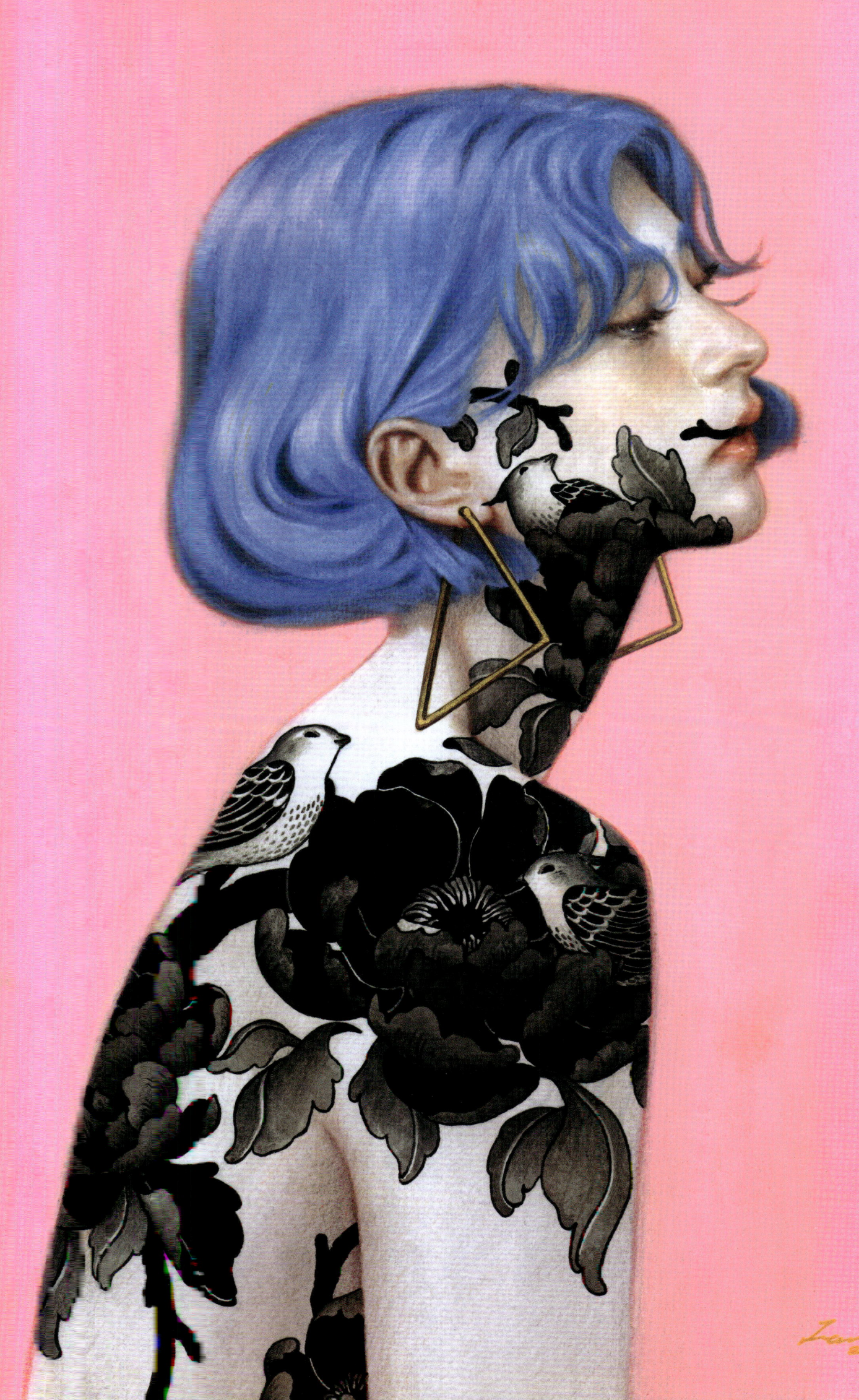

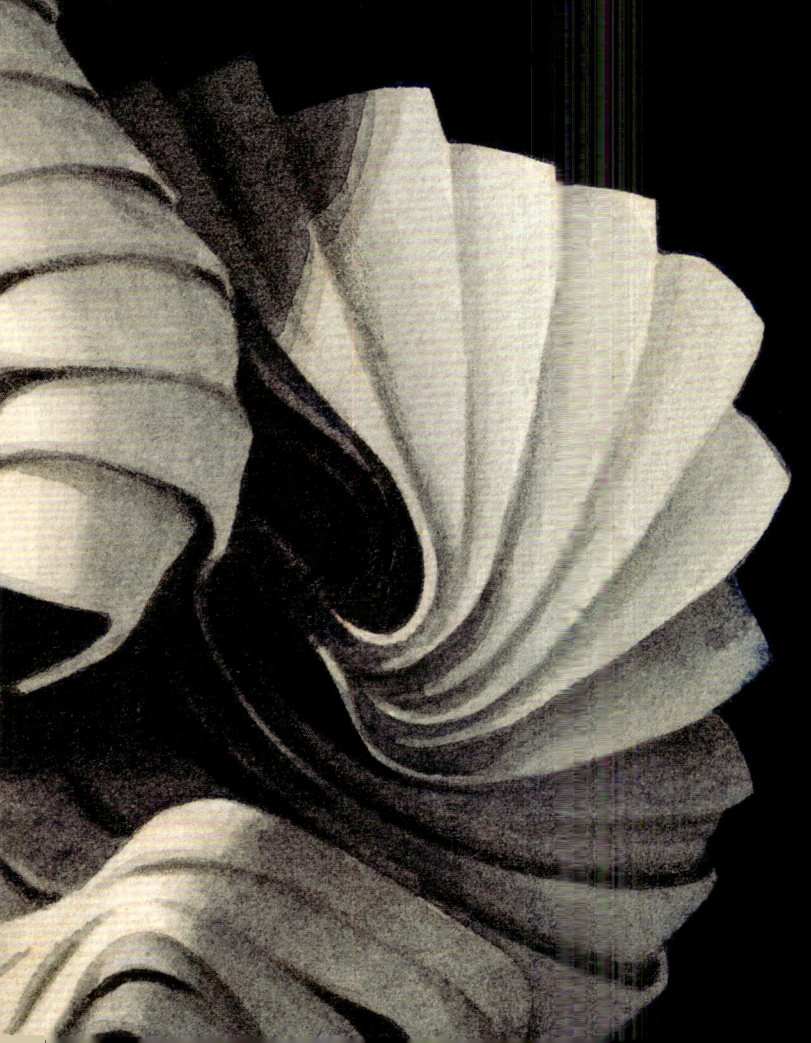

ADVE
& ED

RTISING
ITORIAL

ART CREATED FOR MAGAZINE COVERS AND INTERIORS, TELEVISION, ONLINE JOURNALS, ADS AND PRODUCT PACKAGING.

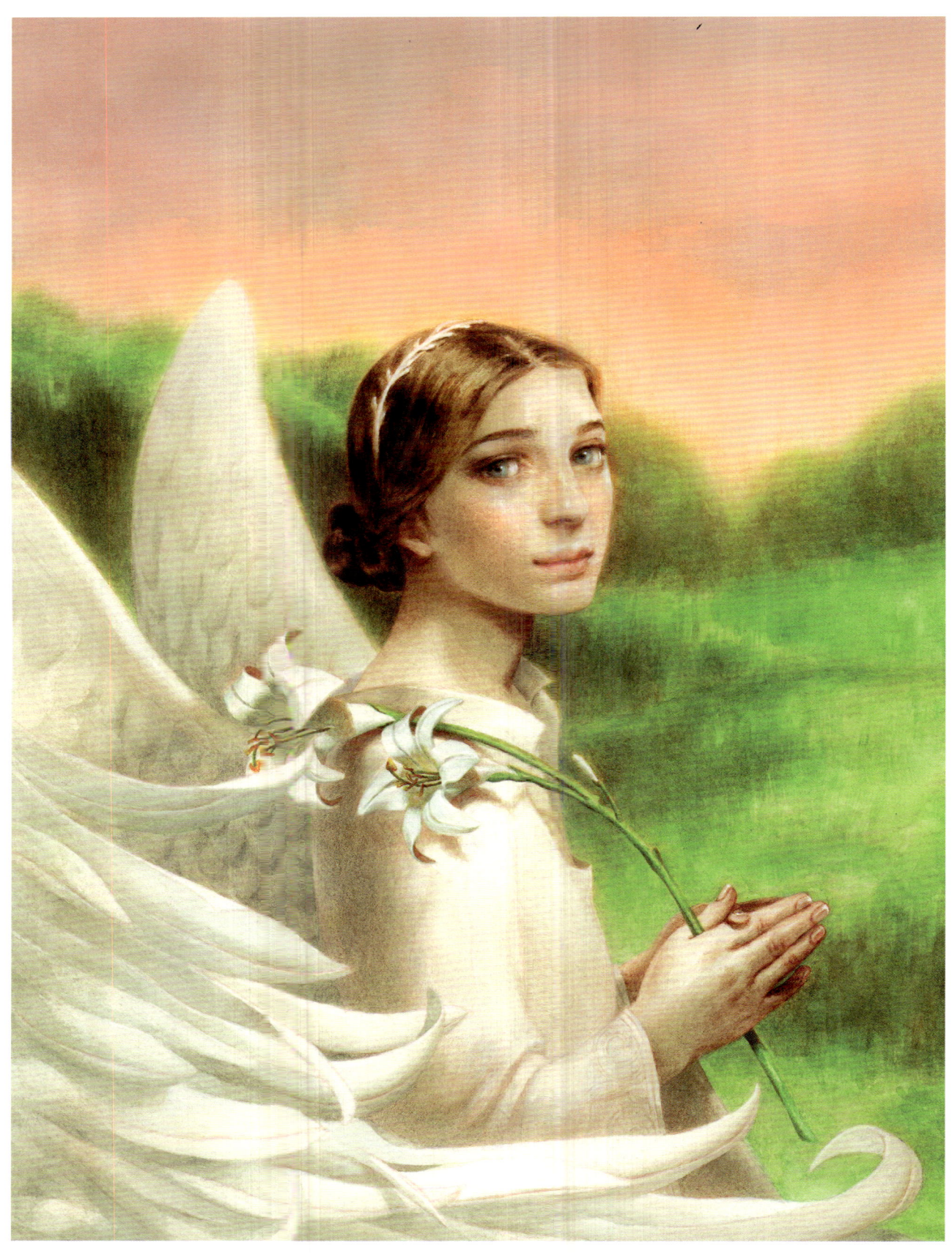

above
ANGELS ON EARTH
Angels On Earth magazine, AD: Olga Jakim, 2012

right
TOWARDS LEADERSHIP
ACC Docket, AD: Jamie Mitchell, 2013

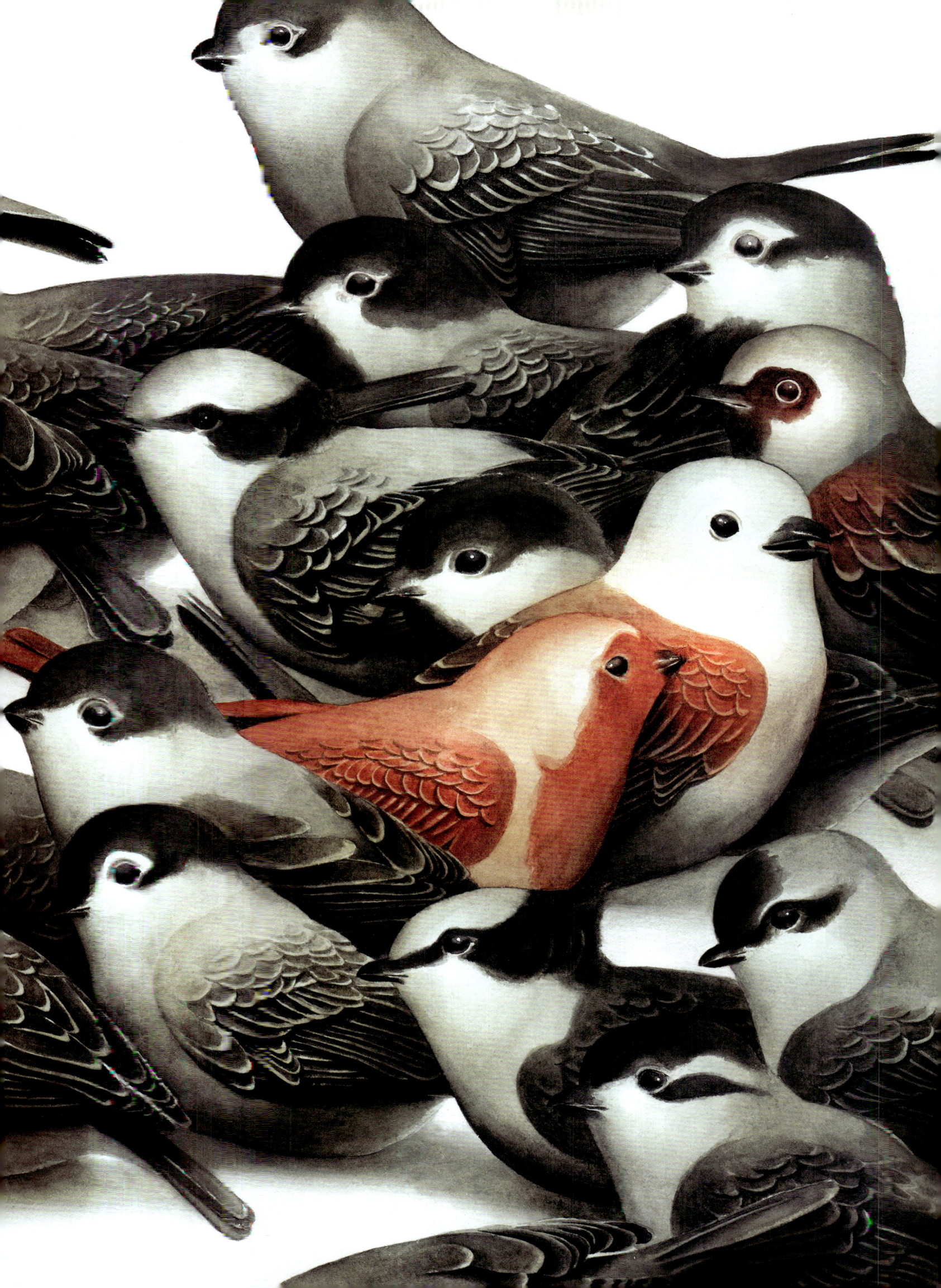

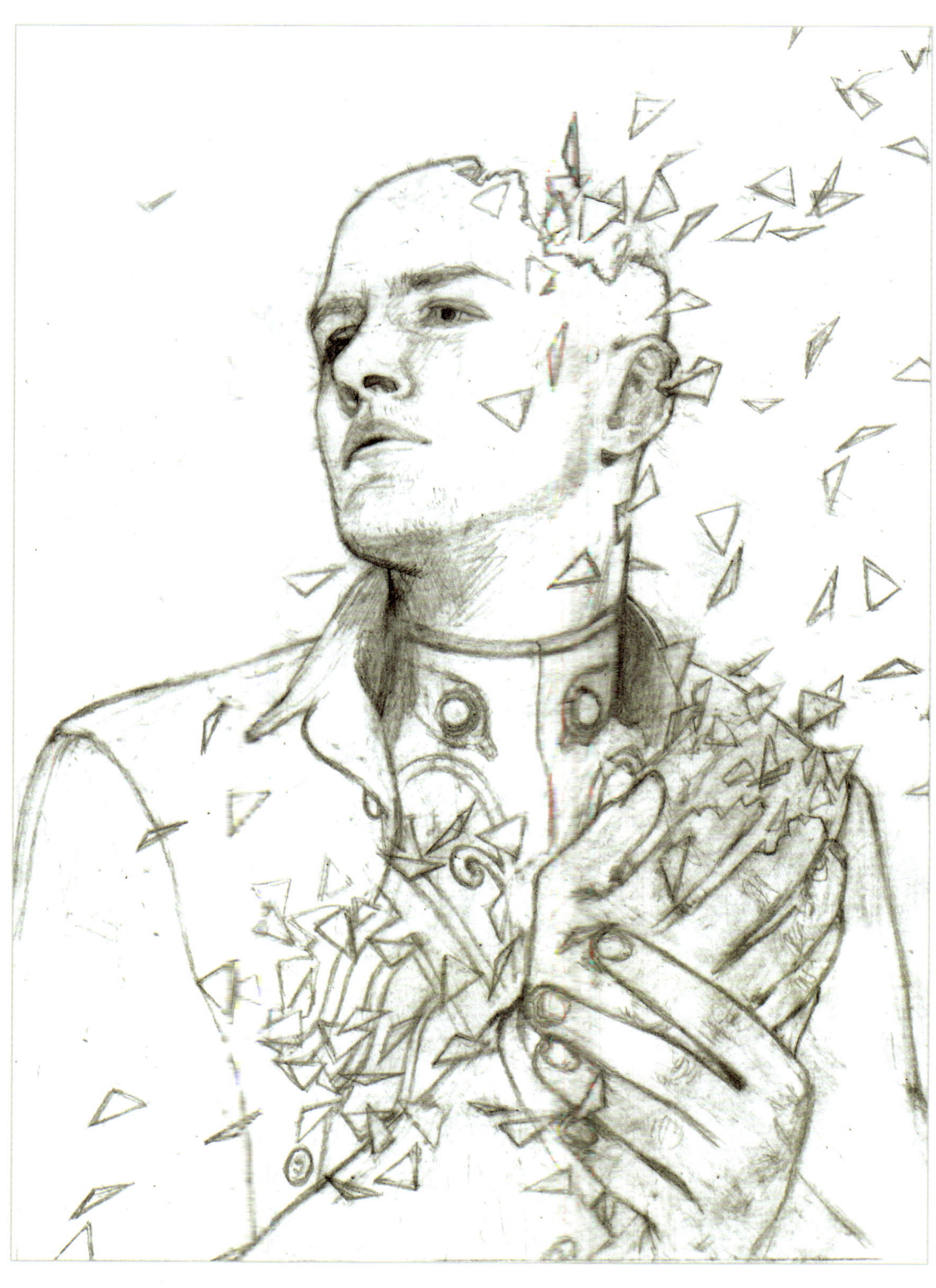

VILERAT
Playboy magazine, AD: Justin Page, 2013

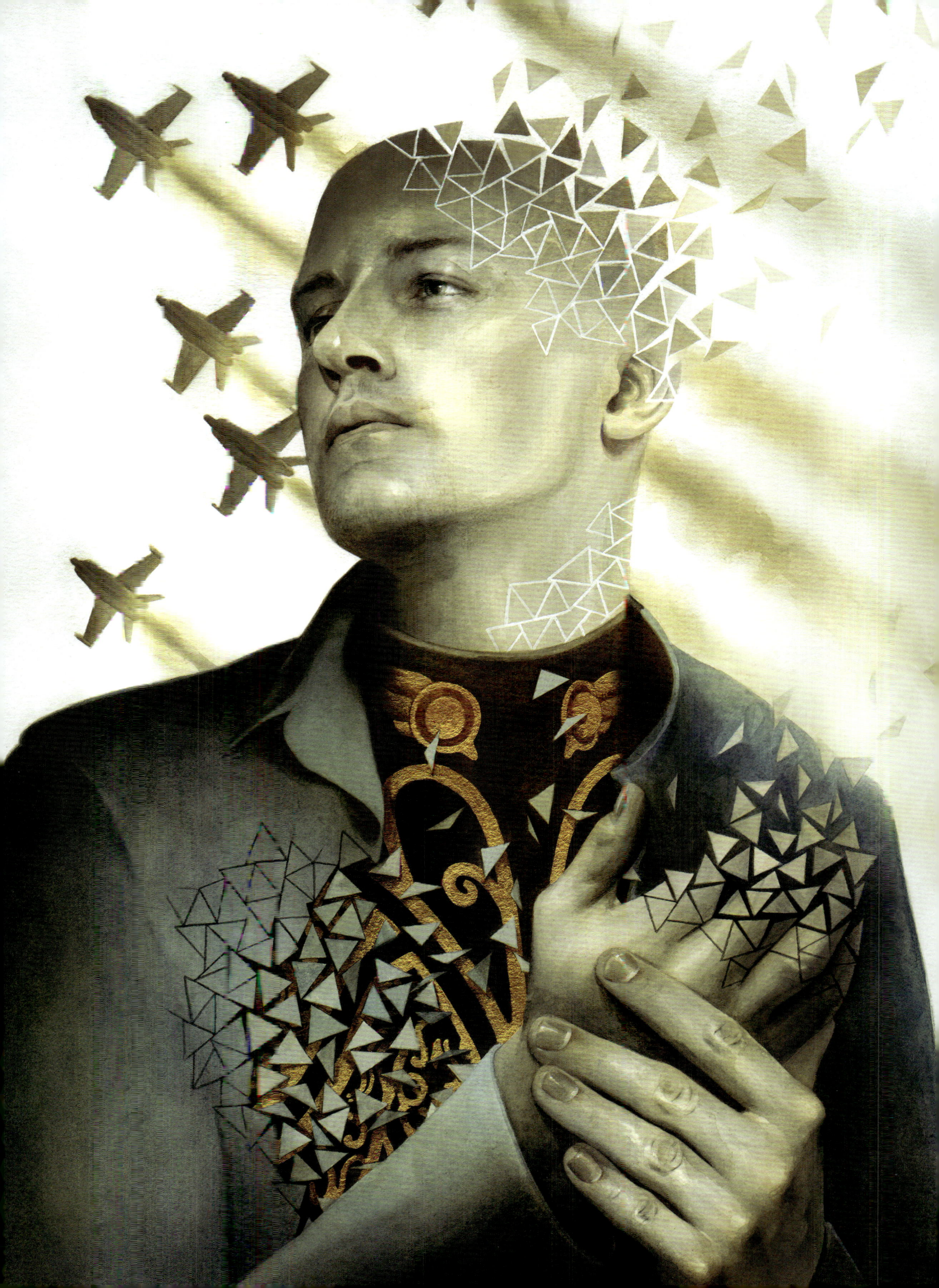

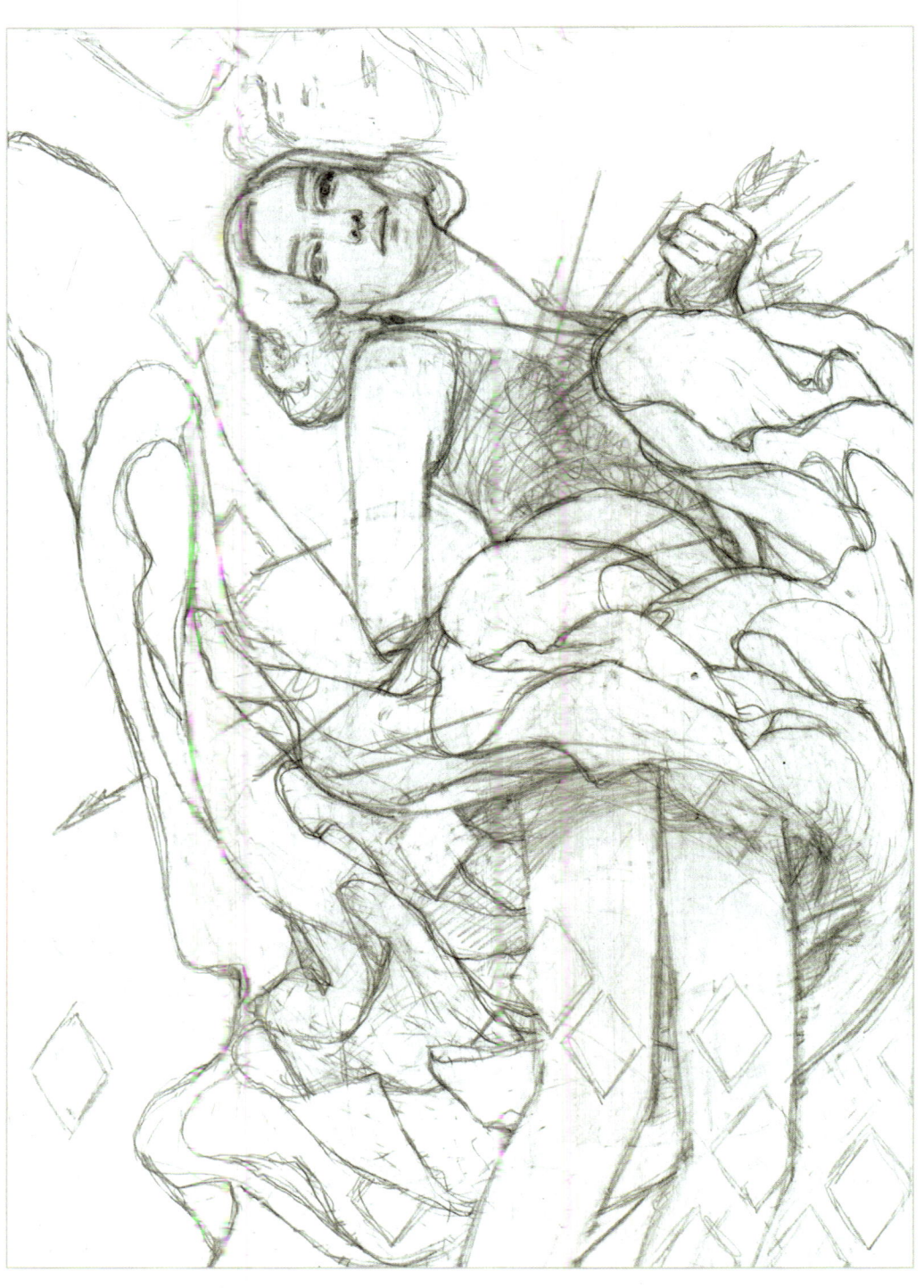

A DISTRESSED DAMSEL
ImagineFX magazine, AD: Claire Howlett, 2014

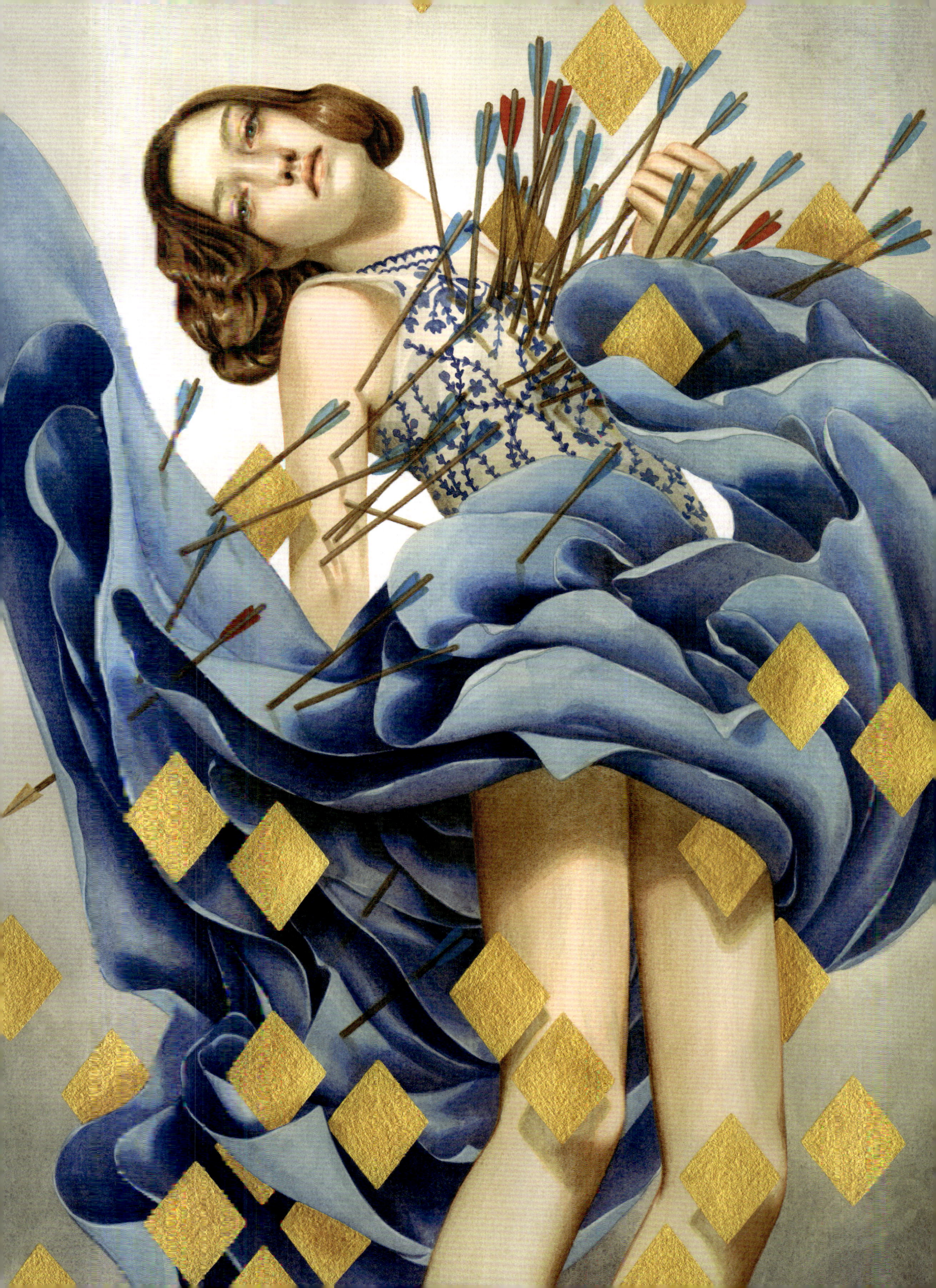

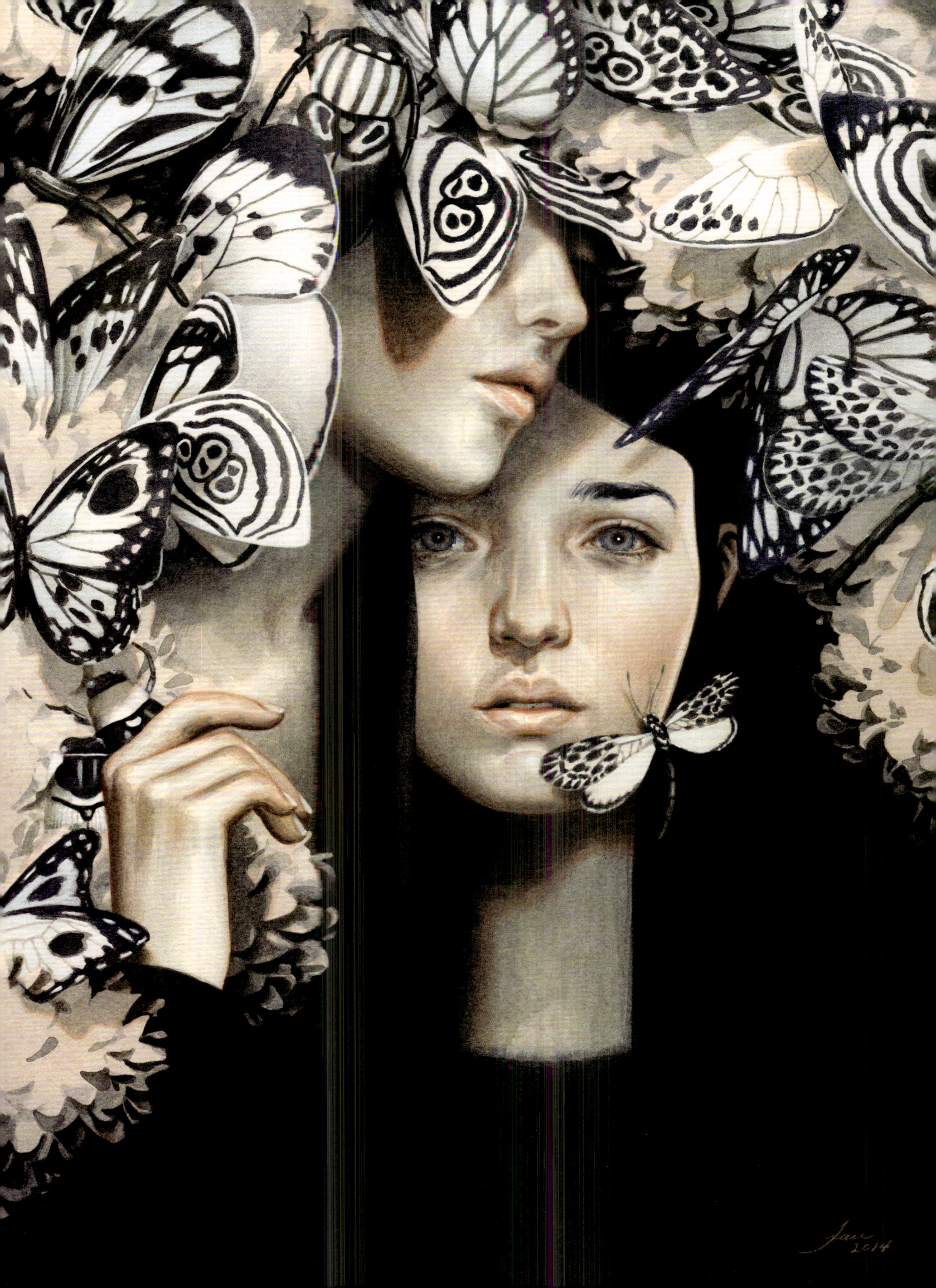

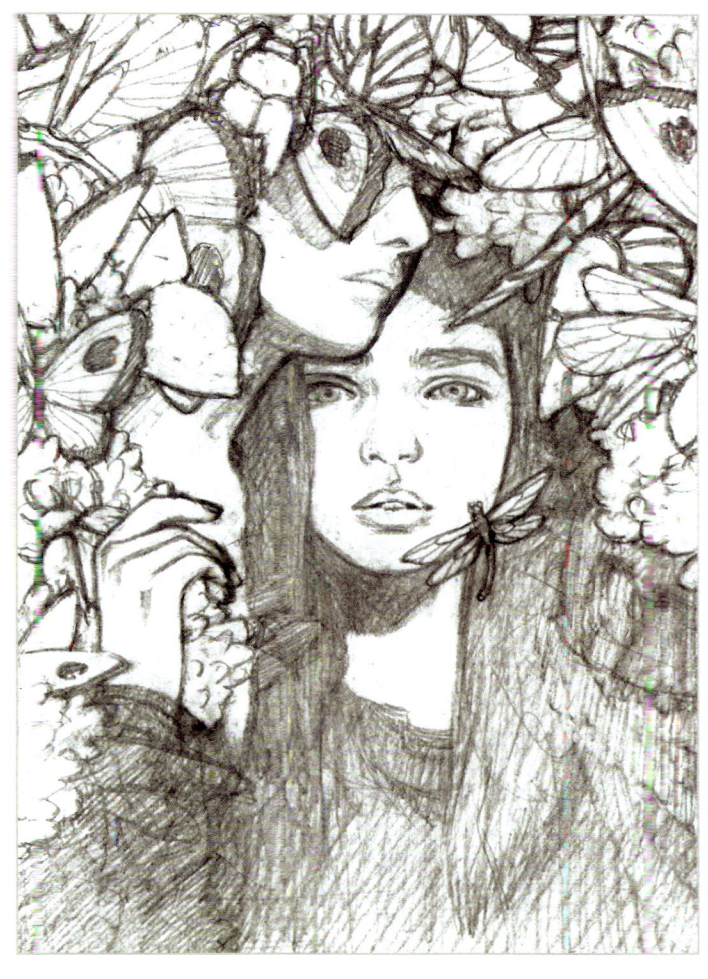

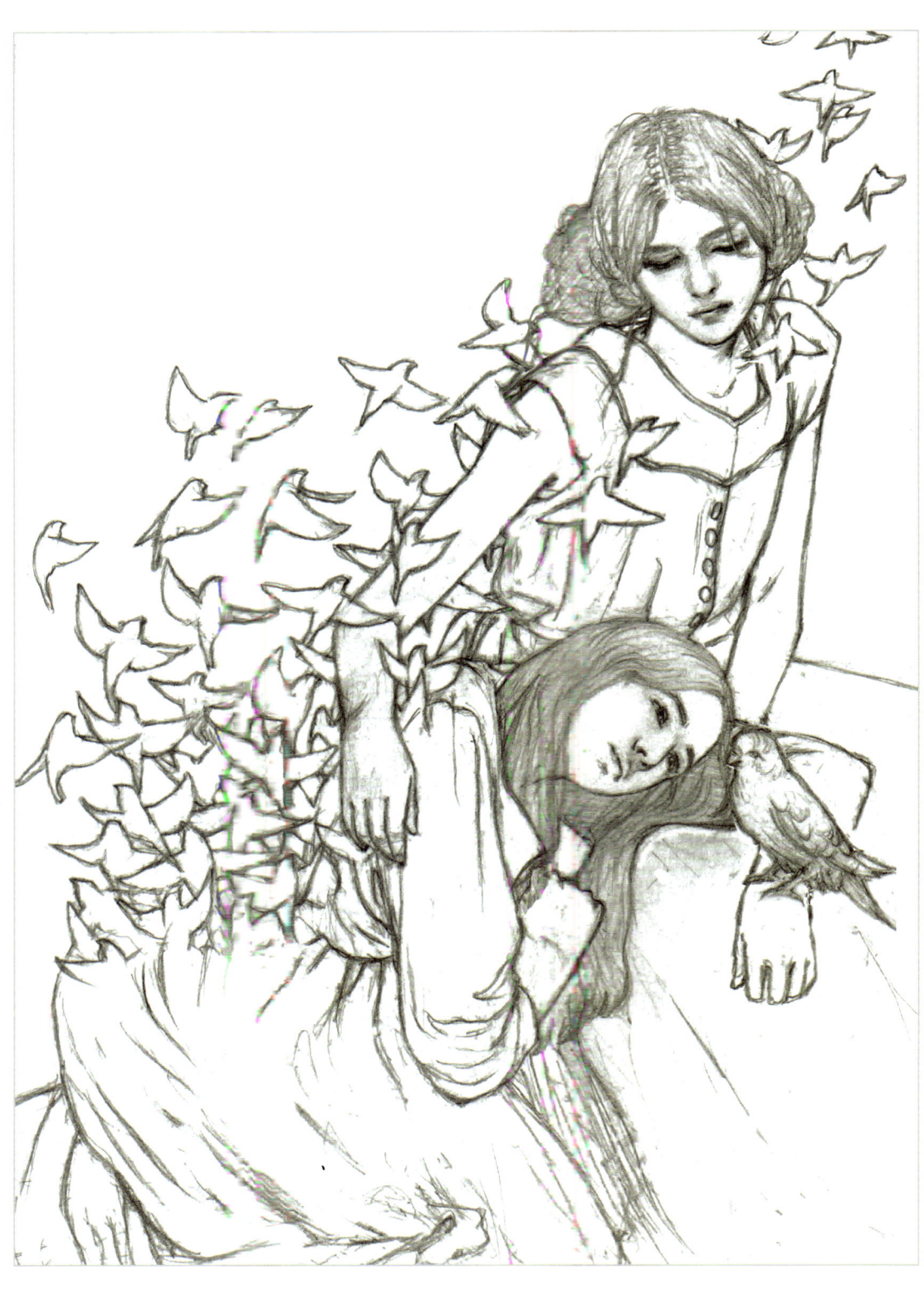

WAY OF WORDS
Tor.com, AD: Irene Gallo, 2014

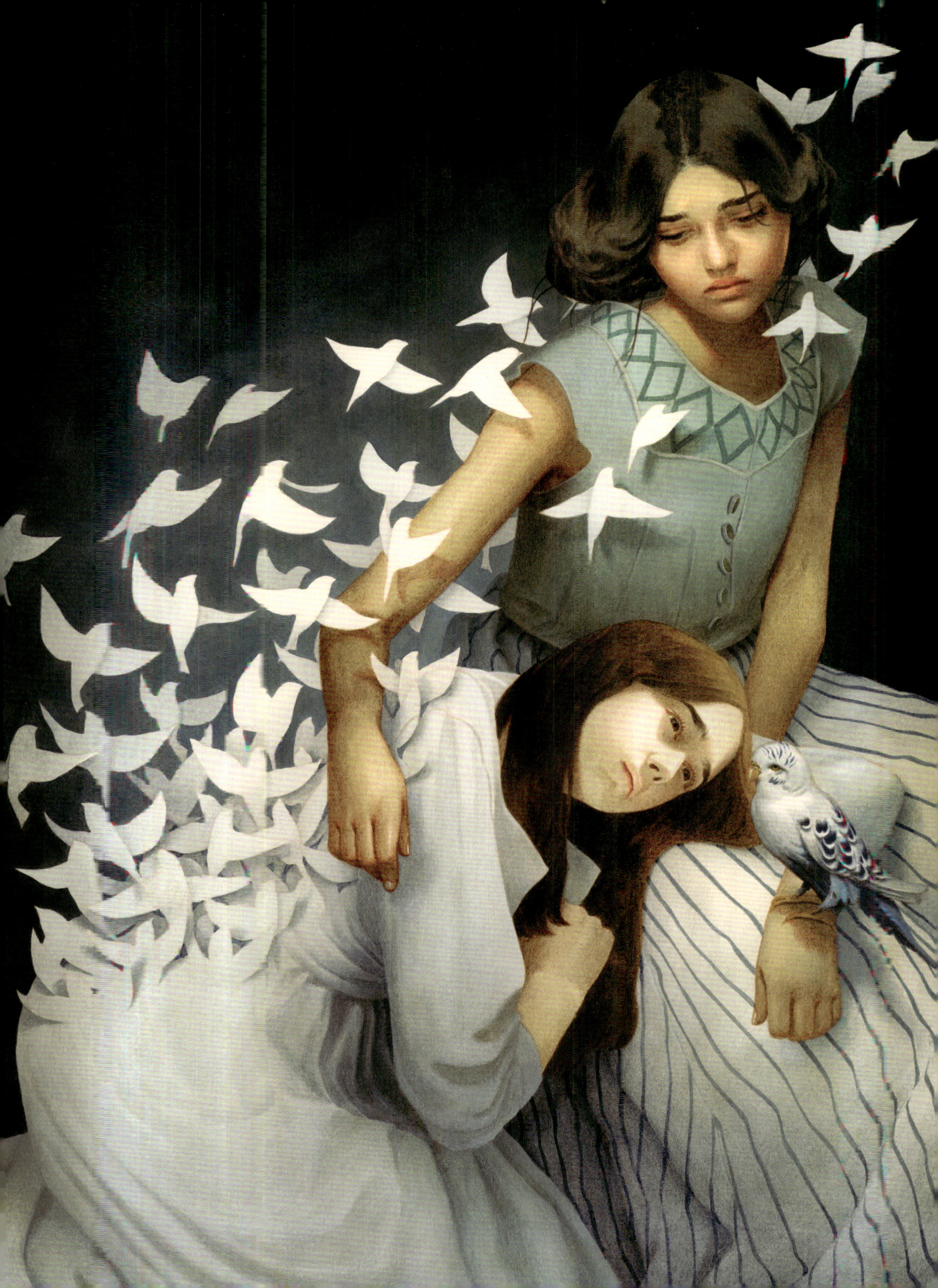

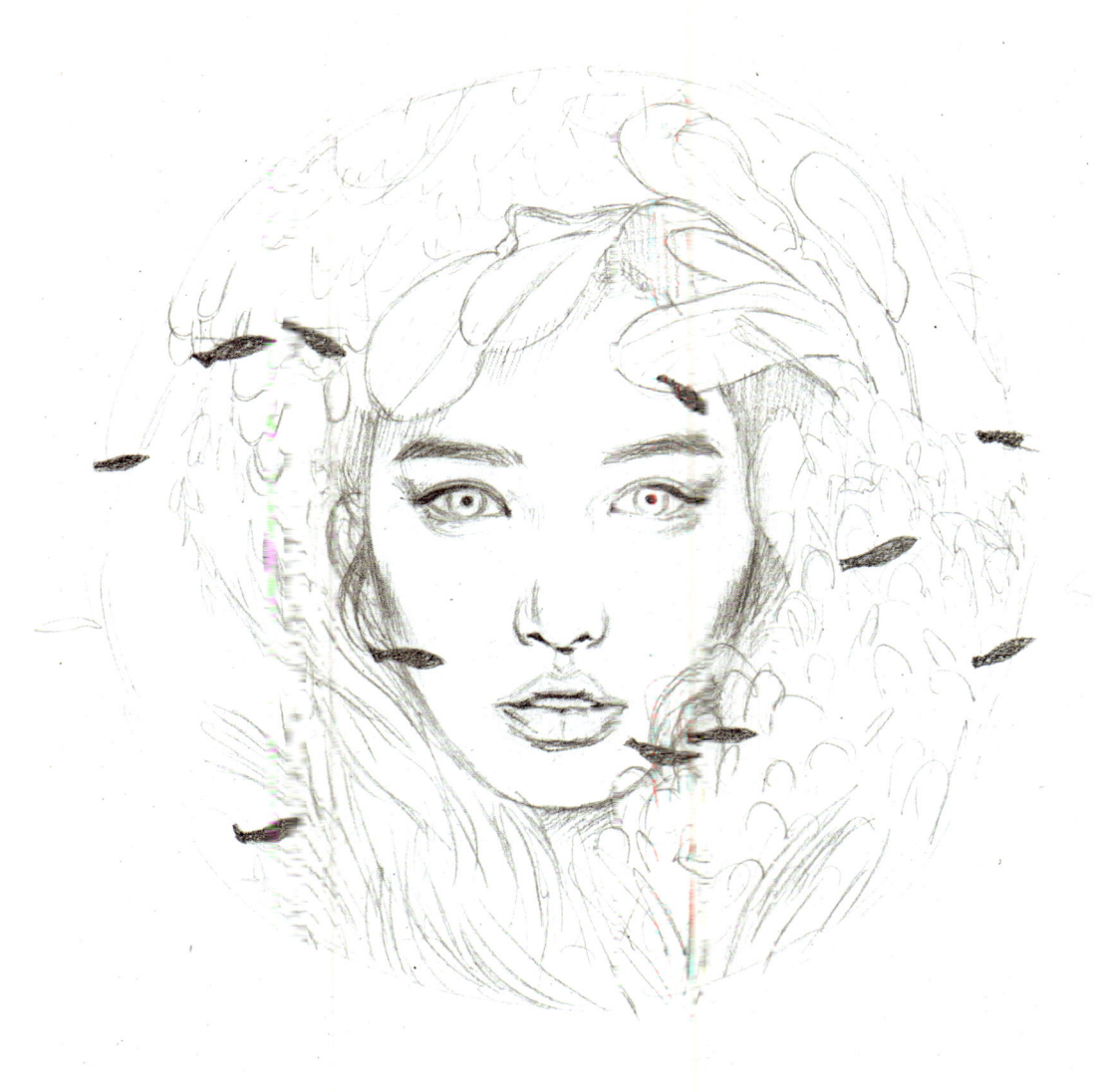

A MERMAID SCAR
ImagineFX magazine, AD: Clifford Hope, 2015

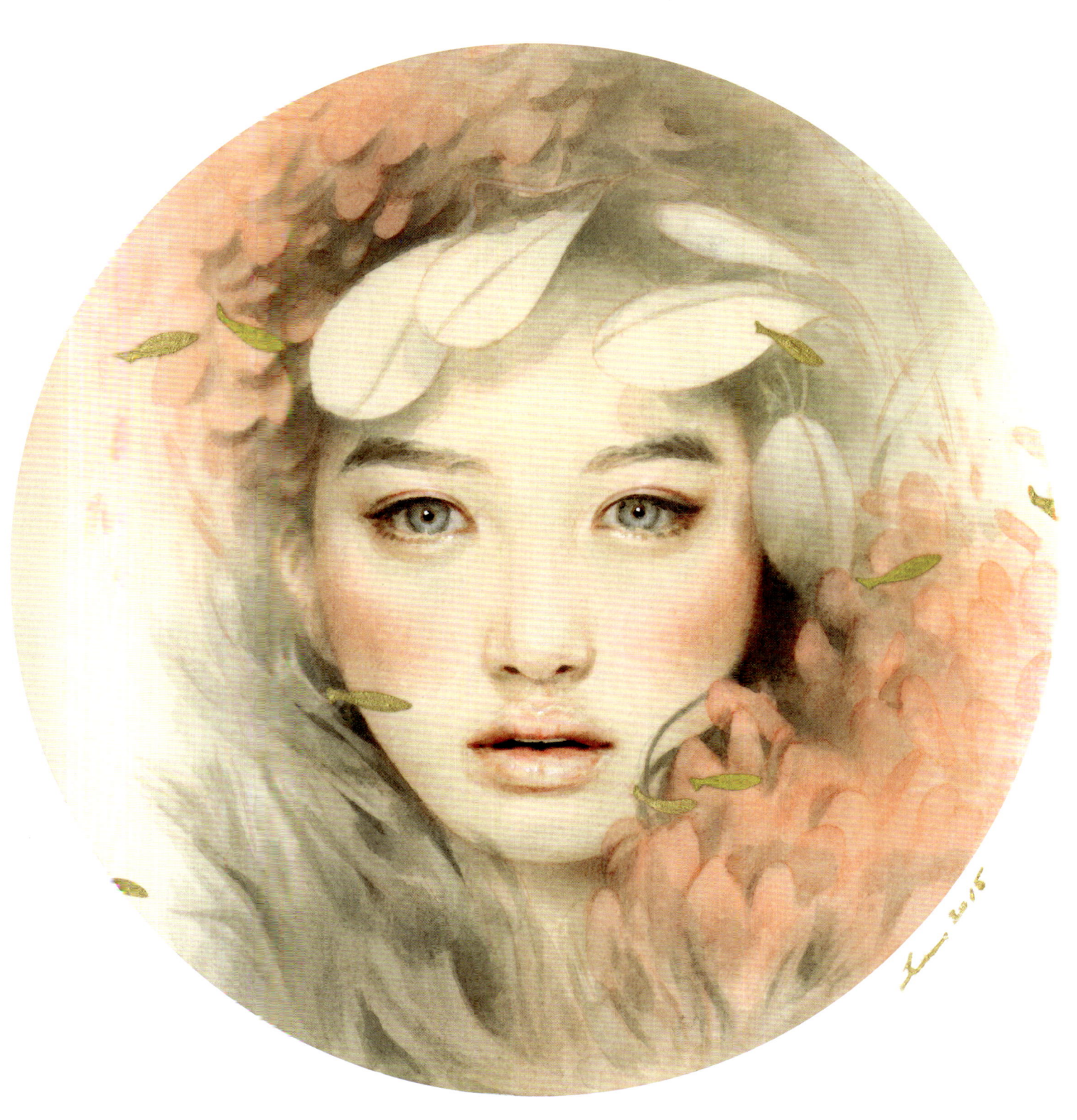

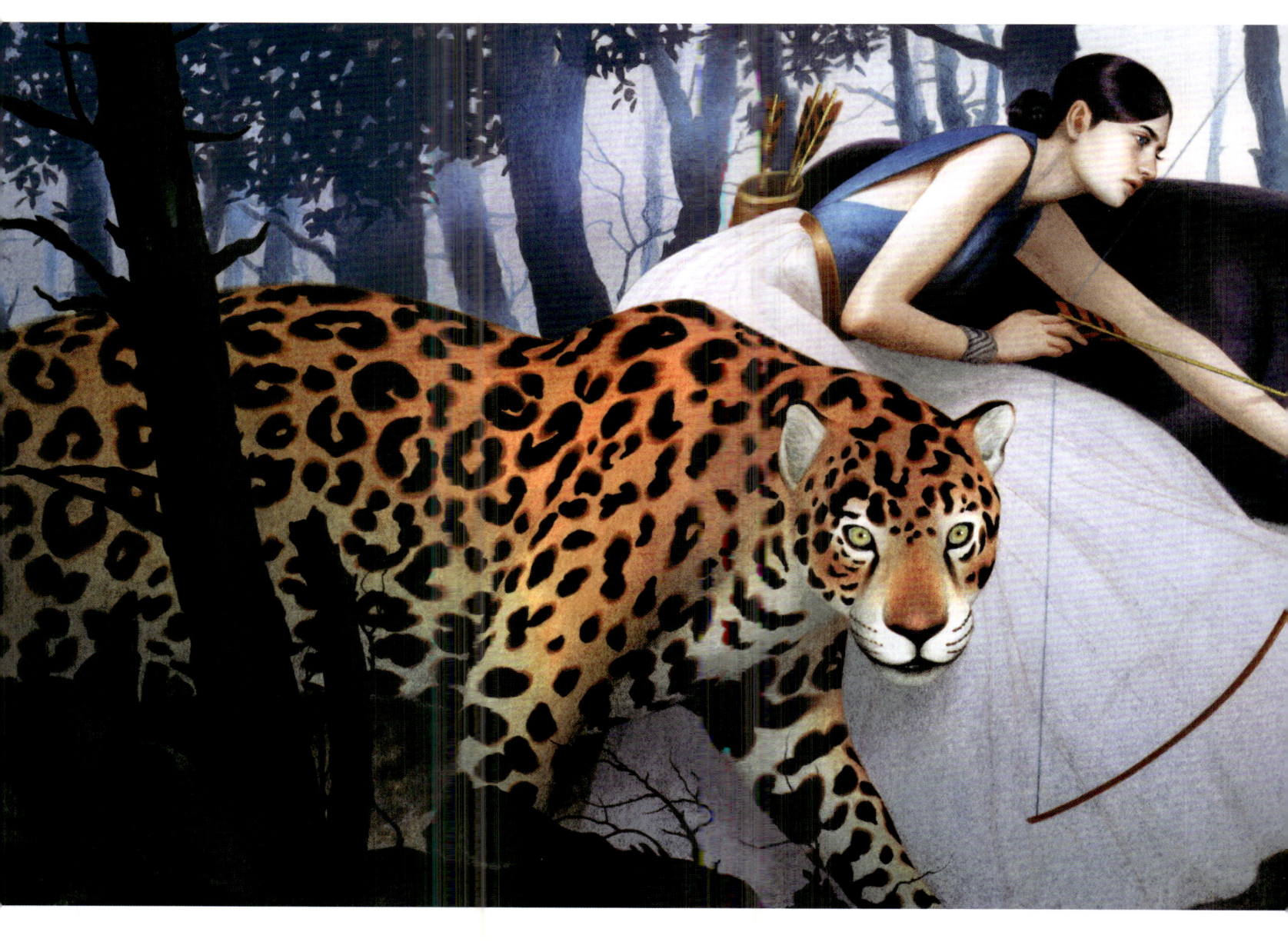

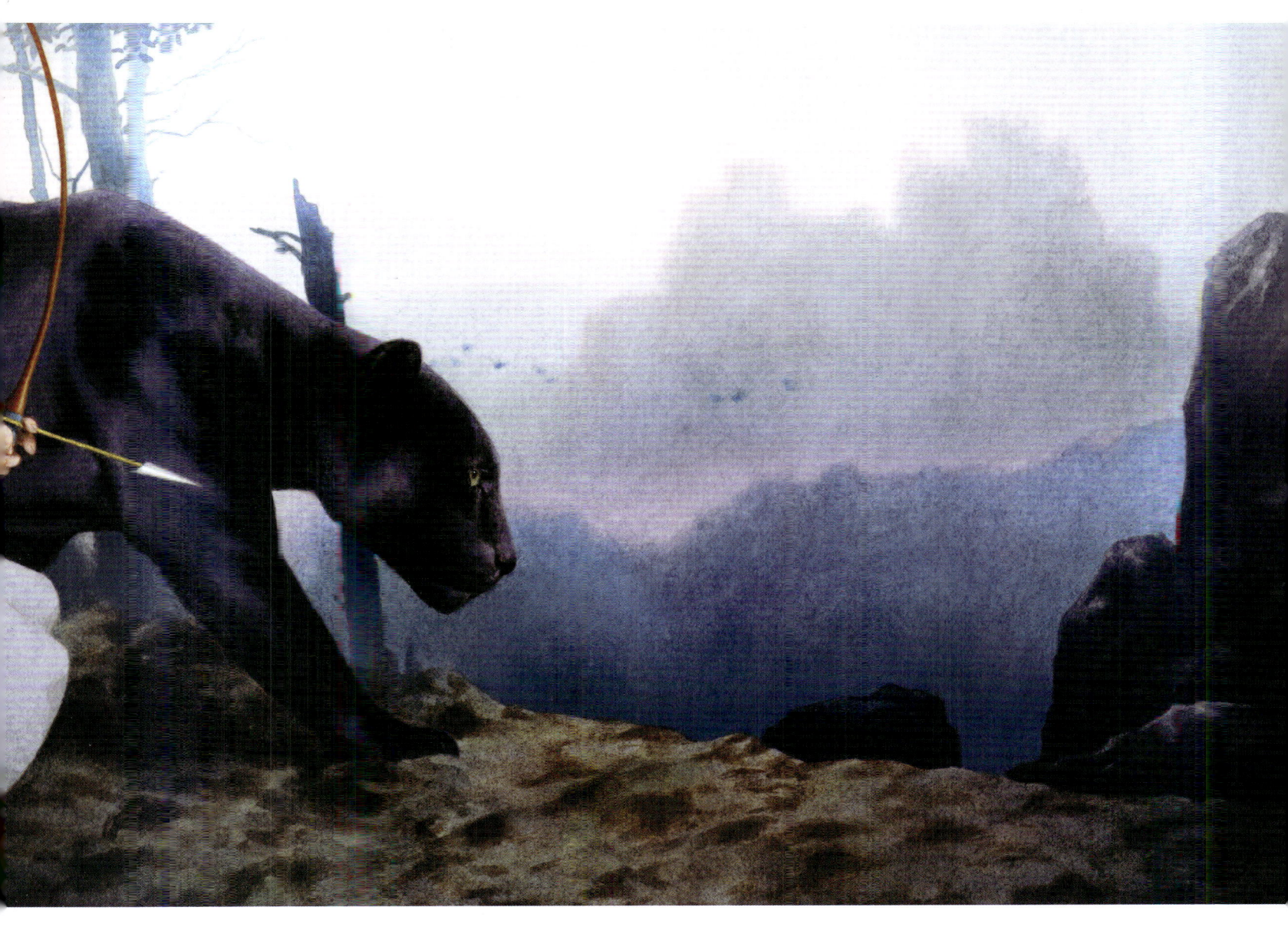

DISCOVERING NEW TERRITORY
Planadviser, AD: SooJin Buzelli, 2015

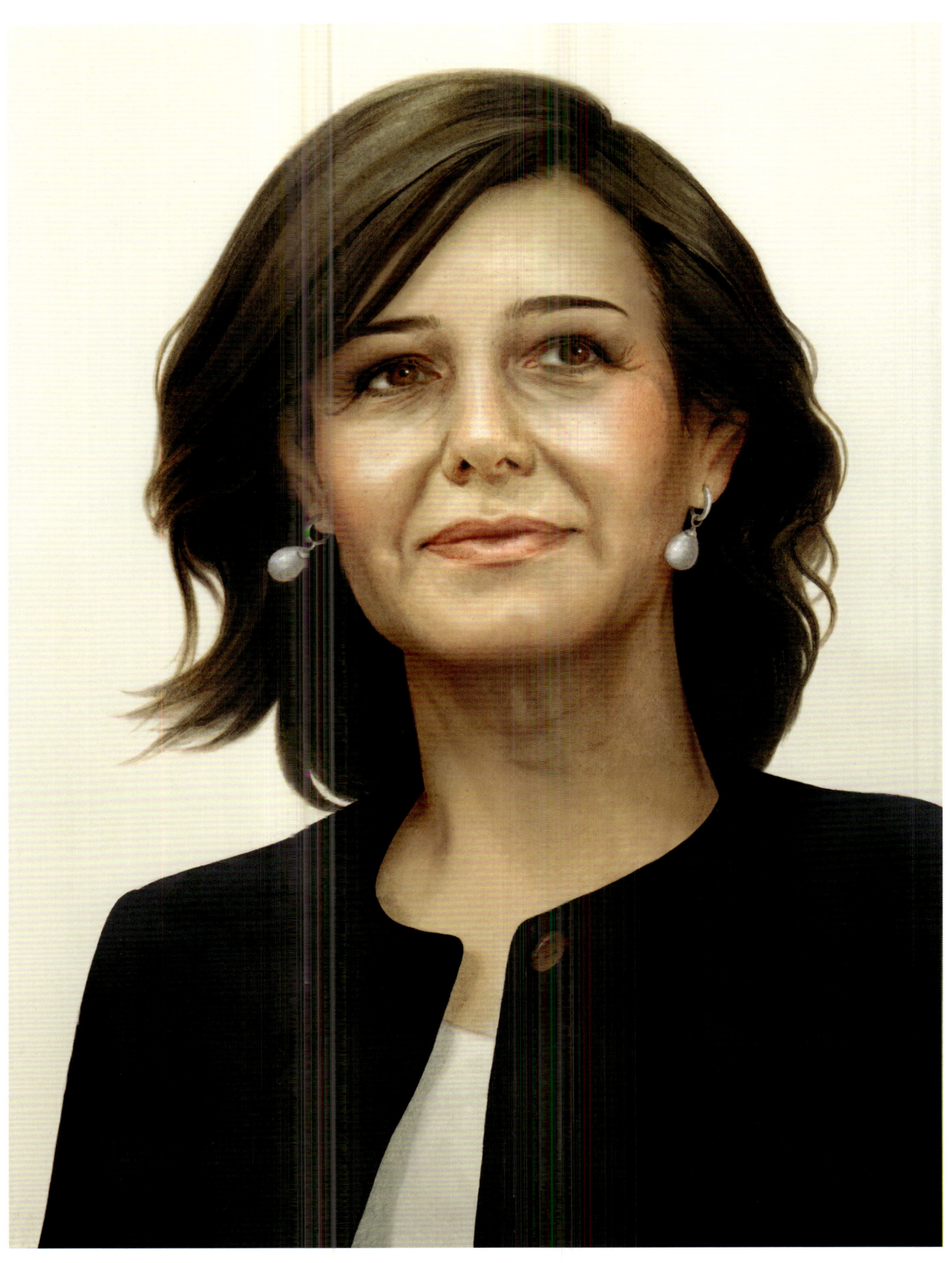

ANA BOTIN
Bloomberg magazine, AD. Siung Tjia, 2015

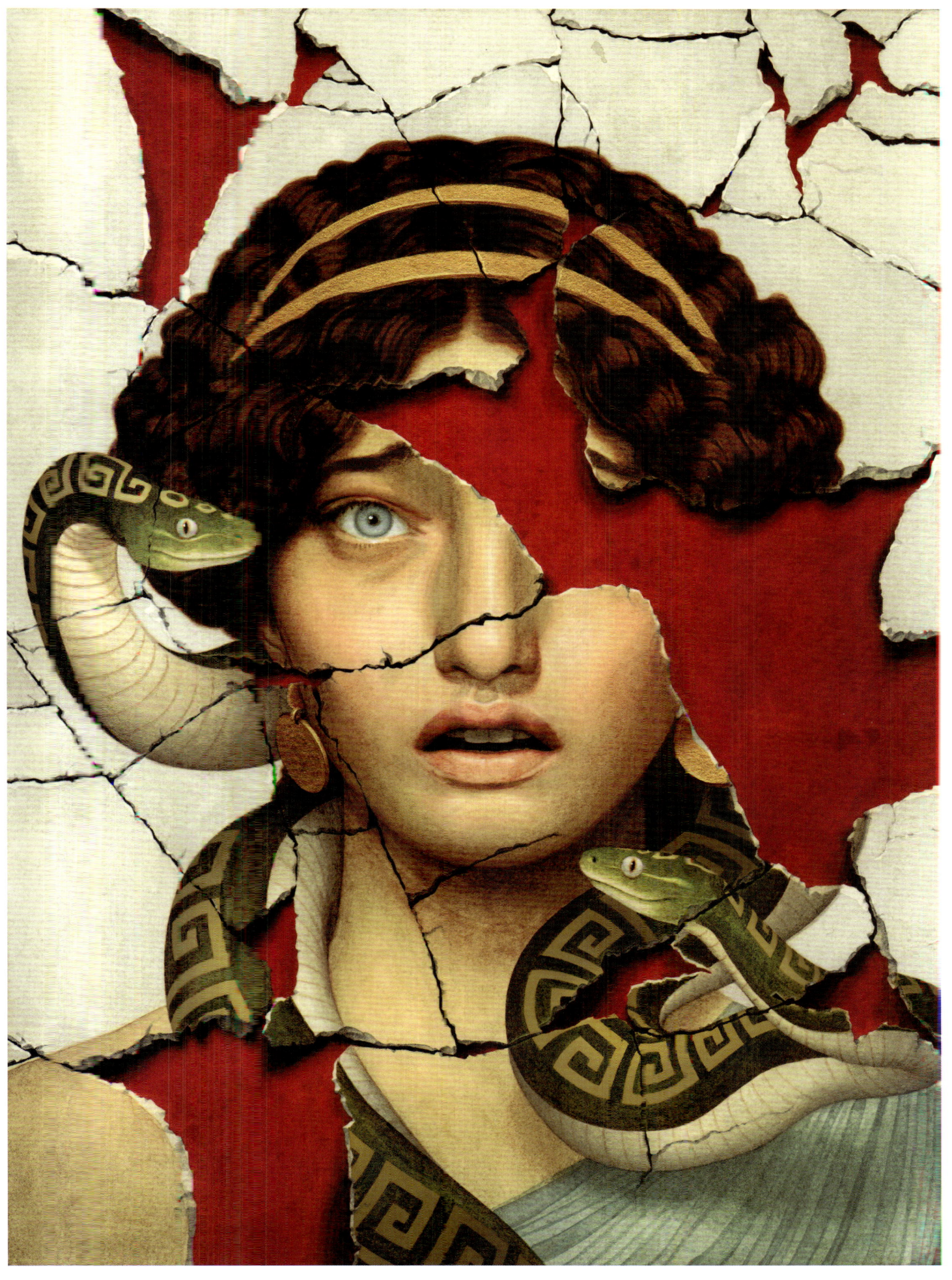

LAID IN A LANDLESS FAÇADE

Smithsonian magazine, AD: Maria Keehan, 2015

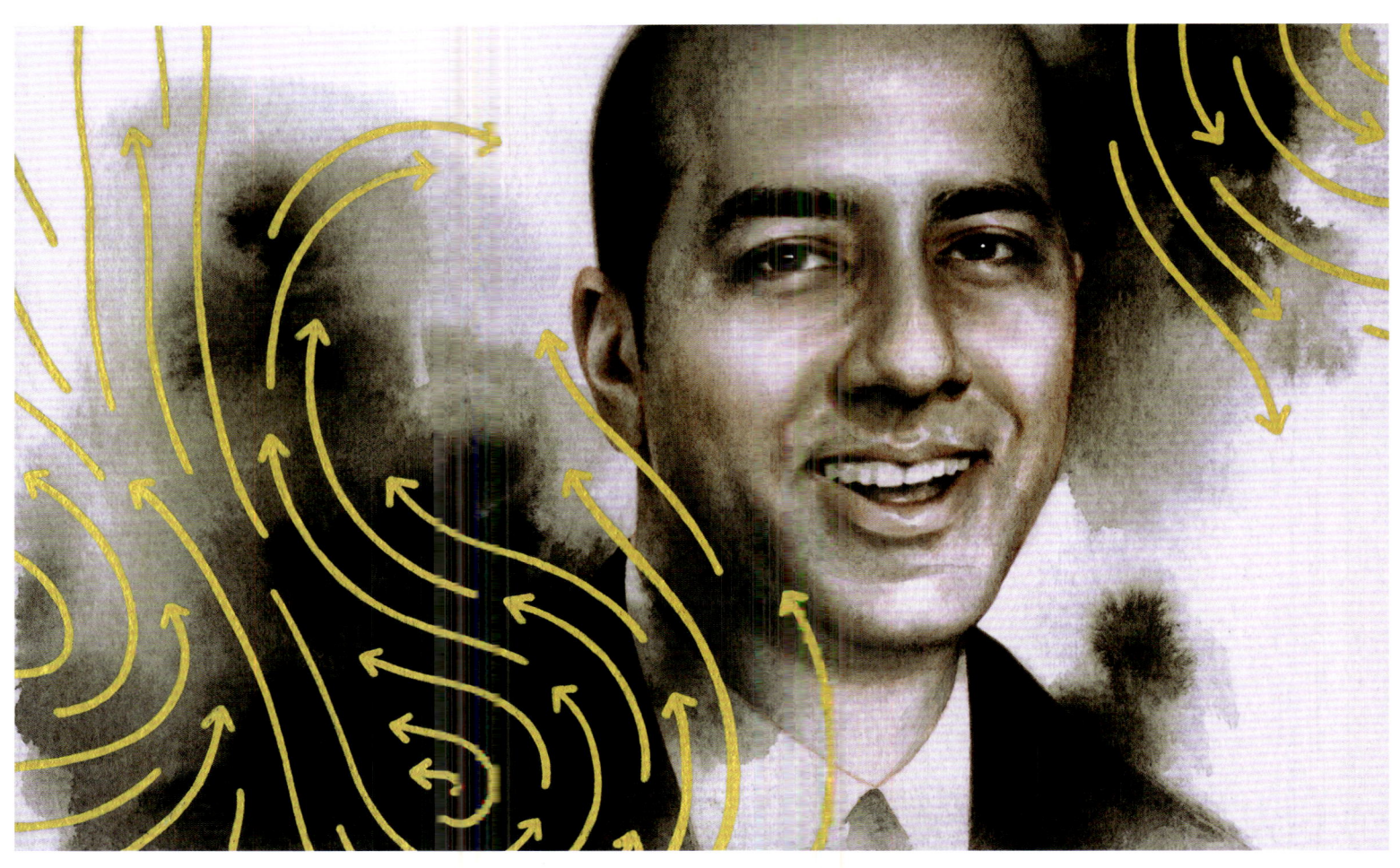

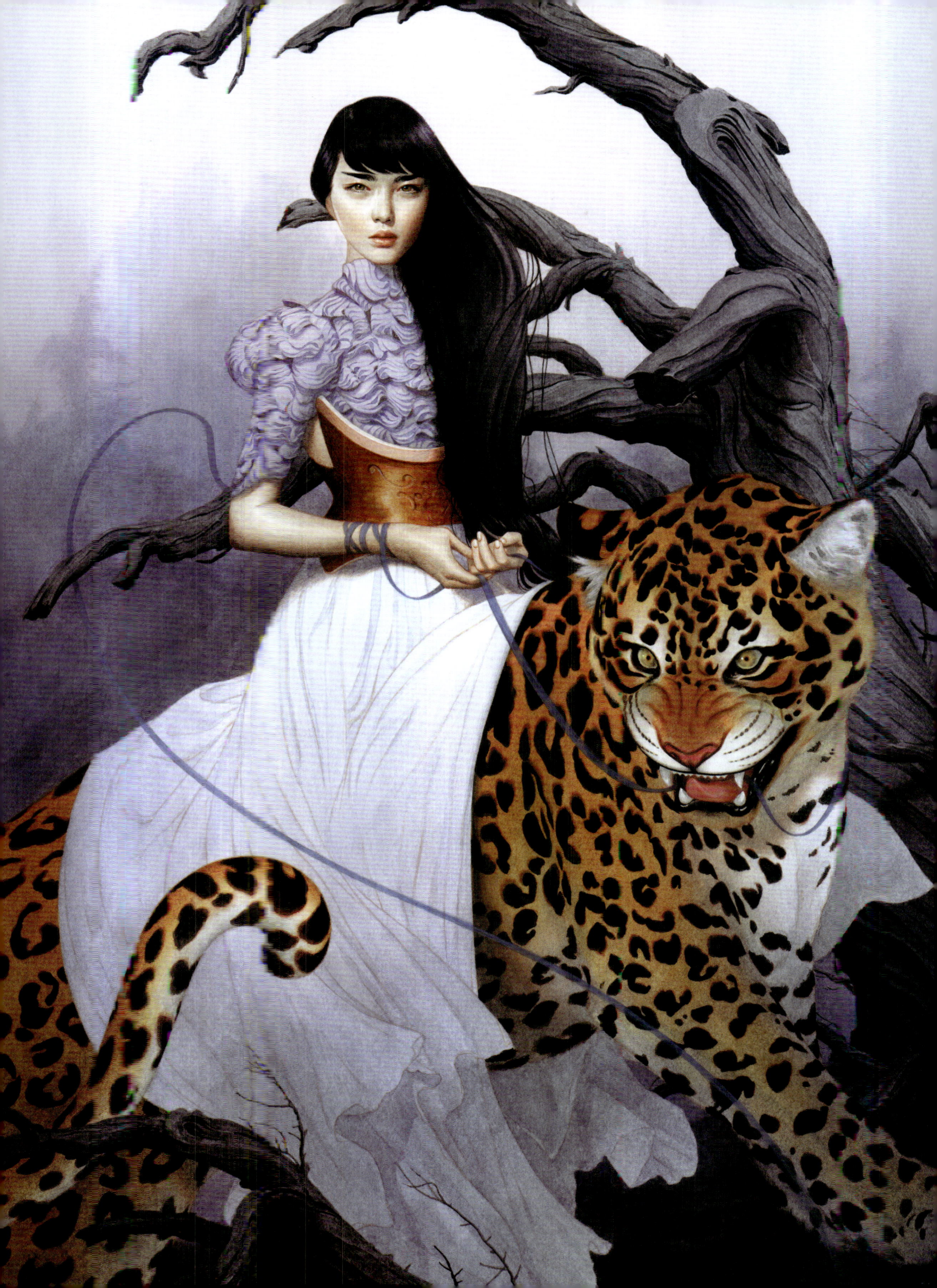

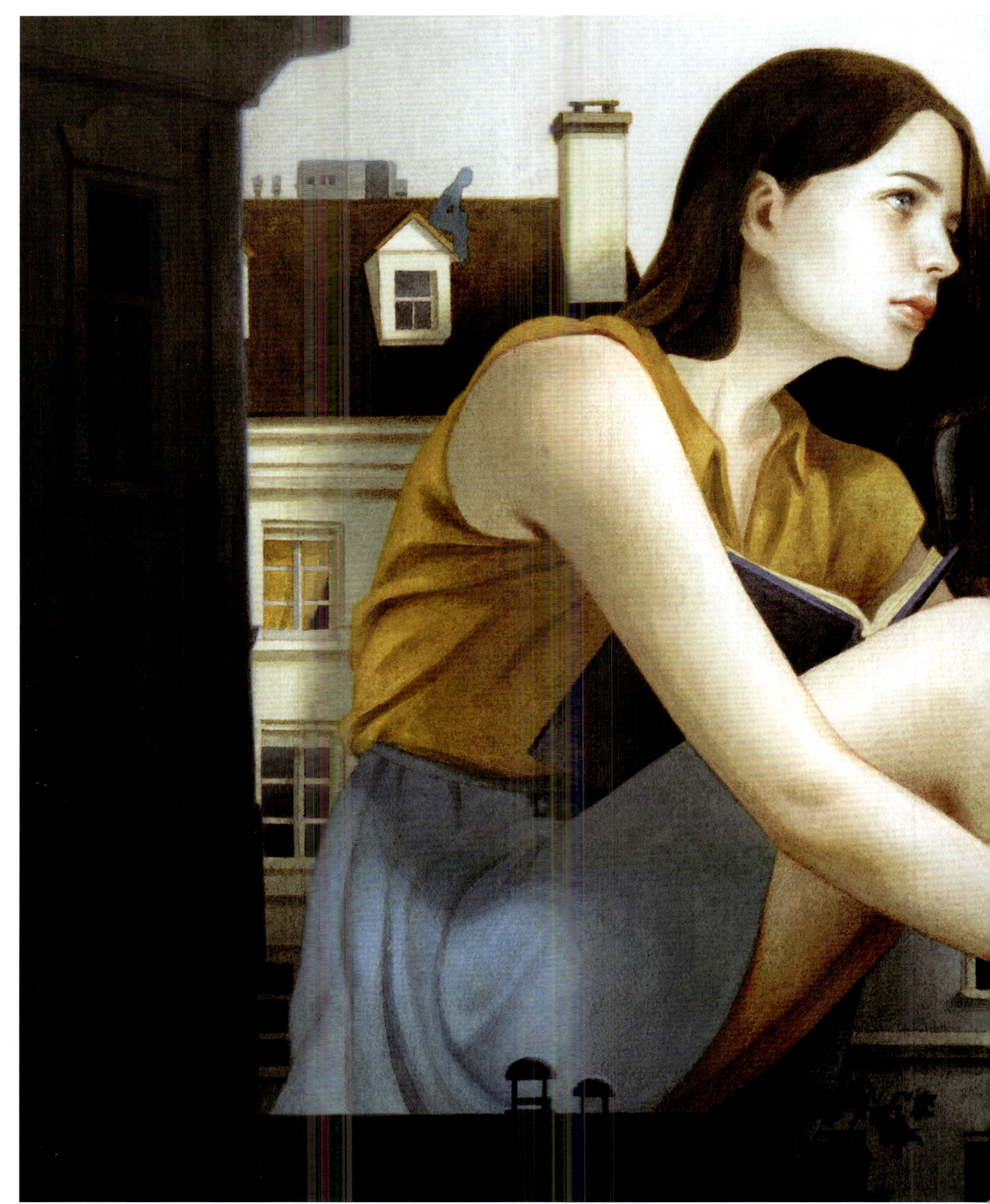

40 ROOMS
O, The Oprah magazine, AD: Jill Armus, 2010

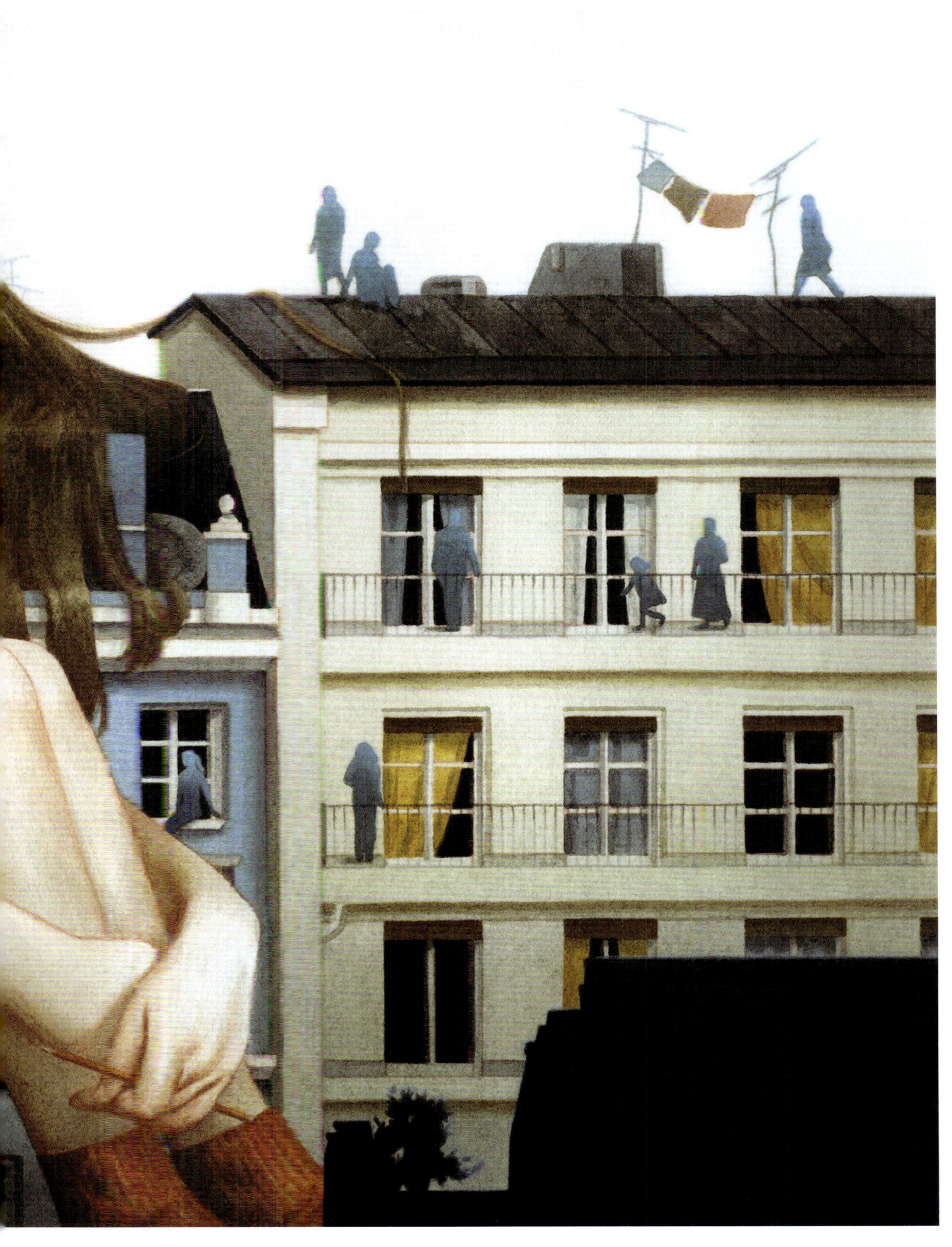

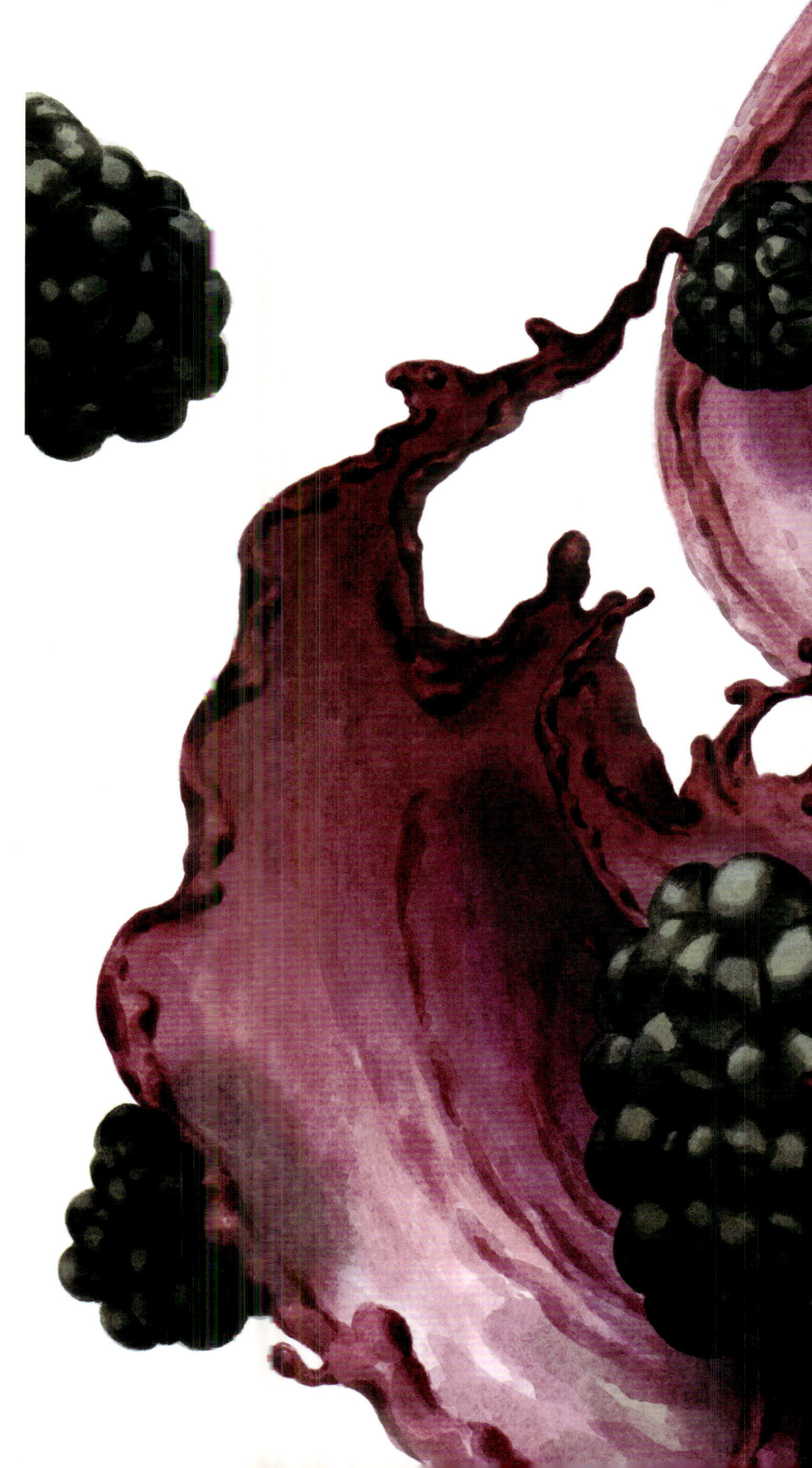

BLACKBERRY
Common Cider, AD: Fran Toves, 2016

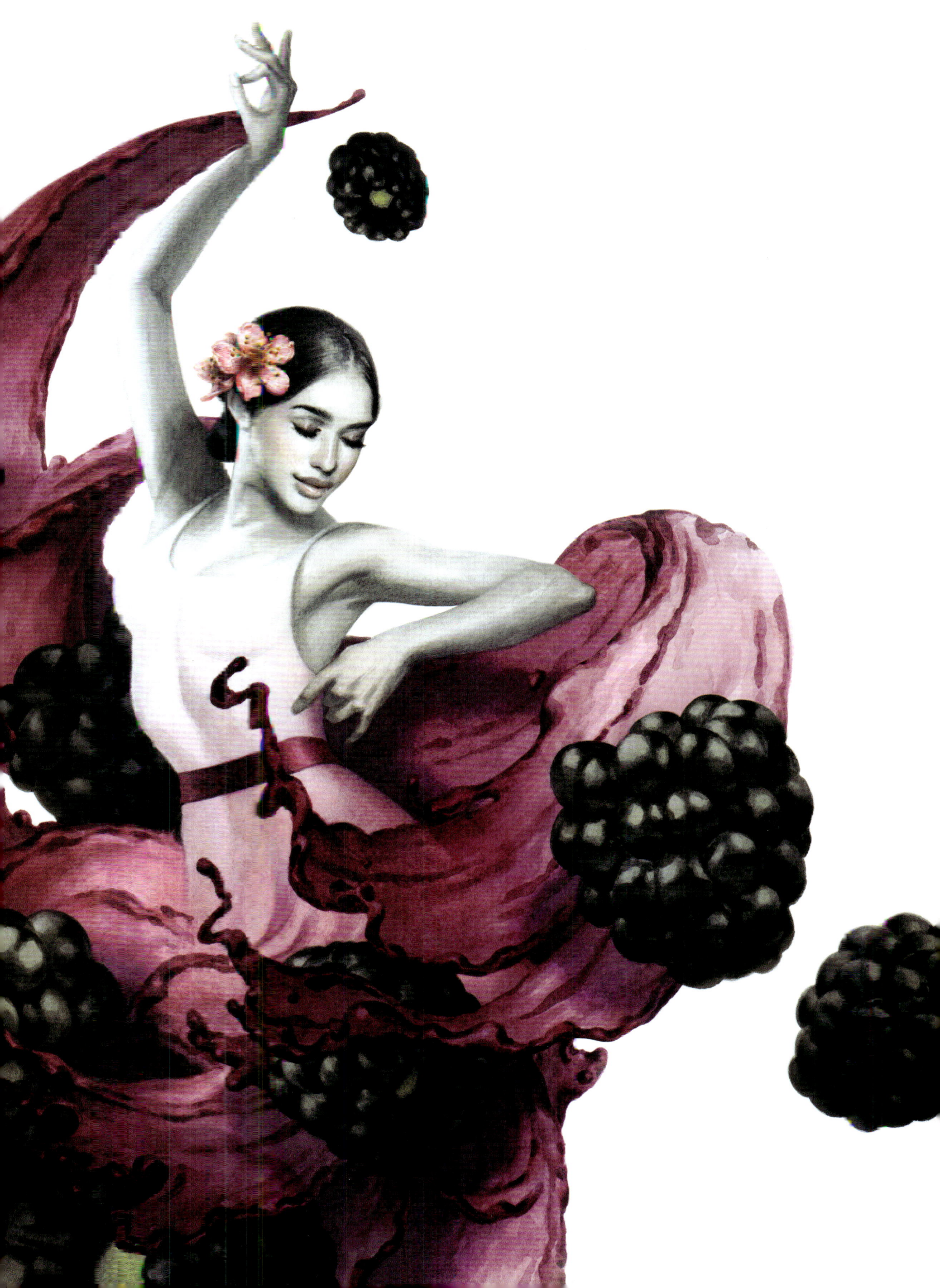

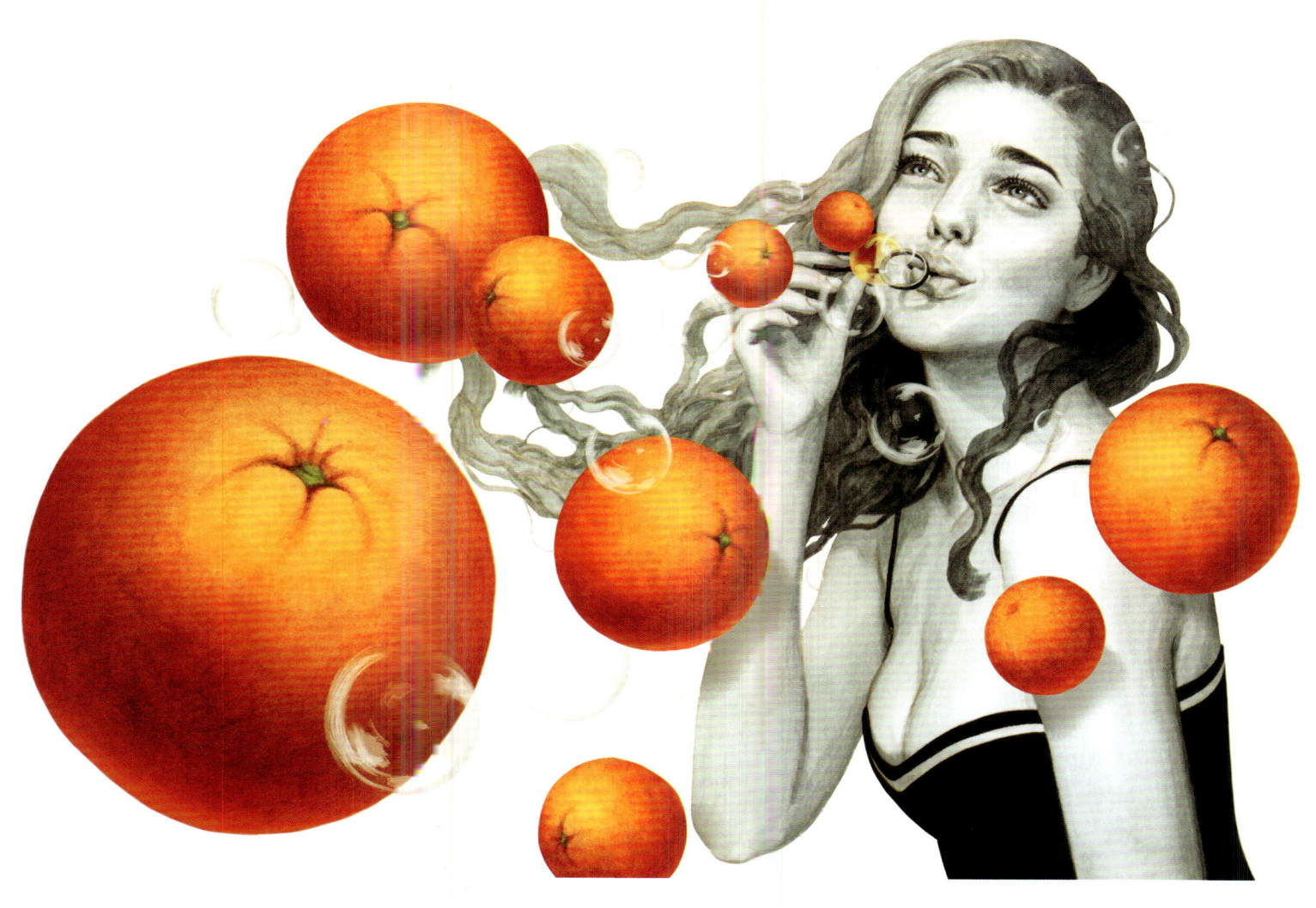

BLOOD ORANGE
Common Cider, AD: Lee Felch, 2016

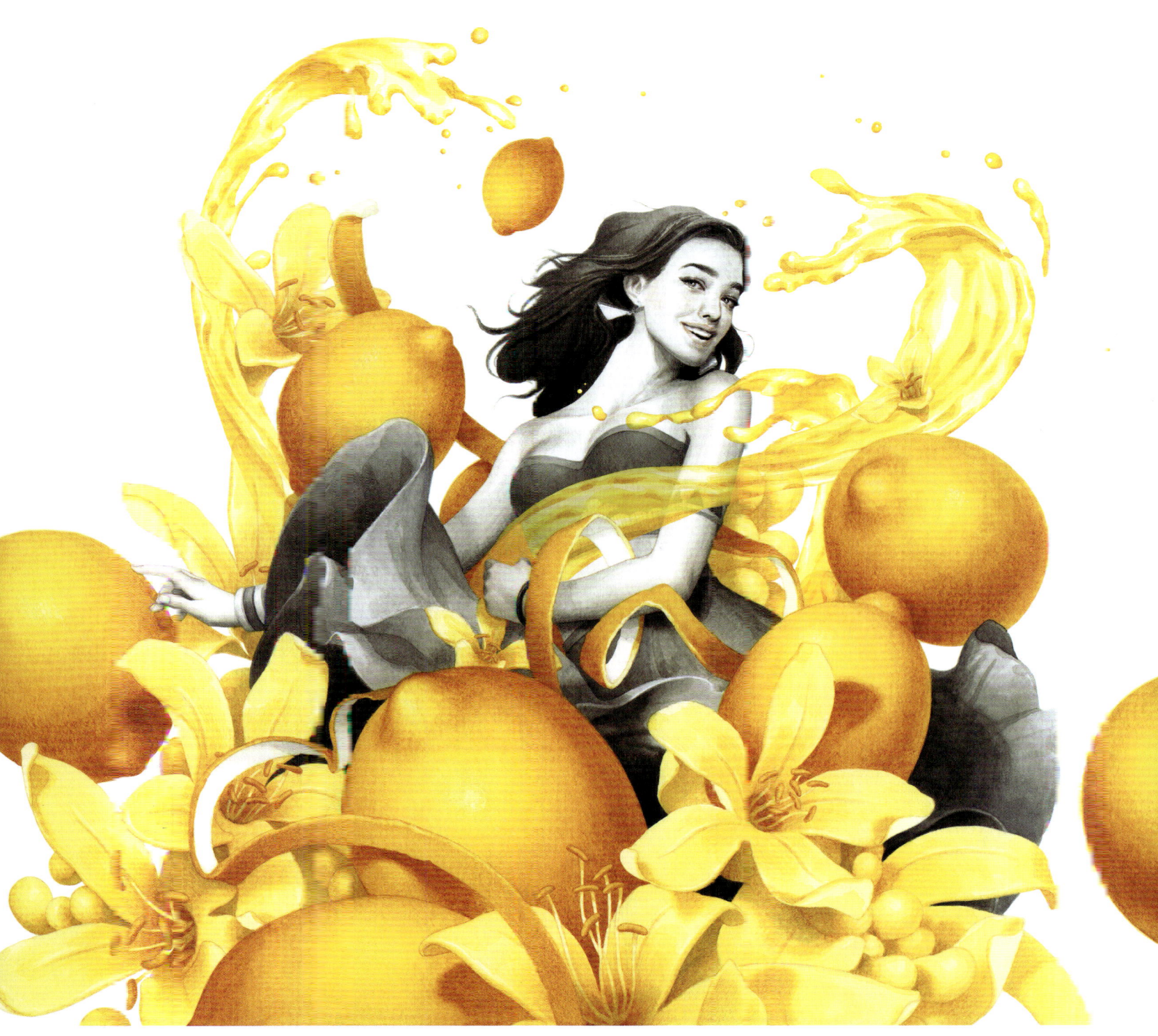

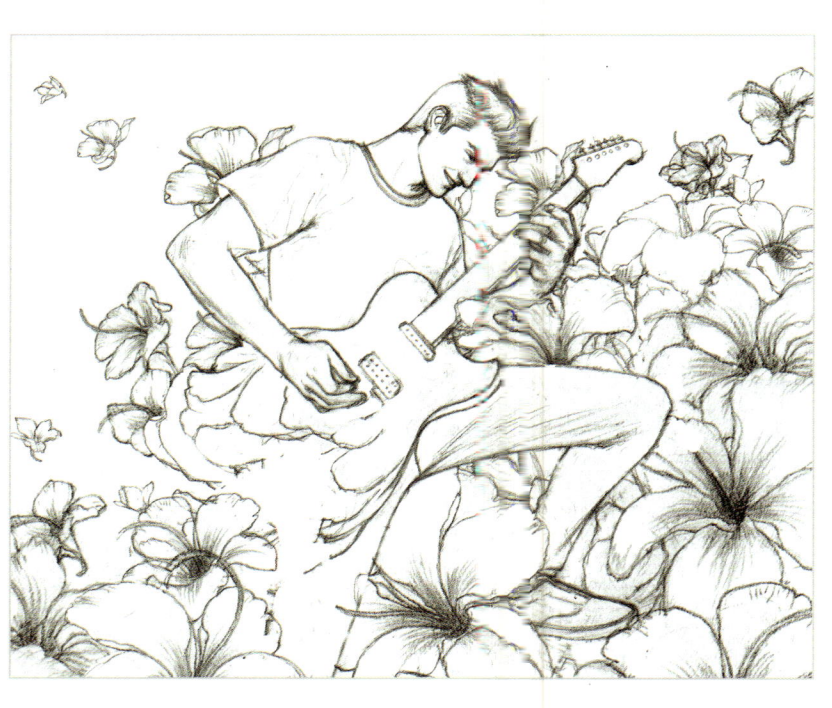

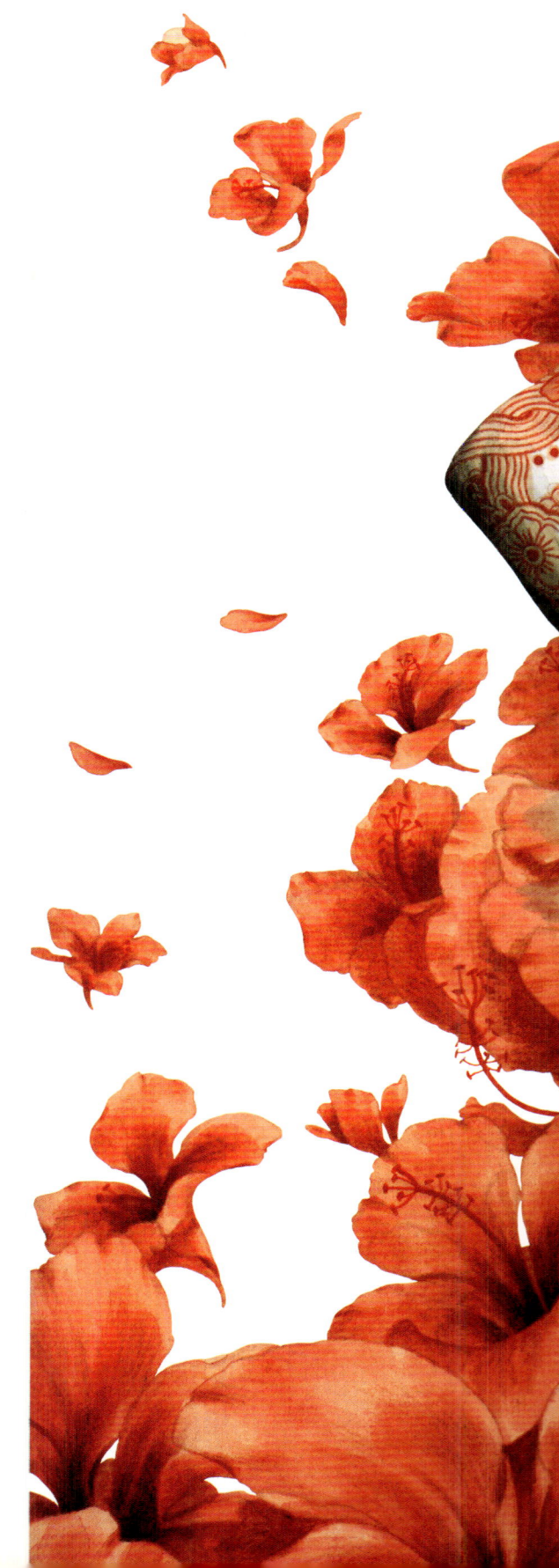

HIBISCUS
Common Cider, AD: Lee Felch, 2016

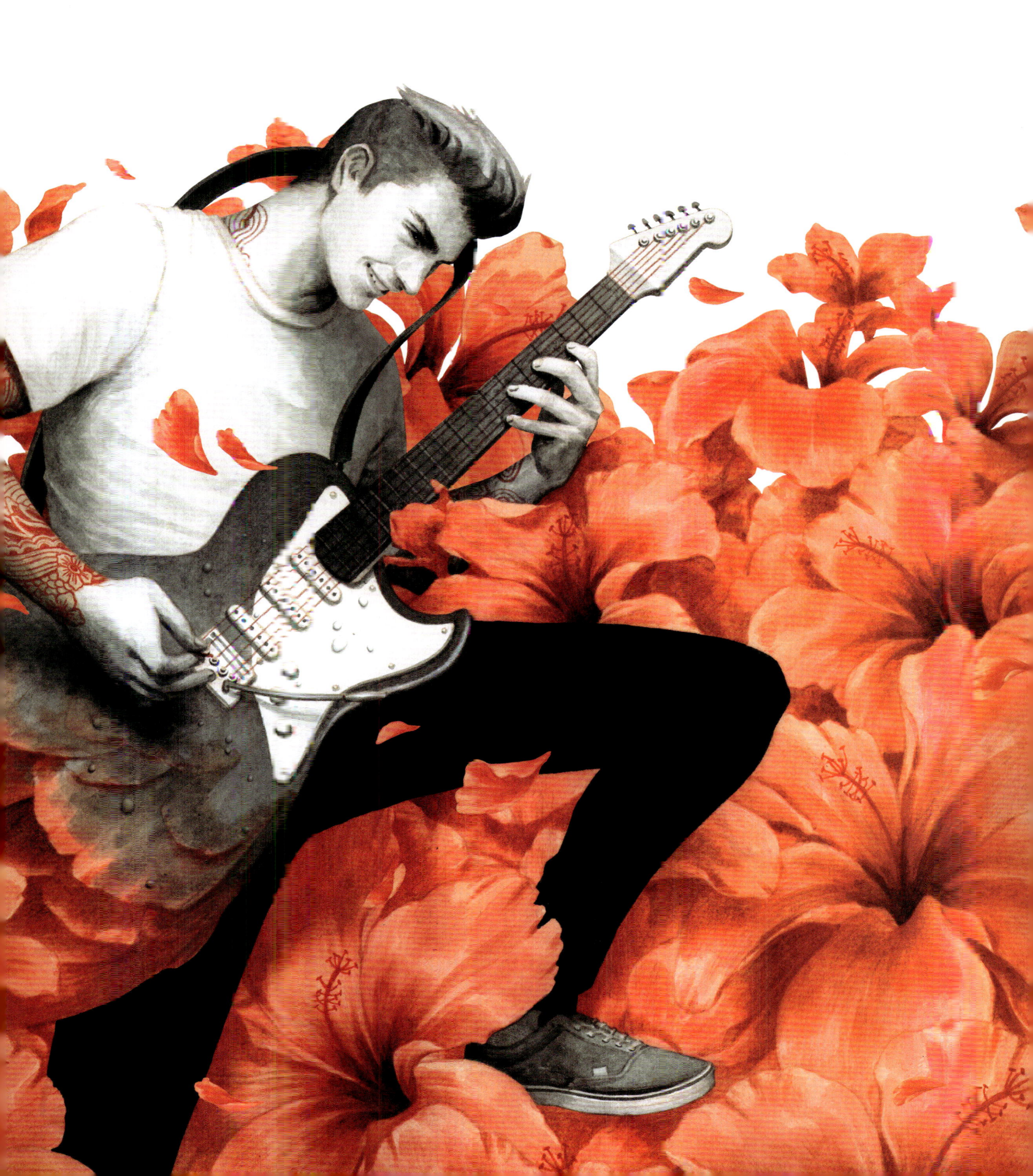

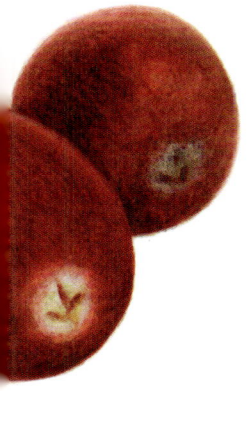

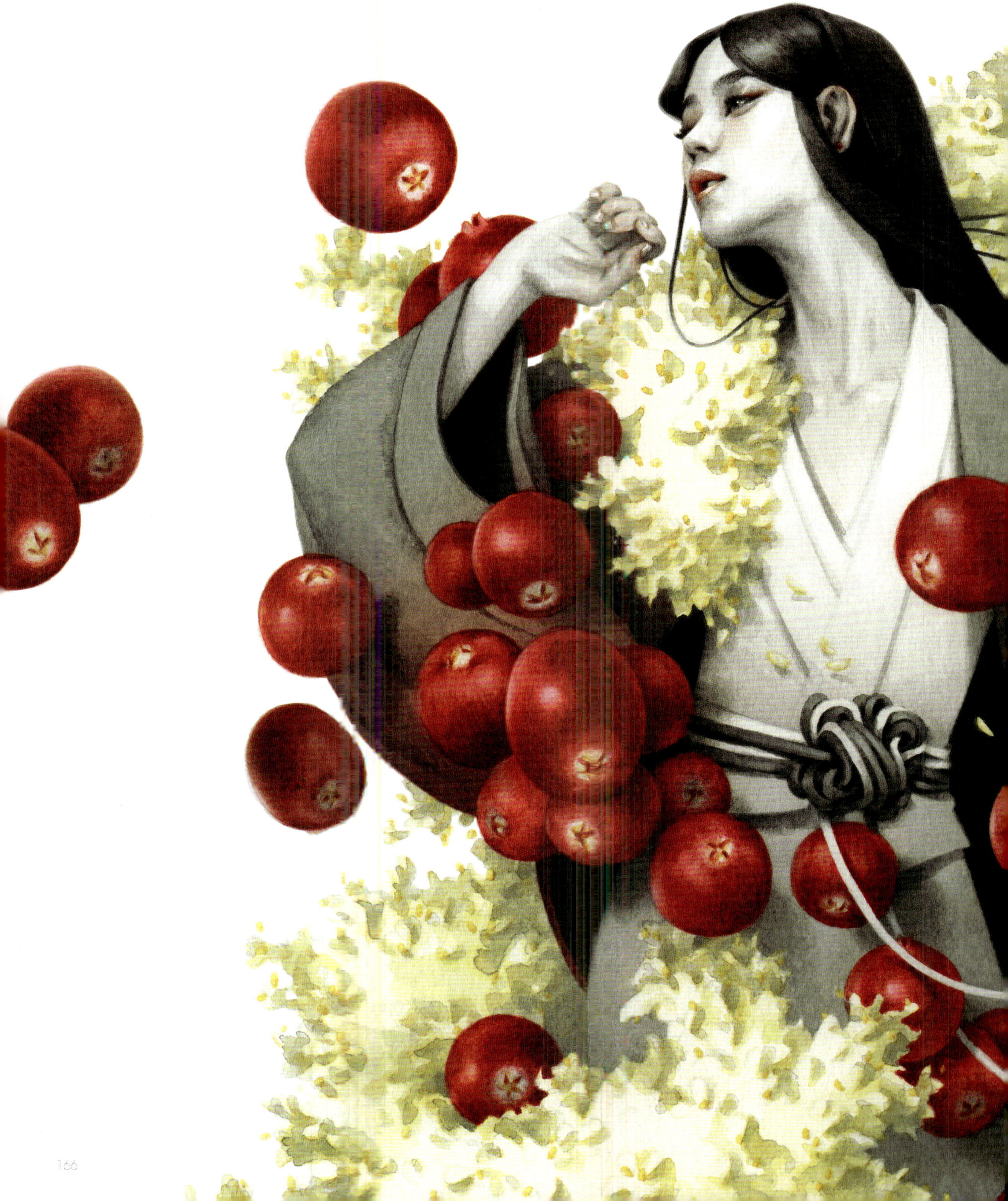

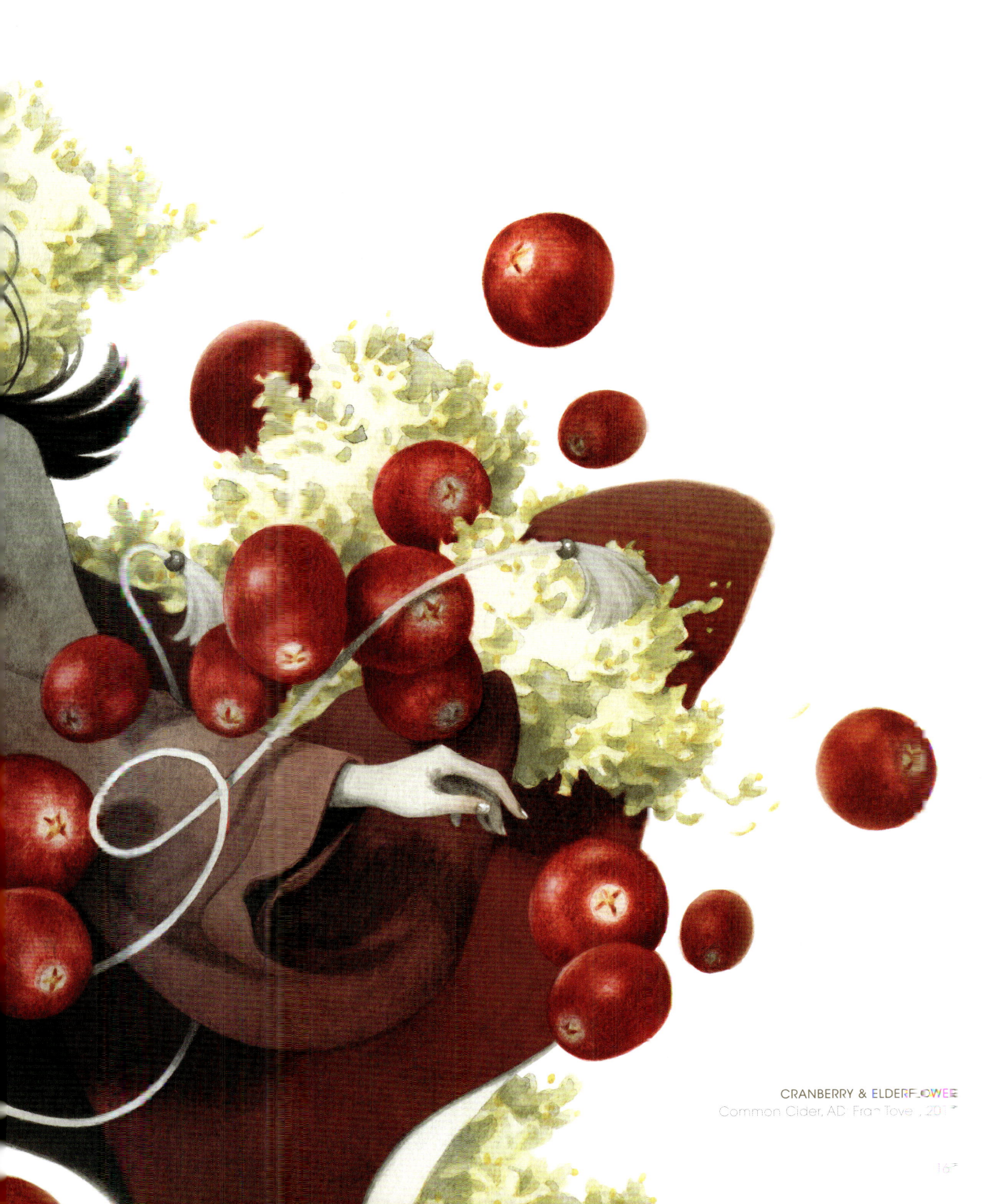

CRANBERRY & ELDERFLOWER
Common Cider, AD: Fran Tover, 2017

169

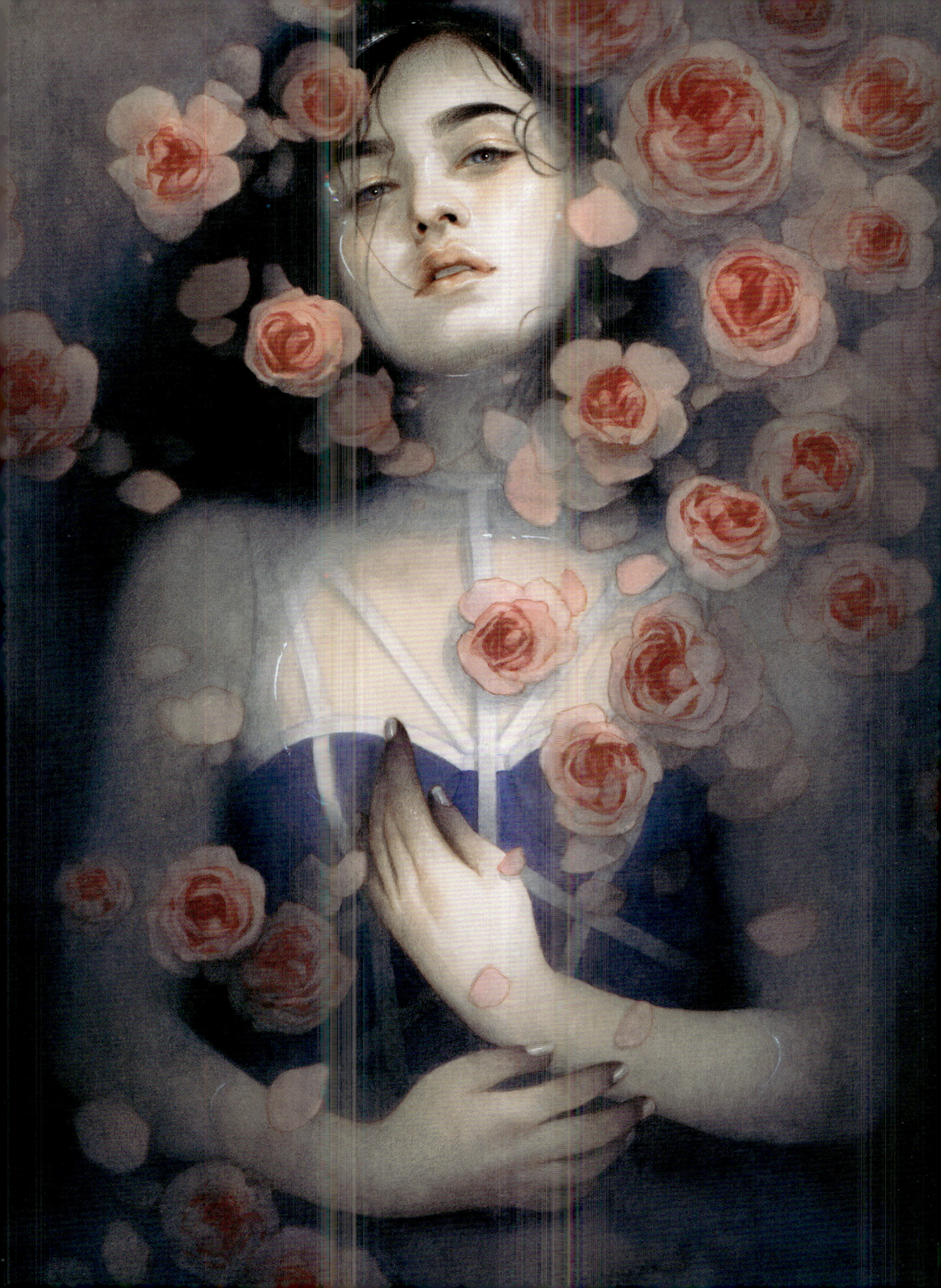

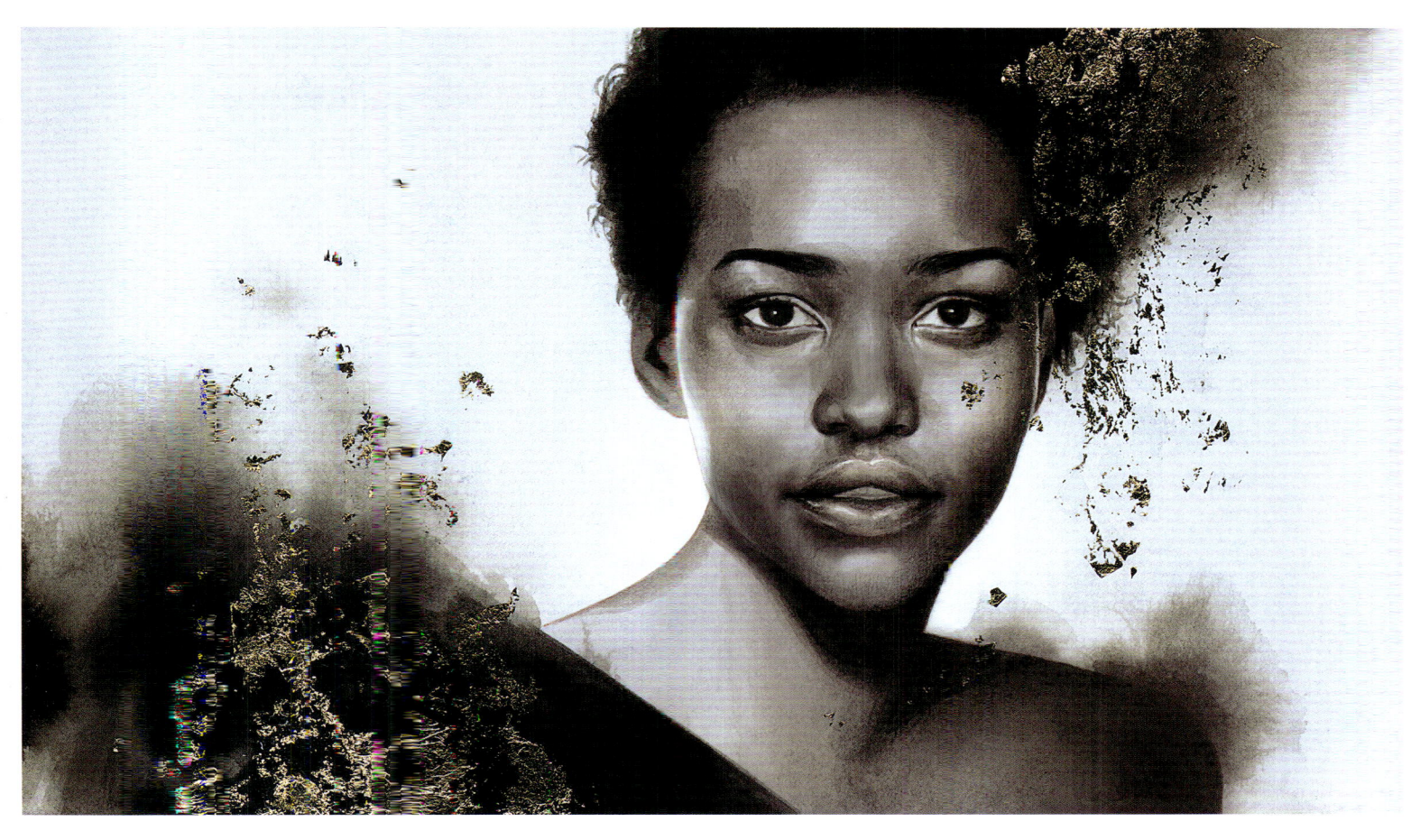

SLEEPLESS ON THE SILK ROAD
Uncanny magazine, AD: Michael & Lynne Thomas, 2017

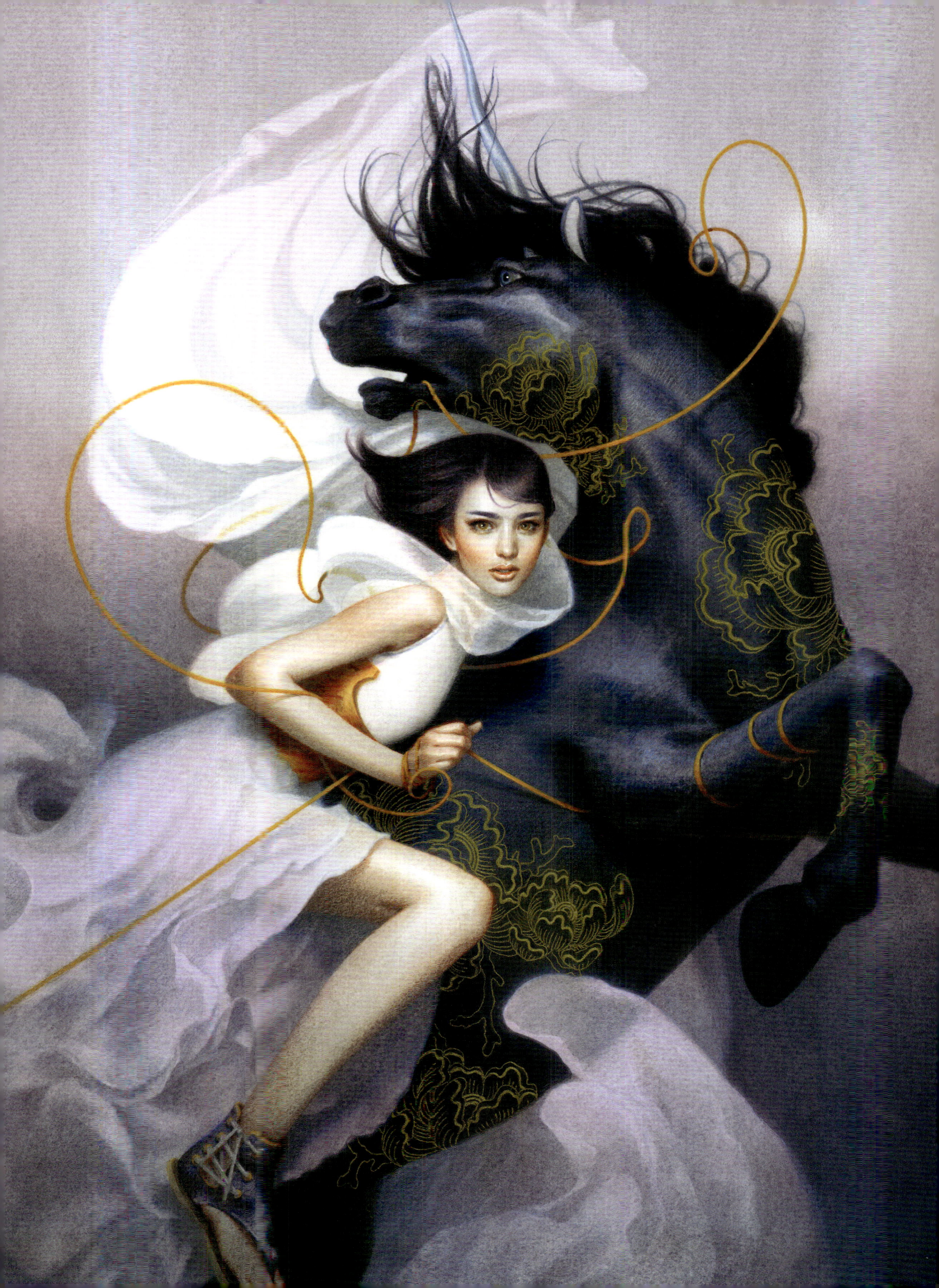

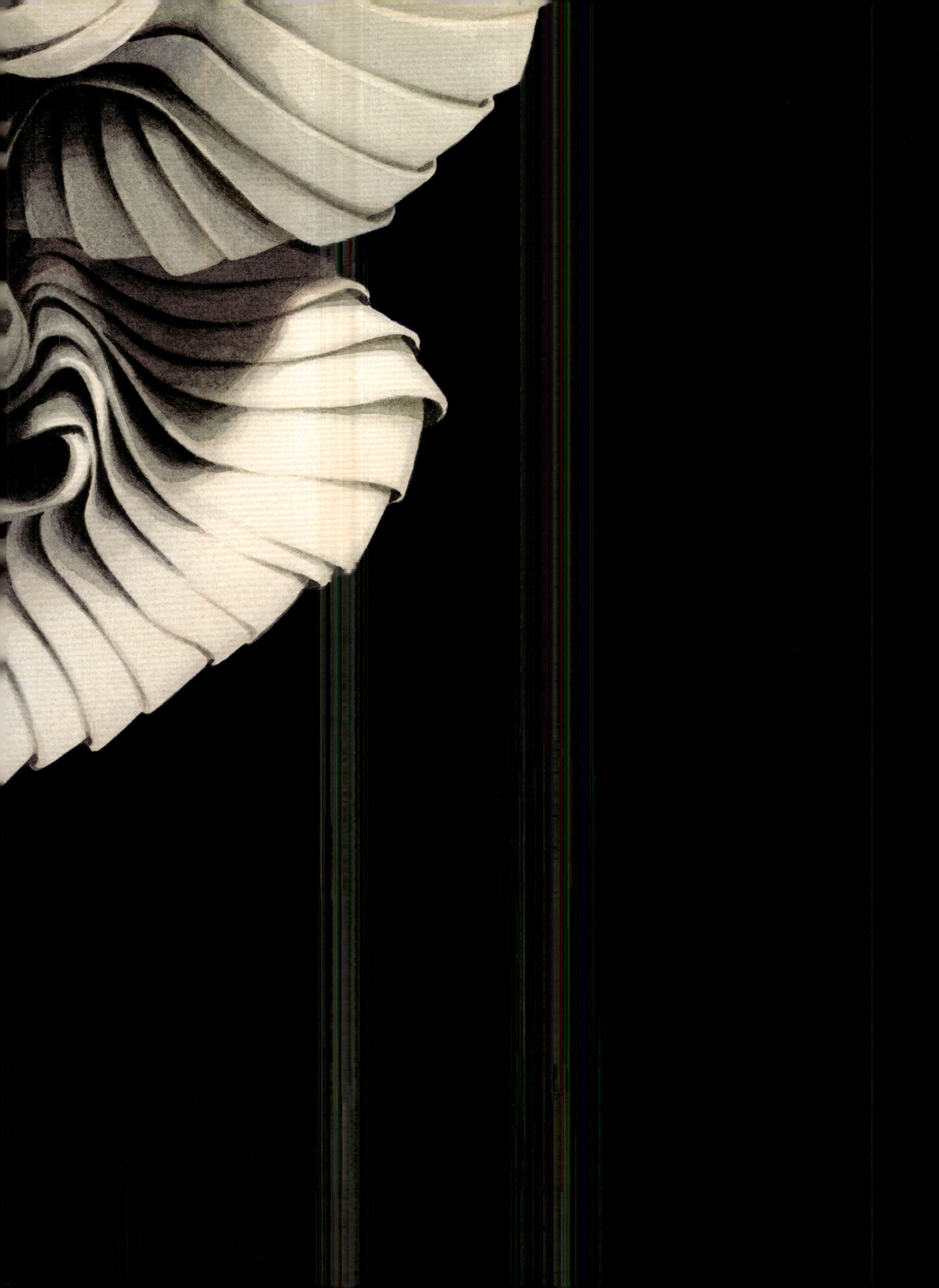

BOOK

ART CREATED FOR HARDBOUND AND PAPERBACK
BOOK COVERS AND INTERIORS

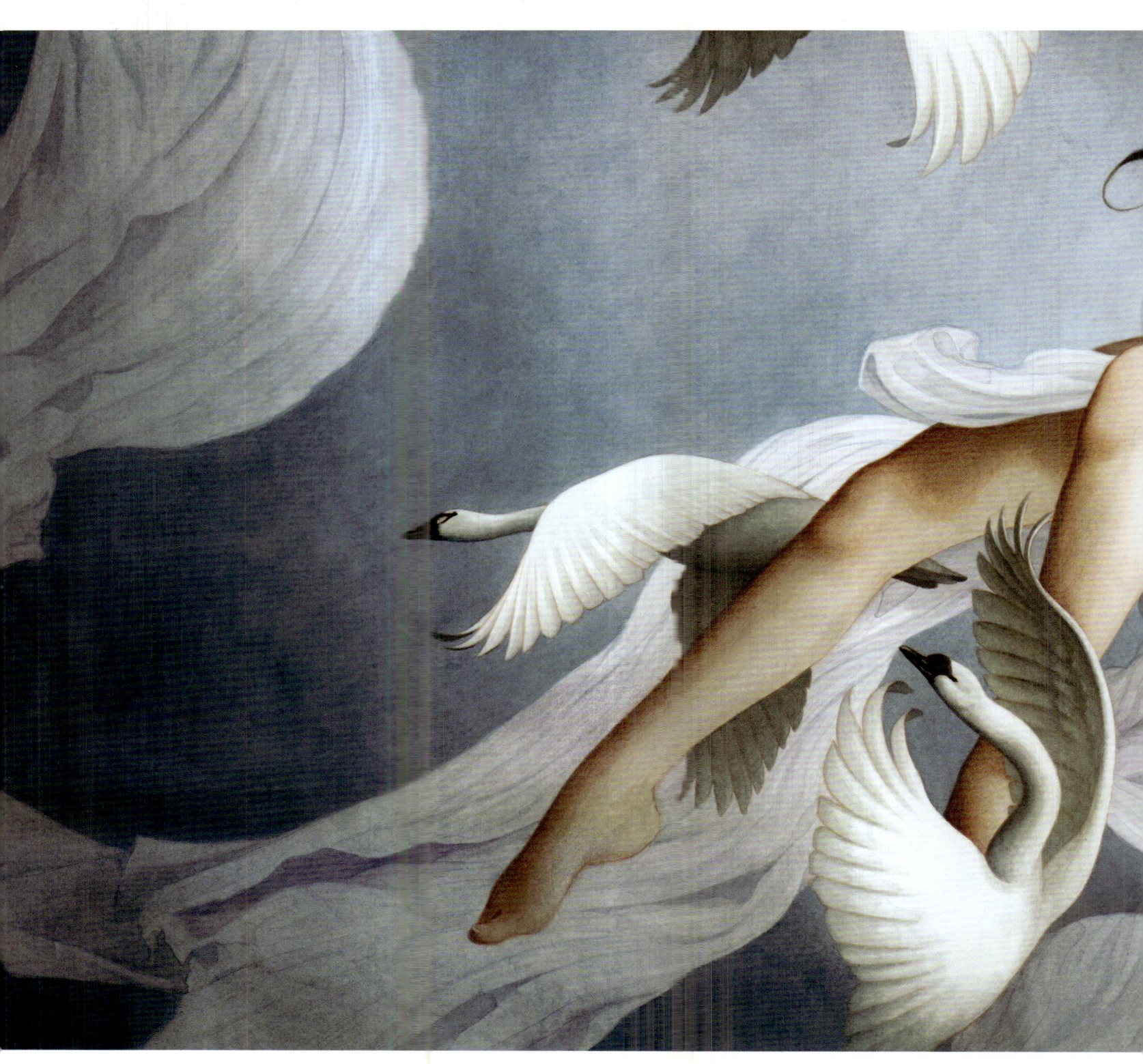

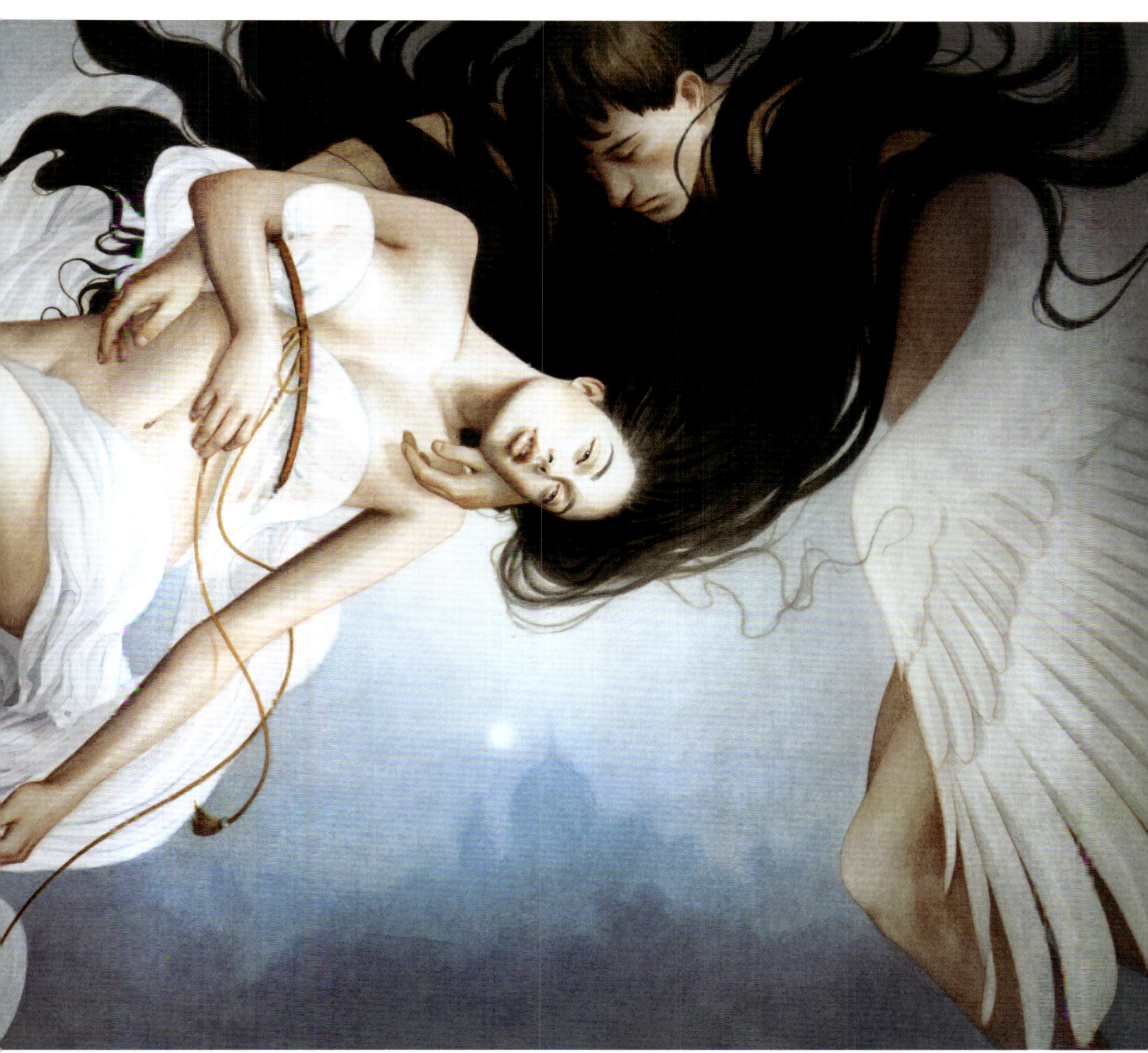

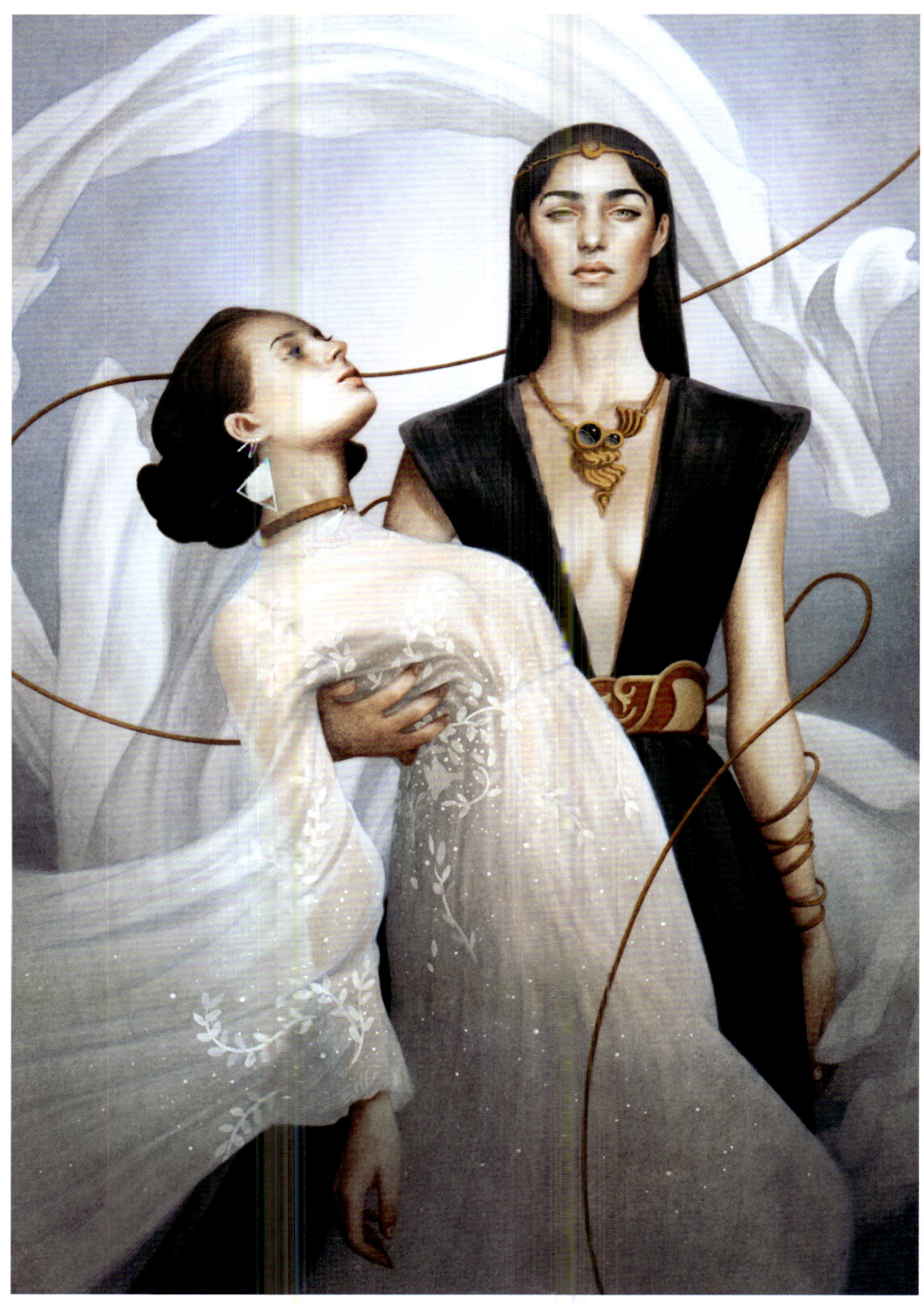

above
KUSHIEL'S DART II
Subterranean Press, AD: Yanni Kuznia, 2016

right
KUSHIEL'S DART III
Subterranean Press, AD: Yanni Kuznia, 2016

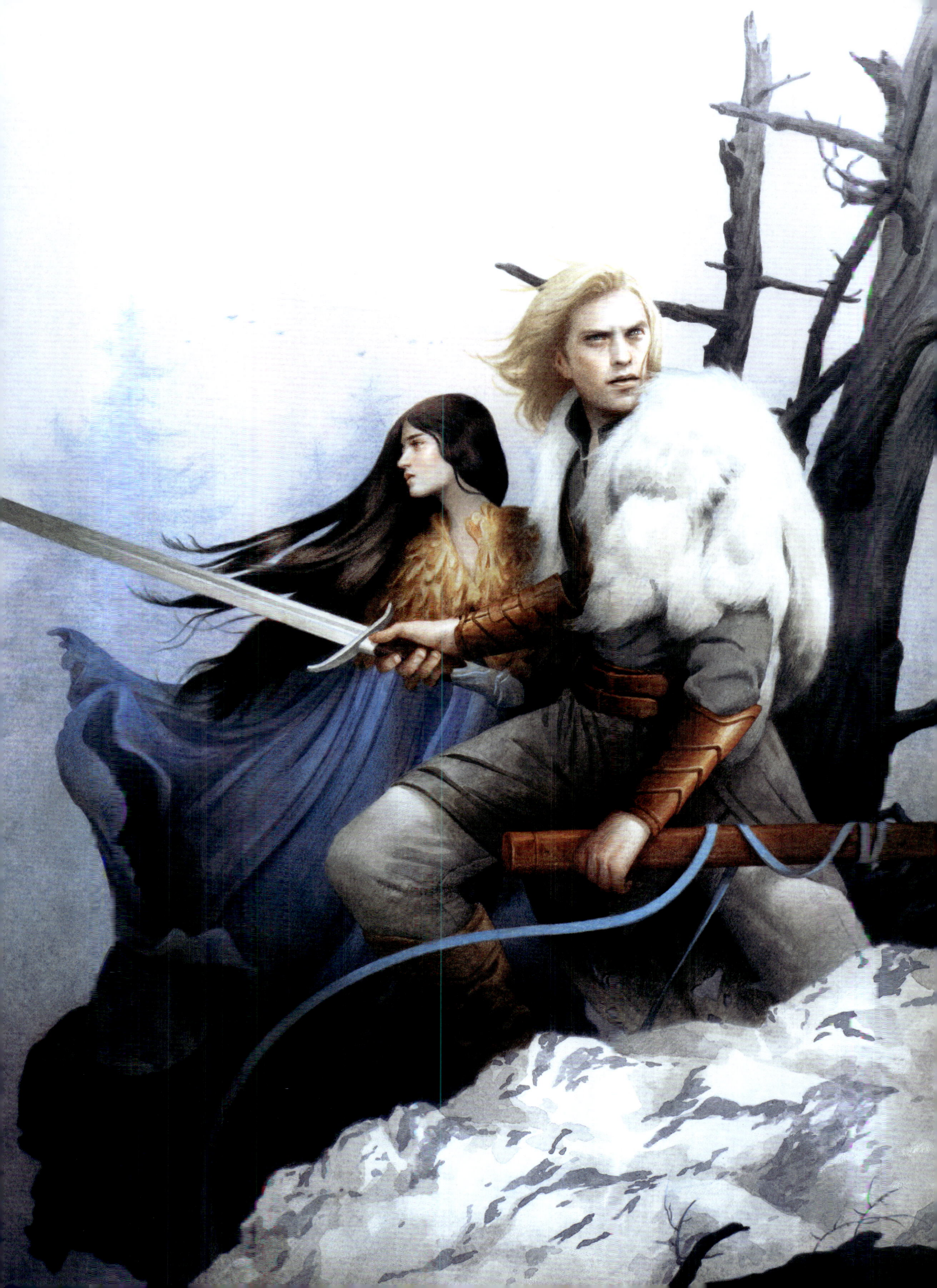

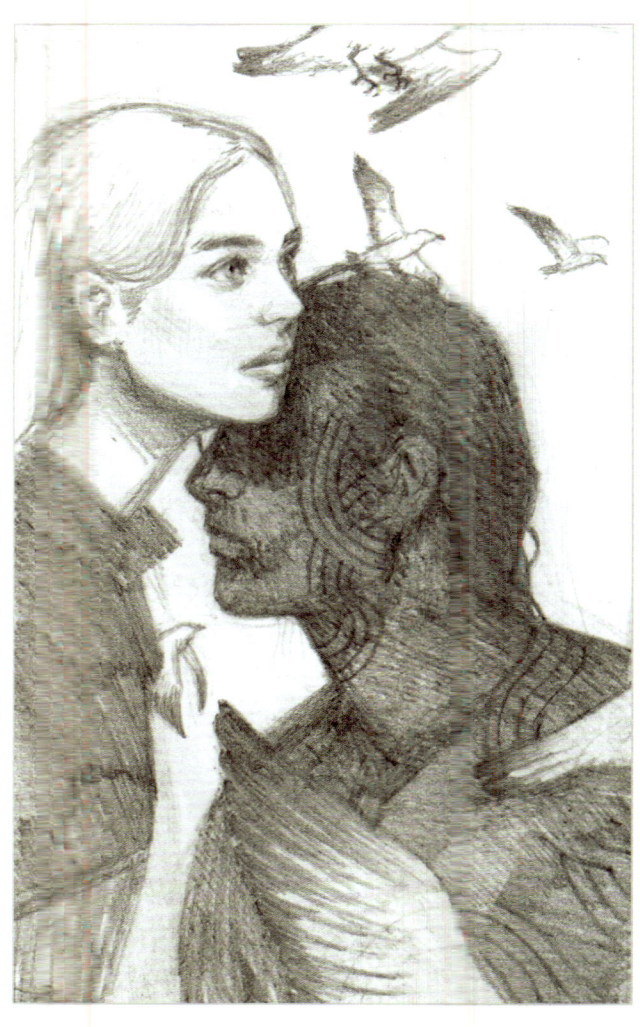

MIRANDA & CALIBAN
Tor Books. AD: Irene Gallo, 2016

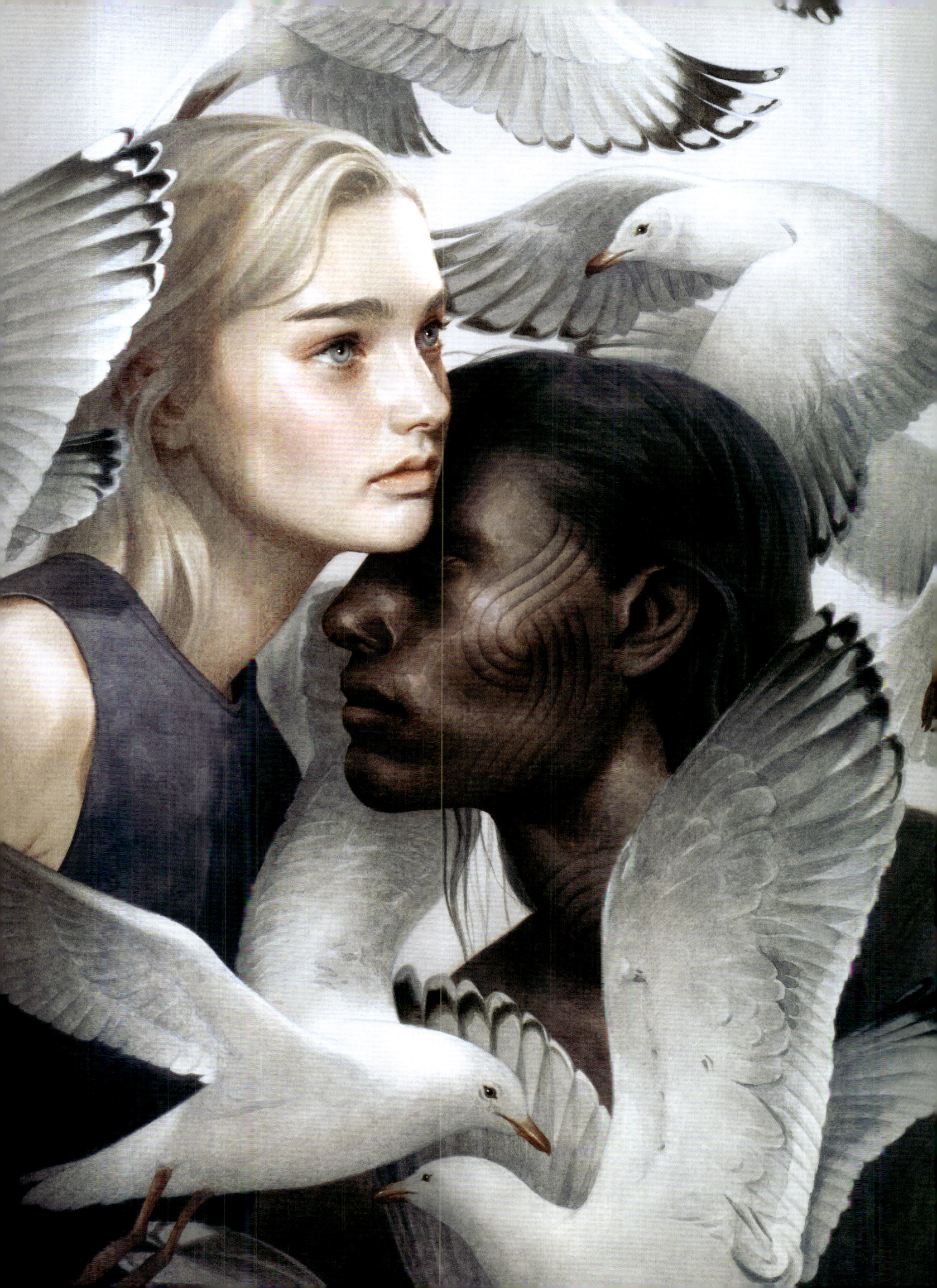

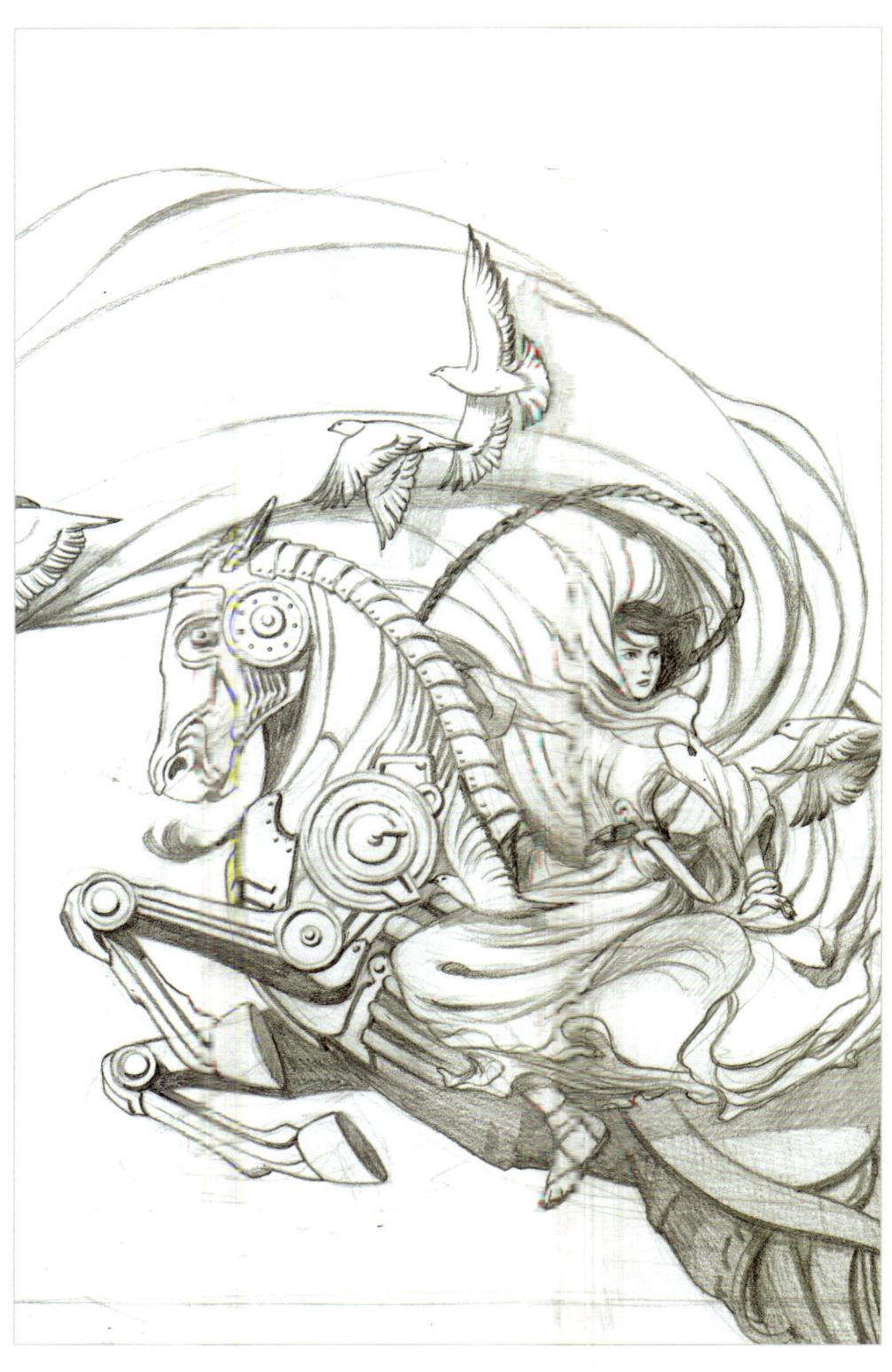

THE BOOK OF ESTHER
Penguin Random House, AD: Michael Morris, 2017

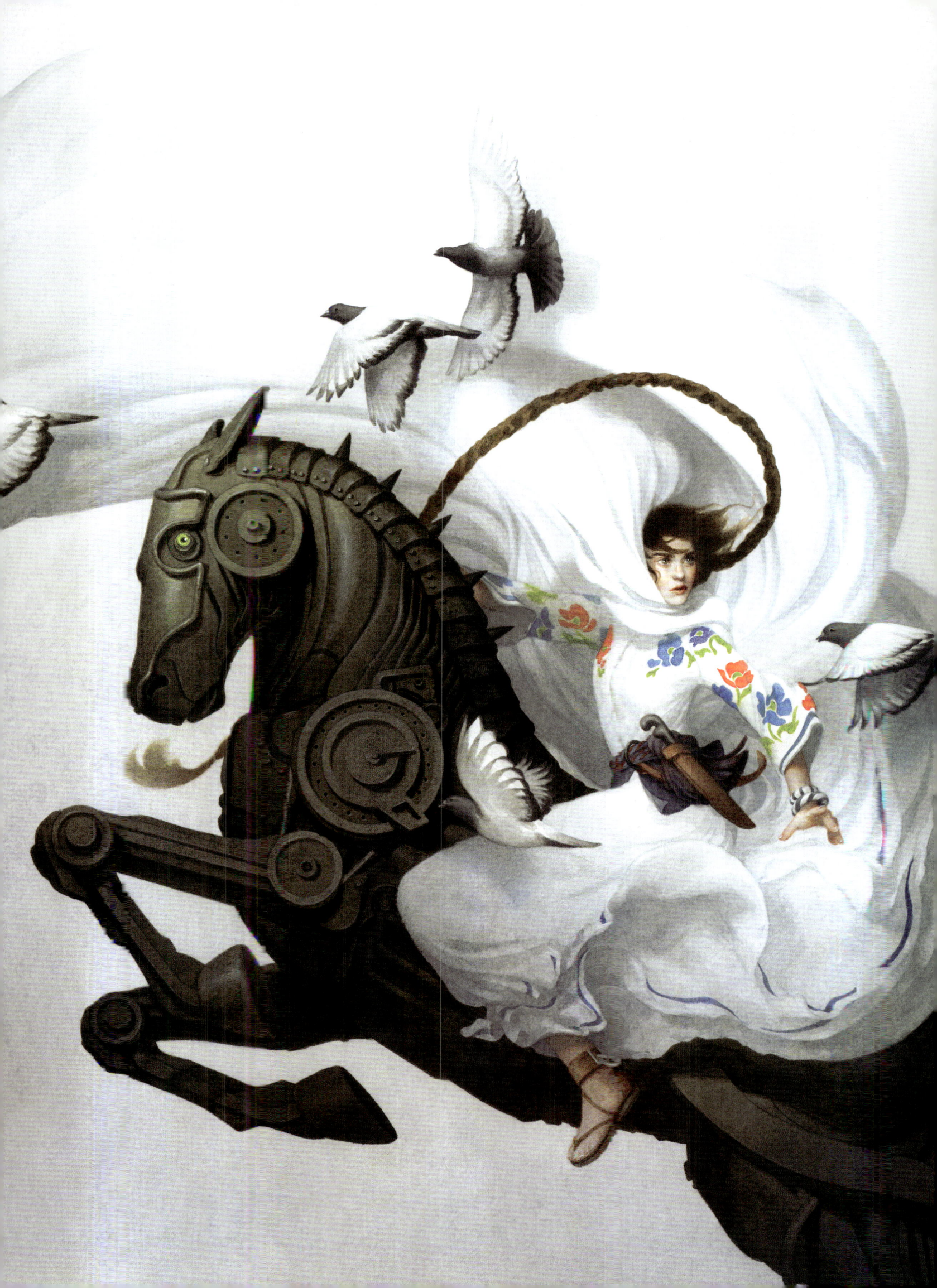

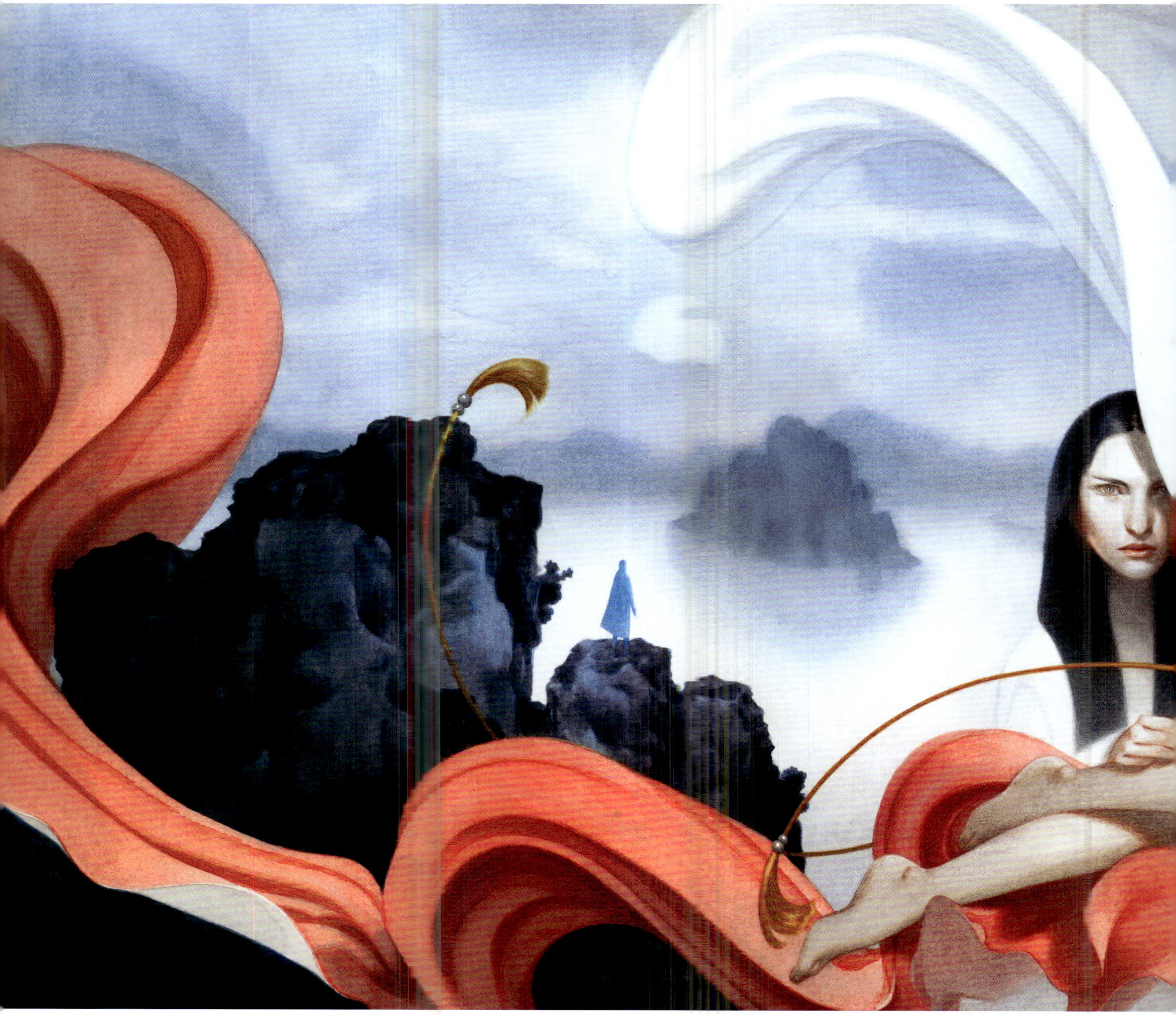

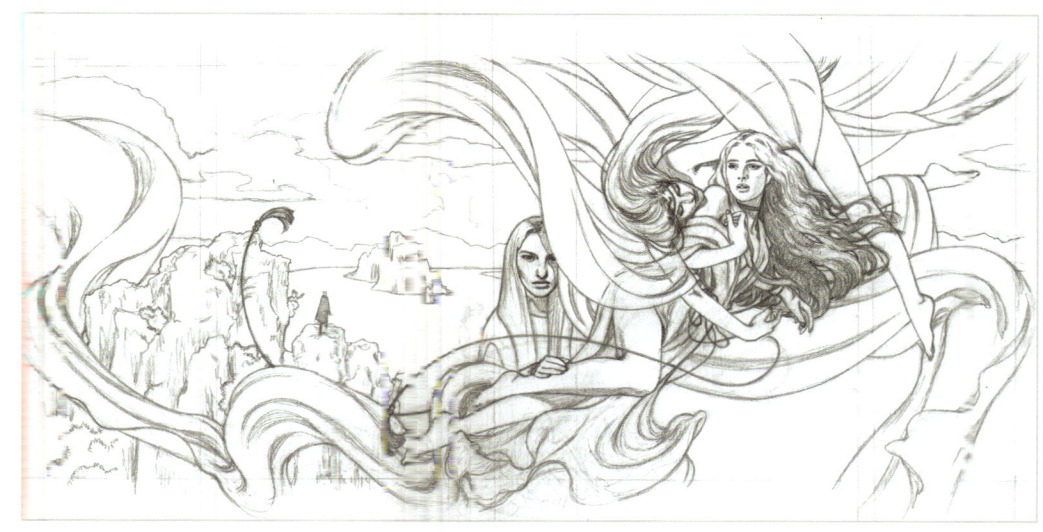

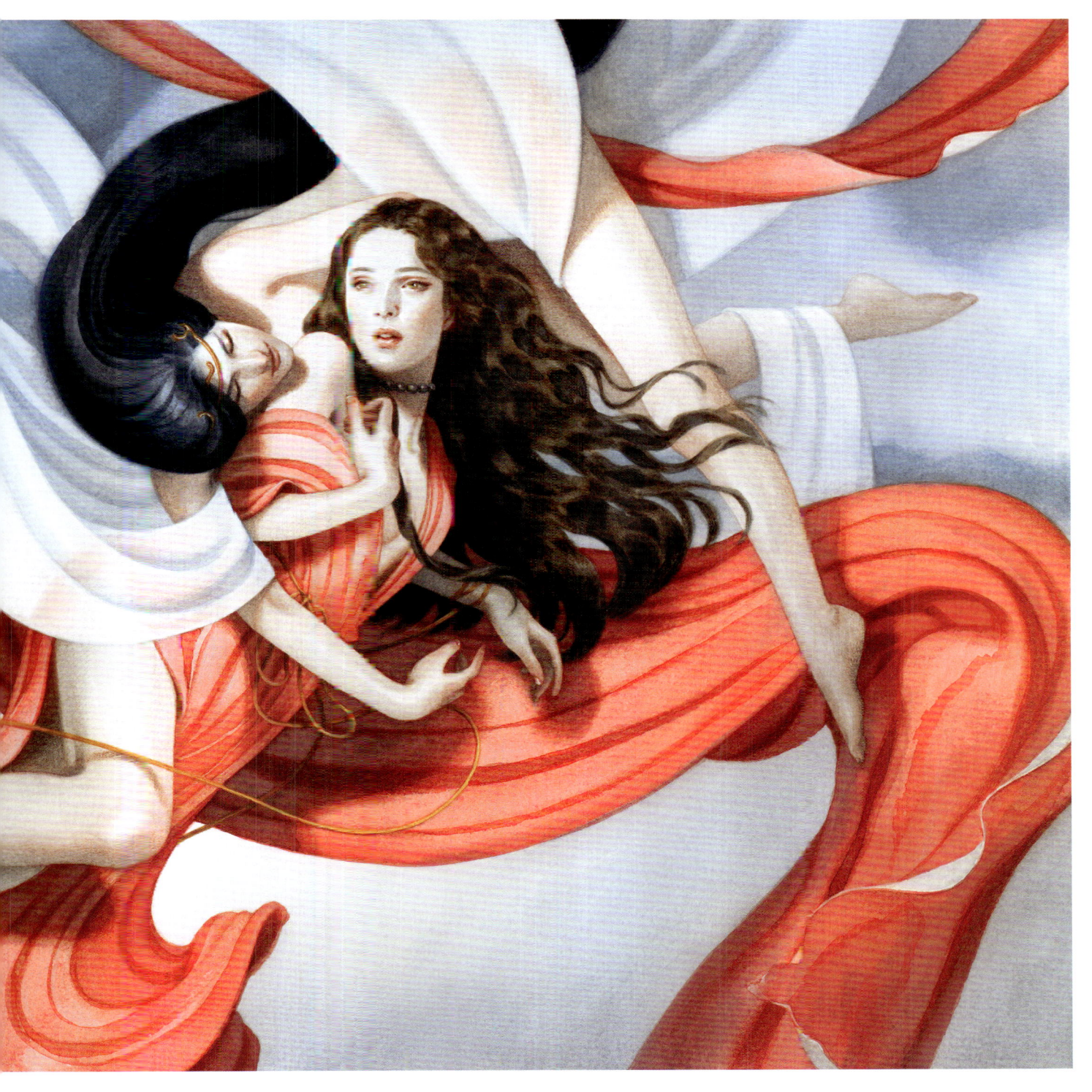

KUSHIEL'S CHOSEN
Subterranean Press, AD: Yanni Kronenberg, 2016

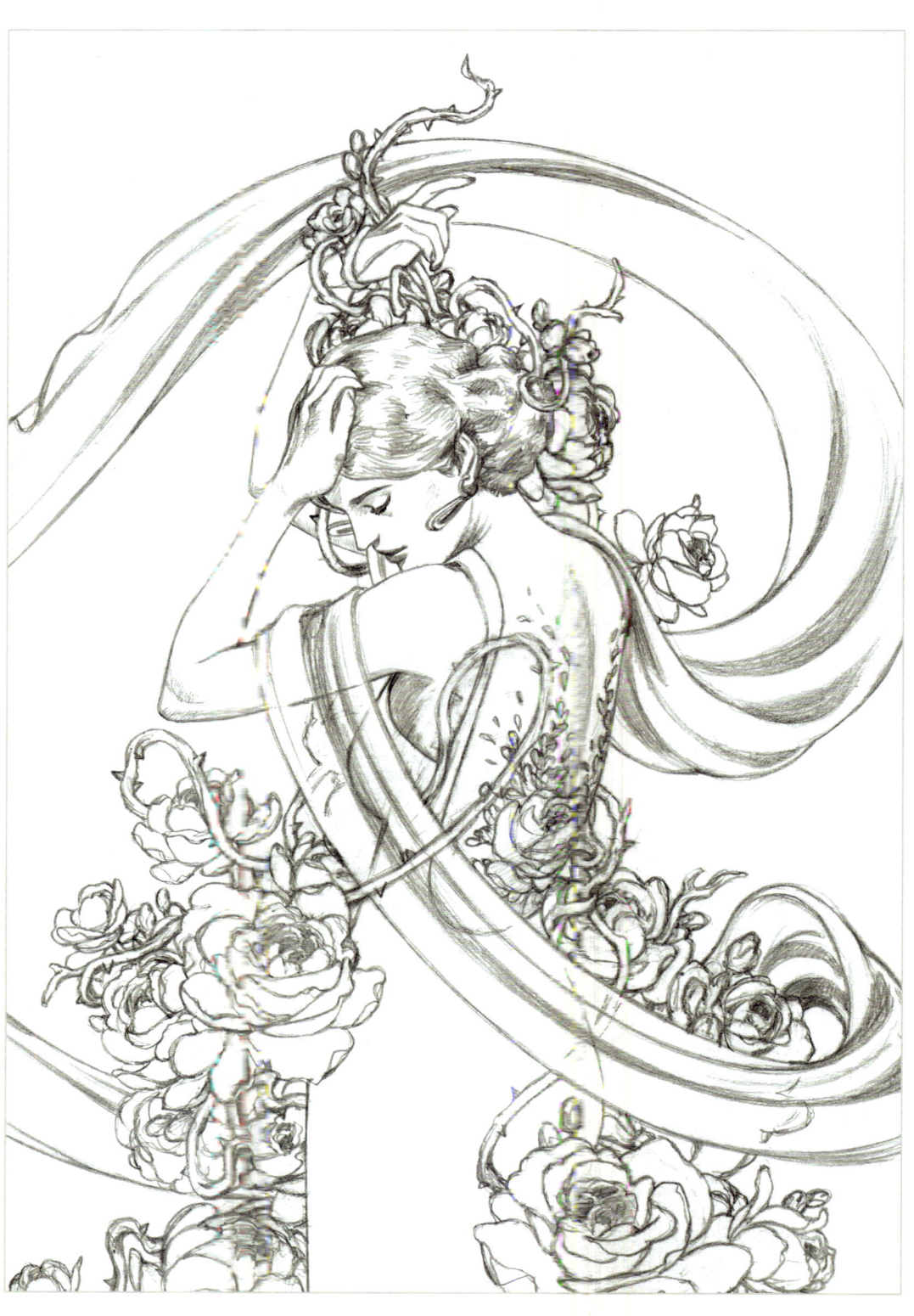

KUSHIEL'S CHOSEN II
Subterranean Press, AD: Yanni Kuznia, 2018

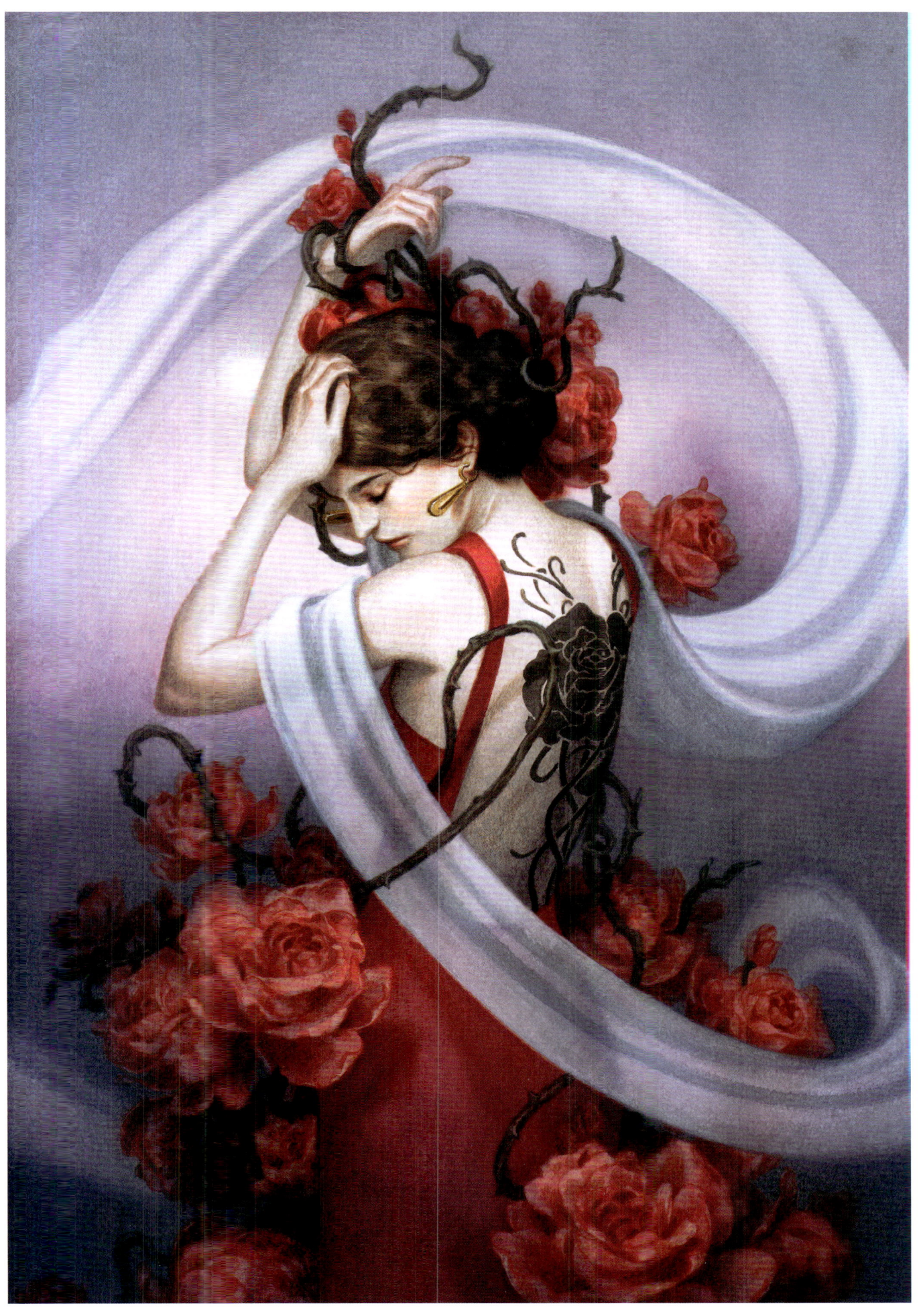

KUSHIEL'S CHOSEN III

Subterranean Press, AD: Yanni Kuznia, 2018

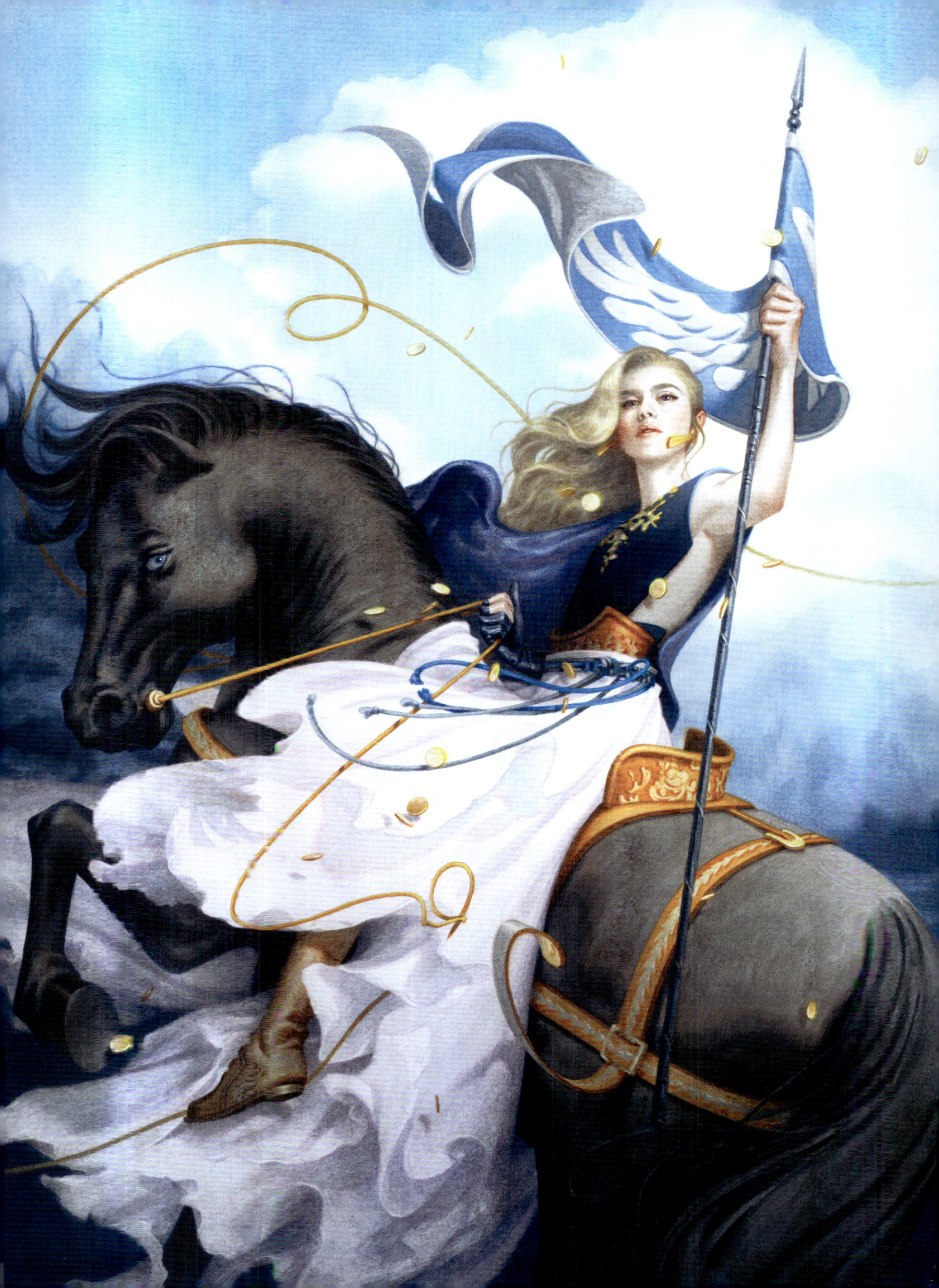

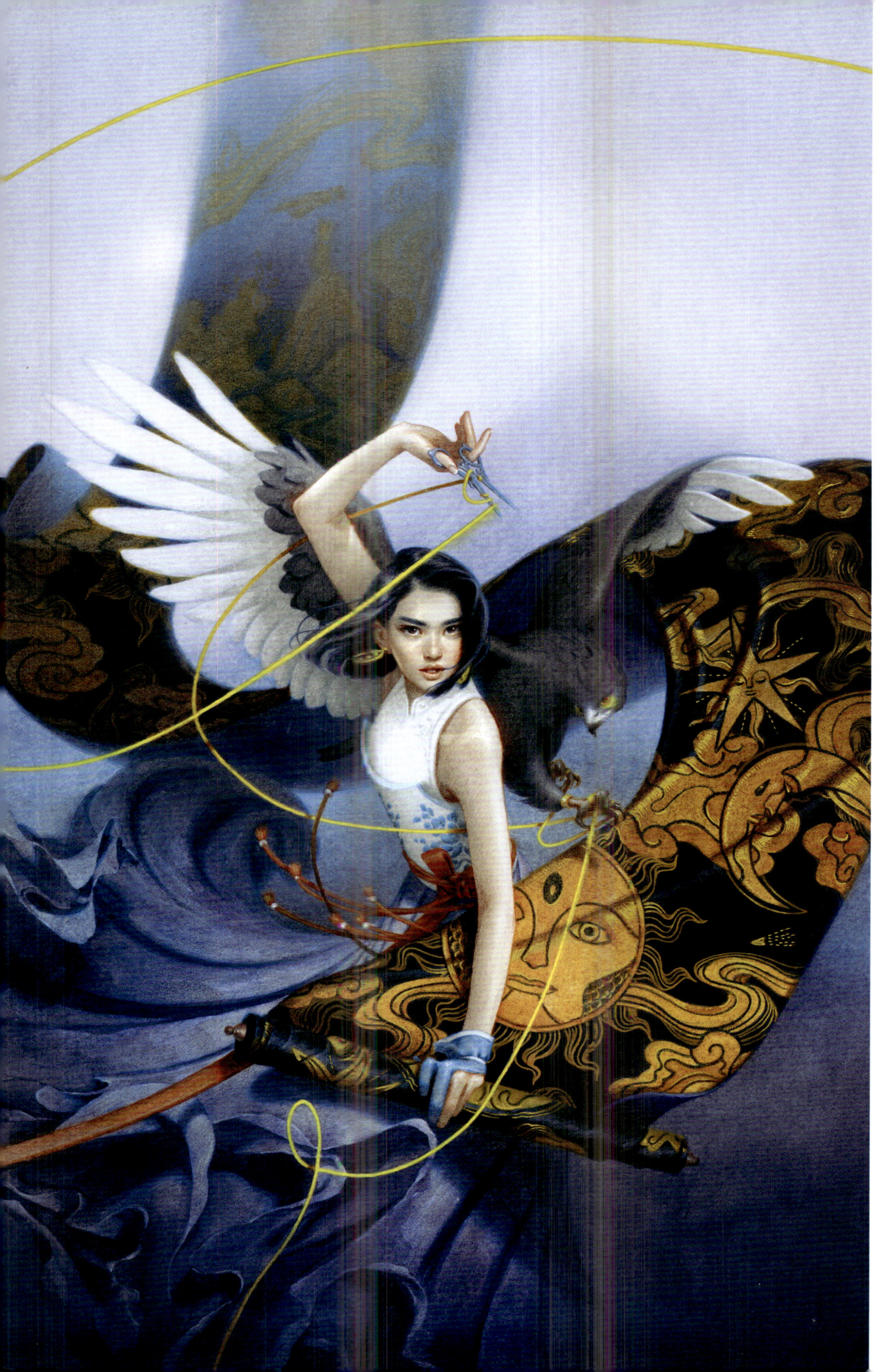

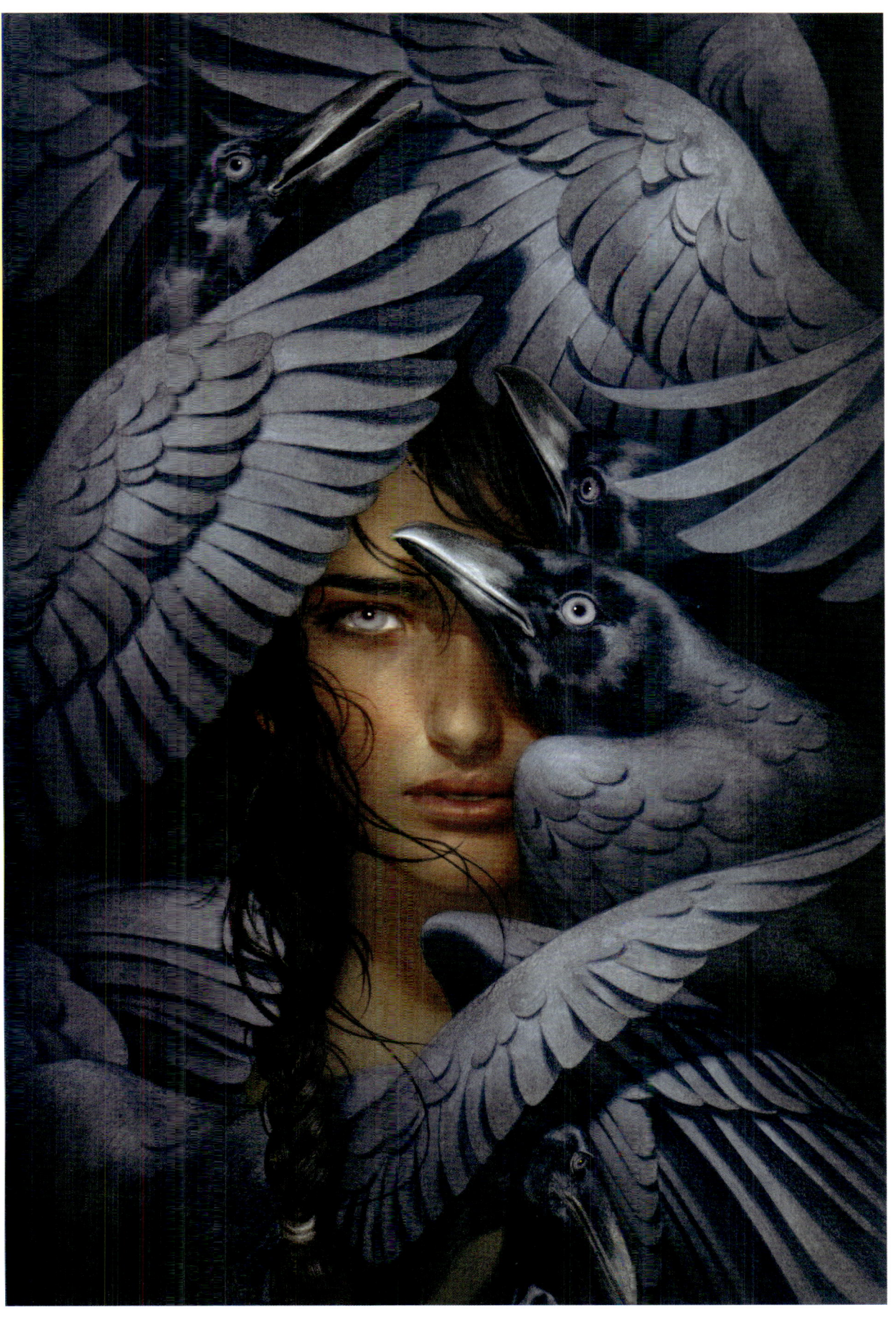

THE STORM CROW
Sourcebooks, AD: Nicole Howe

SPIN THE DAWN
Penguin Random House, AD: Alison Impey

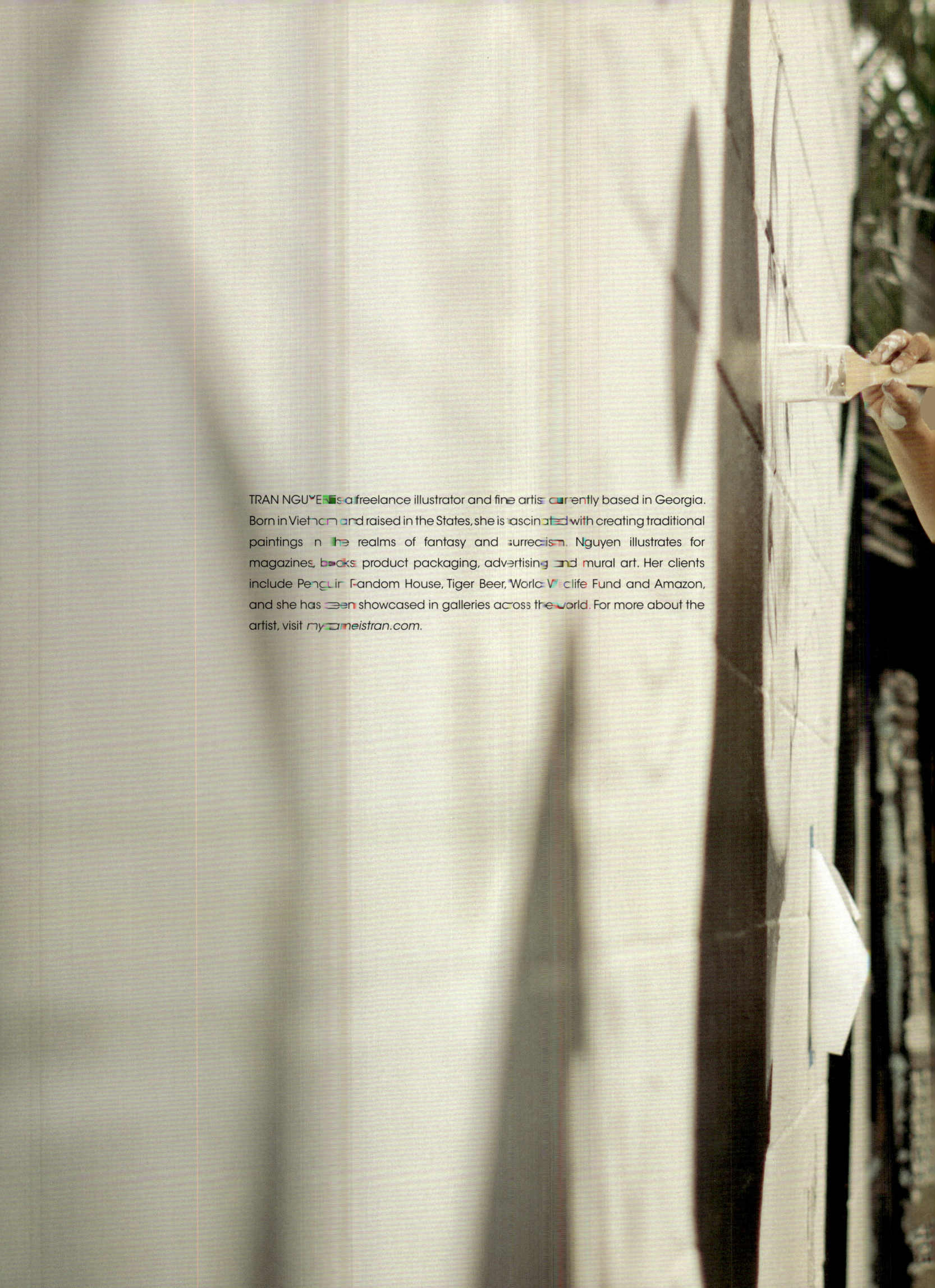

TRAN NGUYEN is a freelance illustrator and fine artist currently based in Georgia. Born in Vietnam and raised in the States, she is fascinated with creating traditional paintings in the realms of fantasy and surrealism. Nguyen illustrates for magazines, books, product packaging, advertising and mural art. Her clients include Penguin Random House, Tiger Beer, World Wildlife Fund and Amazon, and she has been showcased in galleries across the world. For more about the artist, visit mynameistran.com.

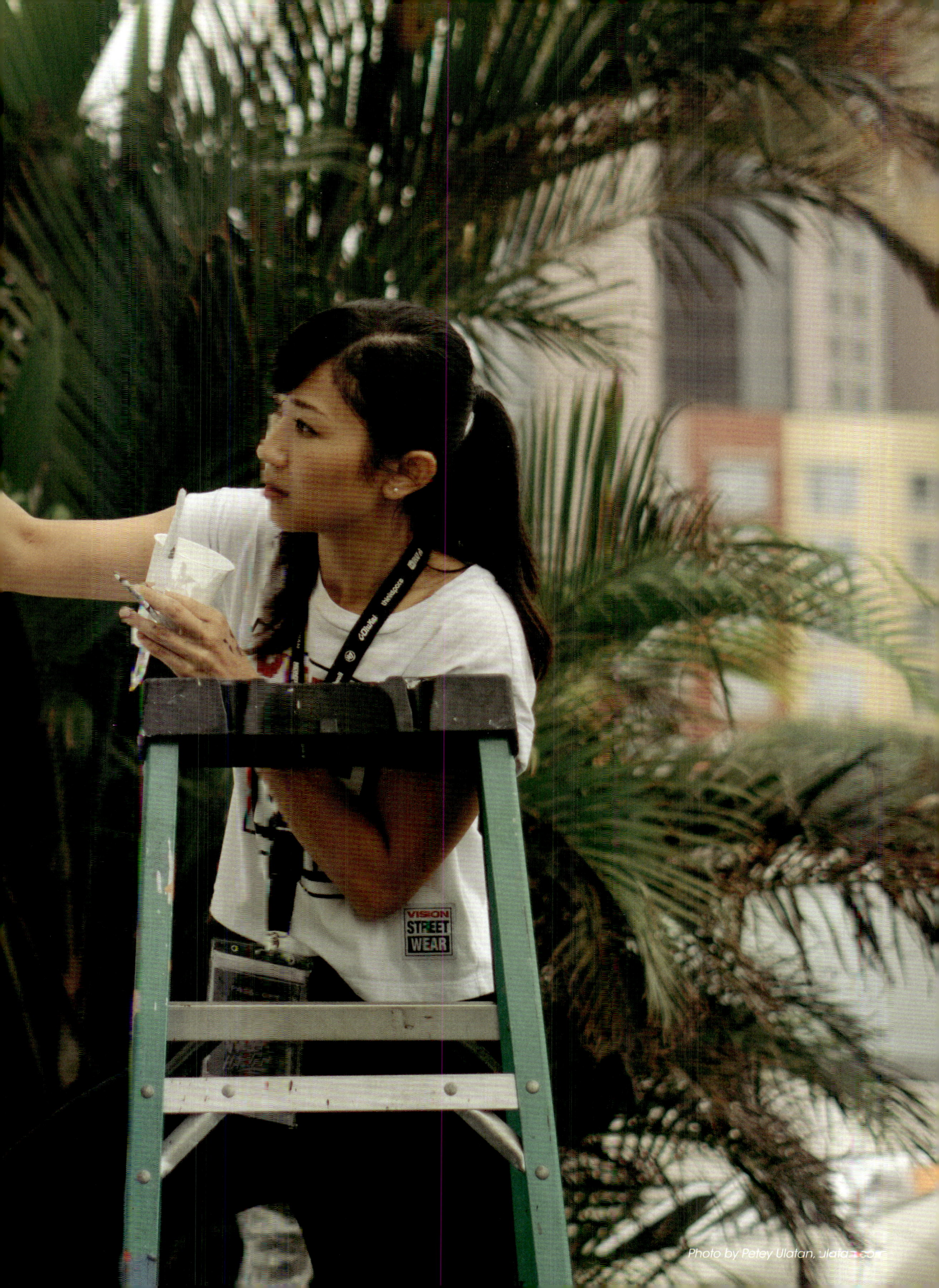

TO MY FAMILY,

FOR ALL THE UNCONDITIONAL LOVE YOU'VE GIVEN ME.